"Clear and compelling. This book combines hard data with touching real-life stories. To win in BRIC, multinational companies must tap into the rich pool of well-qualified, ambitious women: recruit them, empower them, and retain them. Grooming top female talent will become a prerequisite for survival and success in this decade."

—Pully Chau, Chairman and CEO, Draftfcb Greater China

"Hewlett and Rashid fill the gap in our knowledge about the impressive pool of highly qualified women in BRIC countries. They also provide a rich and nuanced understanding of women's ambitions, working conditions, and challenges. *Winning the War for Talent in Emerging Markets* is an invaluable resource for companies intent on finding the best talent in fast-growing emerging markets."

—Dr. Vishakha N. Desai, President, Asia Society

"Written with clarity and conviction, this powerful book will transform how business leaders tackle talent constraints in the growth hubs of the world."

—Lord Michael Hastings of Scarisbrick, Global Head of Citizenship and Diversity, KPMG International

"I recommend *Winning the War for Talent in Emerging Markets* to CEOs everywhere. What company can afford to overlook the vast untapped potential of women in developing economies? From a rolling mill in Russia, to a mine in the Amazon, Alcoa is benefiting tremendously from the contributions of talented women who are eager to take on any challenge."

—Klaus Kleinfeld, Chairman and CEO, Alcoa

"Drawing on an original database and in-depth interviews, this insightful and well-written book demonstrates that women are an important part of the solution to the talent gap that challenges multinational companies in emerging markets."

—Laura D'Andrea Tyson, S.K. and Angela Chan Professor of Global Management, Haas School of Business, University of California, Berkeley

WINNING
THE WAR FOR
TALENT
IN EMERGING
MARKETS

WINNING THE WAR FOR TALENT IN EMERGING MARKETS

✴

WHY
WOMEN
ARE THE
SOLUTION

✴

SYLVIA ANN HEWLETT
RIPA RASHID

Harvard Business Review Press

Boston, Massachusetts

No part of this publication may be reproduced, stored in or introduced into a retrieval
system, or transmitted, in any form, or by any means (electronic, mechanical, pho-
tocopying, recording, or otherwise), without the prior permission of the publisher.
Requests for permission should be directed to permissions@hbsp.harvard.edu, or
mailed to Permissions, Harvard Business School Publishing, 60 Harvard Way, Boston,
Massachusetts 02163.

Library of Congress Cataloging-in-Publication Data

Hewlett, Sylvia Ann, 1946-
  Winning the war for talent in emerging markets : why women are the solution / Sylvia
Ann Hewlett and Ripa Rashid.
      p. cm.
  Includes bibliographical references.
  ISBN 978-1-4221-6060-2 (alk. paper)
  1. Women in the professions—Developing countries. 2. Businesswomen—Developing
countries. 3. Human capital—Developing countries. 4. Employees—Recruiting—
Developing countries. 5. International business enterprises—Personnel management.
I. Rashid, Ripa. II. Title.
  HD6054.2.D44H49 2011
  331.409172'4—dc22

                                                        2011008673

The paper used in this publication meets the requirements of the American National
Standard for Permanence of Paper for Publications and Documents in Libraries and
Archives Z39.48-1992.

CONTENTS

Part Three:
Action Agenda

ACKNOWLEDGMENTS

We owe a particular debt of gratitude to Catherine Fredman, Maggie Jackson, Laura Sherbin, Peggy Shiller, Karen Sumberg, and Jan Alexander. Without their extraordinary writing and research skills, we could not have met the ambitious deadlines of this fast-track book. We are extremely appreciative.

We would like to thank our lead corporate sponsors—Anne Erni and Melinda Wolfe (Bloomberg LP), DeAnne Aguirre (Booz & Company), Rosalind Hudnell (Intel), Susan Silbermann, Tracy Miller, Sandra Bushby (Pfizer), and Denice Kronau (Siemens)—for generous support that goes well beyond funding. Over this past year these corporate leaders have provided precious access, lent wise counsel, and used up chips on our behalf. We are delighted to see this "walking of the talk" and are hugely grateful.

We are grateful to the cochairs of the Hidden Brain Drain Task Force—Barbara Adachi, Joan Amble, Anthony Carter, Deborah Elam, Anne Erni, Gail Fierstein, Patricia Fili-Krushel, Lisa Garcia-Quiroz, Rosalind Hudnell, Annalisa Jenkins, Patricia Langer, Carolyn Buck Luce, Mark McLane, Marilyn Nagel, Annmarie Neal, Kerrie Peraino, Horacio Rozanski, Billie Williamson, and Melinda Wolfe—for their belief in the importance of this study and their ongoing commitment to our work.

A vote of thanks to Melinda Merino and Adi Ignatius of the Harvard Business Review Group, whose inspiration and leadership were critical to this project. Thanks also to Jennifer Waring for valuable contributions to the final draft.

Thanks also to Christine Abdallah, Hector Aguilar, May Al-Dabbagh, Huda Al-Lawati, Aisha al-Suwaidi, Joanne Alam, Lisandra Ambrozio, Dai Min Barclay, Vanessa Bateson, Pamela Berns, Joni Bessler, Veronika Bienert, Pavan Bhatia, Laura Bergerson, Amanda Bennett, Joni Bessler, Fleur Bothwick, Samara Braga, Sandra Bushby, Valentino Carlotti, Jing Cheng, Sunita Cherian, Sharda Cherwoo, Chantale Couture, Tracy Ann Curtis, Ben Dattner, Patricia de Paula Braga, Vishakha Desai, Alicia Dick, Andrey Donets, Lisa Douglass-Doe, Traci Entel, Isabel Fernandez, Polina Gamper, Tais Garcia Martinez, Jill Guarino, Nandita Gurjar, Arine Hadidian, Jean-Michel Halfon, Kewal Handa, Anjali Hazarika, Leila Hoteit, Bharati Jacob, Julia Jia, Rebecca Kellogg, Alpna Khera, Rapti Khurana, Karine Kocharyan, Murali Kuppuswamy, Sara Laschever, Karma Lande, Liza Landicho, Sandra Lawson, David Lobo, Ginny Luo, Christian Malherbe, Anuradha Mathur, Beth McCormick, Anna Michailowa, Tania Mijas, Carolanne Minashi, Stacè Millender, Hiroo Mirchandani, Keerthana Mohan, Sabrina Mondschein, Maria Muller, Radhika Muthukumaran, Sowmya Nanjundaiah, Priya Pandit, Ludmila Petryahina, Azim Premji, Maria Pronina, Viji Rajogopalan, Jayashri Ramamurti, Julia Repryntseva, Yula Rocha, Elluany Rodriguez, Tami Rosen, Rania Rostom, Tony Russell, Karim Sabbagh, Anu Sarkar, Sandra Scharf, Singari Seshadri, Alexandra Shaforost, Ruby Sharma, Liana Slater, Eytan Sosnovich, Lisa Starzyk, Tom Stewart, Carin Taylor, Deborah Tsai-Munster, Edward Tse, Sunita Thawani, Andrea Turner, Nermeen Varawalla, Joy Villagracia, Robin Vince, Heather Wang, Joan Wang, Veronica Wang, Kim Warren, Adeline Wong, Cindy Wright, Jessica Zhang, and Julia Zhu—and all the women and men who took part in focus groups, interviews, and Virtual Strategy Sessions.

We're deeply appreciative of the research support and editorial talents of the CWLP team: Mirembe Birigwa, Joseph Cervone, Courtney Emerson, Diana Forster, Shelley Haynes, Claire Ho, Lauren Leader-Chivee. We also want to thank Bill McCready, Stefan Subias, and the team at Knowledge Networks who fielded the survey and were an invaluable resource throughout the course of this research.

Last but not least, a heartfelt thank you to all sixty-five members of the Hidden Brain Drain Task Force for providing cutting-edge ideas and impressive amounts of collaborative energy: Elaine Aarons, DeAnne Aguirre, Amy Alving, Rohini Anand, Diane Ashley, Subha Barry, Ann Beynon, Esi Eggleston Bracey, Cindy Brinkley, Sheryl Brown-Norman, Brian Bules, Fiona Cannon, Rachel Cheeks-Givan, Ilene Cohn, Desiree Dancy, Nancy Di Dia, Ana Duarte McCarthy, Patricia Fili-Krushel, Melvin Fraser, Edward Gadsden, Michelle Gadsden-Williams, Heide Gardner, Laurie Greeno, Sandra Haji-Ahmed, Kathy Hannan, Henry Hernandez Jr., Ginger Hildebrand, Kathryn Himsworth, Gilli Howarth, LaShana Jackson, Annalisa Jenkins, Nia Joynson-Romanzina, Someera Khokhar, Nancy Killefer, Denice Kronau, Patricia Langer, Frances Laserson, Kedibone Letlaka-Rennert, Yolanda Mangolini, Cindy Martinangelo, Linda Matti, Donna-Marie Maxfield, Cheryl Miller, Judith Nocito, Lynn O'Connor, Juliana Oyegun, Sherryann Plesse, Farrell Redwine, Kari Reston, Ellen Rome, Barbara Ruf, Susan Silbermann, Jeffrey Siminoff, Sarah Stuart, Eileen Taylor, Geri Thomas, Priya Trauber, Lynn Utter, Jo Weiss, Joan Wood, Helen Wyatt, and Meryl Zausner.

In Plain Sight

In the three years since Goldman Sachs launched its business in Brazil, growth has exceeded all expectations. Head count in the São Paulo headquarters has grown from 25 to 250, and Valentino Carlotti, president of Goldman Sachs Bank in Brazil, predicts it will double again in the next two to three years. So what concerns him?

"The growth opportunity is huge," says Carlotti. "We expect Brazil to become a major contributor to the revenue generation of the firm. But we can't get that done without attracting and retaining great talent."

Right now, that's a challenge for Carlotti, who often finds himself playing musical chairs with other firms for in-demand homegrown high performers. Despite the depth of Goldman's bench in developed countries, Carlotti doesn't want to principally rely on expats from the United States or Europe. "Given what has shaped this market, local talent is very sophisticated, very savvy, and, in many ways, more creative and innovative." A shortage of local talent, he fears, could "impact the growth."

Carlotti's concerns are shared by corporate leaders and talent managers throughout the emerging world, where finding, keeping, and maximizing top talent is more than an important issue: for many organizations, it's now an urgent imperative.

With Western countries already weakened by a deep recession, multinational corporations from all countries are pinning their hopes for future growth on developing markets. The four largest of these—Brazil, Russia, India, and China, the so-called BRIC nations—together represent 40 percent of the world's population and have accounted for some 45 percent of global growth since 2007, compared with 20 percent from G-7 economies.[1]

Among burgeoning economies, the dynamic BRIC markets stand out for the speed of their growth and their long-term potential. Their increasing prominence on the global stage is beginning to reshape the way the world does business. Even as Western Europe and the United States struggle to emerge from the recession, the BRICs have remained remarkably resilient. Indeed, in the eyes of many economists, the BRIC markets are actually leading the global recovery.

Yet there is a critical obstacle to their continued expansion: a cutthroat war for high-echelon talent.

A dearth of top talent is often cited as the biggest single barrier to company growth in emerging markets. To meet the talent shortage, multinational corporations have long followed the same well-trodden path: sending homegrown managers overseas, looking for (mostly male) foreign nationals educated in North American and European universities, or, as Carlotti says, "playing musical chairs" with top-quality local talent. All of these options are problematic given the rapid and sustained growth in these new markets. Corporations know they need to get off the beaten path to find and develop a new wellspring of human capital. But they haven't known where to look.

In fact, the answer is hiding in plain sight: large numbers of university-educated women pour into the high echelon job market in the BRIC countries every year. In 2008 alone, the most recent year for which figures for all four countries are available, the number of women in tertiary education programs topped 27 million, and the trend has continued upward in every reporting country.[2] Women now make up 30 to 50 percent of the workforce in these nations.[3]

These women are highly ambitious; they want to make the most of their credentials. According to research from the Center for Work-Life Policy, more than 80 percent of educated women in Brazil and India aspire to top jobs; in China, the figure is more than 75 percent. In comparison, a mere 52 percent of highly qualified women in the United States are shooting for top jobs.

What is the implication of these numbers? As we enter the second decade of the new millennium, the face of top talent in emerging economies is most likely to be that of a woman.

This is a revolutionary thought that flies in the face of conventional wisdom. Observers in the West tend to see third world women as victims. In their recent best seller *Half the Sky*, Nicholas Kristof and Sheryl WuDunn, for instance, focus on illiteracy and oppression and point to micro credit as one of the few rays of hope for women in emerging markets.[4]

In a similar vein, business leaders tend not to have women on their radar screen. Almost all multinational companies, whether they be headquartered in the United States or in China or India, hope to reap rich rewards in the BRIC geographies, but few recognize the crucial contributions that educated local women make in these markets. Fewer still understand the nature of this rich talent pool or know how to make the most of it. As a result, the brainpower that women from the BRIC countries bring to the workforce has been overlooked and underutilized.

The fact is that no company can afford to ignore highly qualified female talent if it wants to compete in these fast-expanding economies—and win.

THE TALENT GAP IN EMERGING ECONOMIES

The BRICs' surge represents a pivotal point in the history of globalization: following centuries of dominance by the West, the economic balance of power is steadily shifting towards "the rest." The enormous leaps in productivity, purchasing power, and consumer demand in the BRIC nations recently led Goldman Sachs's chief economist Jim O'Neill, who coined the term "BRIC," to predict that their combined GDP could exceed that of the G-7 economies within the next twenty years, with China projected to be the world's largest economy by 2027.[5] Some economists put China, now the world's second largest economy, in first place as soon as 2020.[6] Others estimate that India, now ranked eleventh, could leapfrog slow-growing Japan into third place in the individual country GDP rankings as early as 2012 (see figure I-1).

In short, emerging markets are now the growth engine of the world.

As the BRICs power out of the global slowdown, the demand for—and shortage of—top talent is more pronounced than ever before. Businesses worldwide are heatedly competing for people who, often for the first time in their lives, "have numerous options and high expectations," wrote Douglas A. Ready, Linda Hill, and Jay Conger in 2008.[7] The problem is especially dire at top ranks. At the very moment when many

FIGURE I-1

BRICs will have a larger GDP than the G-7 in less than forty years

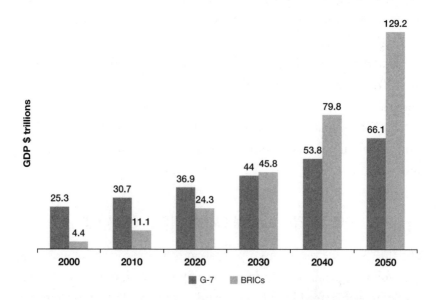

Source: Projection data from Goldman Sachs, most recent available as of May 17, 2010.

FIGURE I-2

Global distribution of the talent pipeline

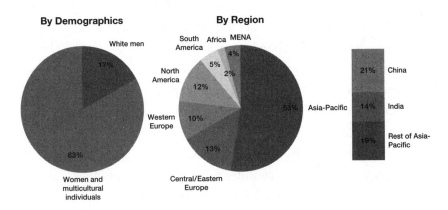

Source: Sylvia Ann Hewlett et al., "The Athena Factor," *Harvard Business Review* (June 2008); Booz & Company analysis; OECD & UNESCO 2000–2006 (based on availability) Education Database, Tertiary Completion Levels; India, Pakistan, and Peru, 2002 UNESCO Education Database, Tertiary Enrollment reduced, assuming 33% completion rate.

Global talent pool is defined as all individuals around the world who were enrolled in tertiary education (college or university level) in the year 2006.

multinationals are setting aside the ingrained "corporate imperialism" that led them to ignore local managers, they face limited rosters of local talent to promote (see figure I-2).

Melinda Wolfe, Bloomberg's head of professional development, explains the situation: "Bloomberg is now in 146 countries and growing at a rapid pace. We have an urgent need to draw upon a deep pool of talent to deliver excellence."

It's time to turn the spotlight on highly qualified women.

EDUCATED BRIC WOMEN: A NEW NARRATIVE

Why has it taken so long to notice them?

The main reason: despite an expanding body of work on women in emerging economies, few studies consider the potential of educated, ambitious women. Much of the existing research casts them in a narrative of victimhood. Books like the aforementioned *Half the Sky* and *From Outrage to Courage* by Anne Firth Murray, as well as highly publicized reports and initiatives from the United Nations and the World Bank, promulgate the notion that *all* women in developing countries are oppressed, their potential obscured by poverty and their presence relegated to the sidelines of male-dominated cultures.

Our research shows this to be untrue.

Just as in the United States and in other developed economies, women in emerging markets are enrolling in and graduating from universities and graduate schools at rates that match and often outstrip those of men. Furthermore, these women are highly ambitious; according to our surveys, nearly two-thirds of women in China and Russia and 85 percent of women in India consider themselves very ambitious—almost twice as many as in the United States. As opportunities undreamed of a generation ago open up in BRIC countries, one regional expert remarks, "Women no longer have to apologize for their ambition."

Educated women from the BRIC countries who step out of the shadows of their less-fortunate sisters encounter another misconception: that their ability to participate in today's workforce lags behind that of their American and European counterparts because of the persistence of traditional attitudes, explicit discrimination, or an absence of opportunities. In reality, under Communism, women in Russia and China were encouraged to help build their nation's economies and were put to work in numbers equal to men. In the Soviet Union, for example, 90 percent of working-age women were in the paid labor force.[8] In Brazil, India, and the dynamic economies of the Middle East, traditionally close-knit extended families and the availability of inexpensive domestic help enable ambitious women to mitigate the child care issues that cripple the careers of many Western women professionals.

THE BENEFITS BRIC WOMEN BRING

In addition to providing much-needed qualified talent to growth-minded companies, from Shanghai to São Paulo, from Moscow to Mumbai, educated women have much to offer their employers.

Those markets are increasingly dominated by women. As women flood into management positions, a surprising number are earning salaries greater than their spouses. Women now control two-thirds of all consumer spending. Married women are overwhelmingly the primary decision makers for their family's purchases of food, clothing, health care, education, and household products.

Educated women in emerging markets bring a keen sense of the consumer marketplace to their employers. When translating product development and marketing strategy into emerging markets, the mandate to "think globally and act locally" in pragmatic terms means "hire more women." Lisandra Ambrozio, Pfizer's human resources director in Brazil, doesn't need convincing. "More than fifty percent of doctors here in Brazil are women. Seventy-five percent of the health decisions made in the family are made by women, not by men. We need to understand what is in the mind of a female doctor, or we need to better understand women, because they are the ones who make the health care decisions in a family." She continues, "Gender diversity is not a social issue. It's a business issue, not only for Pfizer but for each company in the market."

Ambrozio's comments are echoed by Hiroo Mirchandani, business unit director at Pfizer, India: "We know women are good at engaging customers, nurturing relationships, and communicating product features. Tapping in to this talent pool provides a competitive advantage."

In the entrepreneurial economies of emerging markets, women are key to connecting with the main engine of growth: the small-to-medium business market. "The SMB market in emerging markets is *the* market," explains Tracy Ann Curtis, Cisco Systems' head of inclusion and diversity for Asia-Pacific and Japan. "It's not the big enterprise market any longer. We're servicing small entrepreneurial companies, and 33 percent of them in Asia are owned by women. If we want to sell into that market, we've got to understand who those women are and how they reflect on the marketplace."

The diversity of thought, perspective, and experience that educated women add to any organization is multiplied in developing markets.

Because of the obstacles they've often had to overcome, they bring a determination and a "can do, leave no stone unturned, we'll find a way" approach to coming up with solutions, says Goldman Sachs's Carlotti. When they solve problems, it sends a signal of "openness, creativity, forward thinking, and an innovative approach" to potential hires as well as clients. He concludes, "For me, when you look at who's coming into the workforce and what they can mean for the development of human capital, it's a no-brainer that women are a competitive advantage."

AN INTRICATE WEB OF PUSHES AND PULLS

Deeply entrenched stereotypes make it difficult for Western employers to have a clear view of this new tranche of talent. But behind the images—the cliches of the girl from Ipanema with the world's smallest string bikini, the doe-eyed Bollywood heroine, and the docile Asian wife who collects Ferragamo shoes and Chanel jackets by the closetful—is a generation of well-educated women determined to forge a new identity. Thanks to the Internet, movies, and TV, their role models are drawn not from traditional cultural archetypes or national heroines but from around the world. They have a global perspective, a view that includes their role in helping their country develop *its* new identity.

Even though the potent pool of highly qualified women professionals in emerging markets is composed of neither victims of oppression nor cultural caricatures, organizations should not make the other mistake of assuming that these women are BRIC clones of their counterparts in advanced industrialized economies. In fact, their career dynamics—both the opportunities they aspire to and the challenges they encounter—are complex, fundamentally different, and, says Subha Barry, former global head of diversity at Merrill Lynch, "so nuanced that it's easy to miss the multitude of issues these women are dealing with."

Among them are these challenges:

- The maternal guilt that frequently derails Western women's careers is less onerous among female professionals in the BRICs and the United Arab Emirates (UAE), but they carry a heavy load of "daughterly guilt." In countries like India, China, and the UAE, where notions of filial piety underpin cultural values and where demographers project an explosion in the percentage of the population over the age of sixty, elder care responsibilities are a ticking time bomb.

- Although "extreme jobs"—characterized by extended work weeks, an always-on 24/7 culture, and intense performance pressure—are the norm among highly qualified and ambitious women worldwide, the average workweek for employees of multinational corporations (MNCs) in BRIC nations is especially onerous. Moreover, the demands of work have intensified over the past few years; more than a quarter of the women surveyed by the CWLP report working, on average, eight to eighteen hours more per week than three years ago, additional time that amounts to *one to two extra workdays*.

- Workplace biases faced by professional women in these markets are overt and explicit. At least 40 percent of the women surveyed in Brazil, India, and China have encountered prejudice severe enough to make them consider scaling back their career goals or quitting altogether.

- Biases in the workplace are magnified outside. In many emerging market countries, there is such strong social disapproval of—and occasionally outright danger for—women traveling alone that women often avoid industry sectors that require significant travel, such as pharmaceutical sales, and gravitate toward those based in urban, modern environs.

If we do not closely examine and understand the intricate web of pushes and pulls that can downsize ambition and stall promising careers, the full potential of this rich talent pool will remain untapped.

METHODOLOGY AND THEMATIC FOCUS

The ever-expanding body of work on the "BRIC phenomenon"— exemplified by such recent publications as *Imagining India* by Nandan M. Nilekani, *The China Strategy* by Edward Tse, *Billions of Entrepreneurs* by Tarun Khanna, or *When China Rules the World* by Martin Jacques— typically focuses on individual countries and adopts a broad-brush approach to the business or economic landscape. Analyses of the talent issues that are critical to the continued growth momentum of the BRIC economies remain primarily qualitative in approach and fragmentary in scope. Most of these studies, which rely exclusively on opinions gathered through interviews, are limited to business leaders and senior managers and focus exclusively on men.[9] Without exception, even those that spotlight the war for talent and the looming skills shortage make no reference to a key segment of the talent pool: highly qualified, ambitious women. Indeed, Nilekani, in his well-regarded book *Imagining India*, devotes a mere four pages to the opportunities and challenges facing women, and Khanna, in his high-profile book *Winning in Emerging Markets*, fails to mention women at all.

This book fills a fundamental gap in the research. It is based on a robust combination of quantitative data collection and in-depth qualitative research gathered through the Center for Work-Life Policy's proprietary multipronged methodology.

Quantitative data was gathered through surveys of 4,350 college-educated men and women in Brazil, Russia, India, China, the United Arab Emirates, and, for comparison, nearly 3,000 respondents in the United States. Qualitative data was collected through focus groups, our Virtual Strategy Session online interview tool, and in-depth one-on-one interviews involving hundreds of high-echelon men and women across the targeted geographies. The research spanned interviewees of varying levels and experience, ranging from those new to the workforce to senior managers and business leaders. Data was collected between February 2009 and December 2010 and is, to our knowledge, unparalleled in scope and scale.

In addition to the BRIC countries, the UAE was included in the research as a lens into the talent landscape in the Middle East. Despite recent economic setbacks in business hubs such as Dubai, the Emirates continue to play an important role as a gateway to the region for many multinational organizations. Insights into the specific opportunities and challenges of managing talent in the UAE add a valuable dimension to the rich and complex themes we uncover for BRIC countries.

One other key point: the managers interviewed—male and female— work at a wide range of multinational corporations, including global giants with roots in China, India, and Europe as well as the United States. The insights and advice, therefore, are aimed at *all* multinationals and not only established Western corporations.

THE LESSON FOR GLOBAL COMPANIES

As companies position themselves for global expansion, one fact is clear: educated women in the BRIC nations and the UAE are already a force to be reckoned with. They are enormously ambitious and passionate about their work and are determined to play an ever-expanding role in the economic progress of their countries. Together with their female peers in other parts of the world, they are fundamentally altering the talent equation. But they will not be able to deliver their full potential until and unless their employers help them overcome the cultural limitations and organizational constraints that dampen their ambitions and derail their careers.

As global organizations build their presence in emerging markets, they have a unique opportunity to get it right—that is, to establish systems and processes for managing talent that allow highly qualified and ambitious women to flourish and contribute as fully as their male peers.

Some forward-thinking companies have already begun to experiment with their talent models and strategies. In part three, Action Agenda, we showcase thirty of these cutting-edge initiatives, spotlighting the issues each program addresses, exploring the challenges along the road to successful implementation, describing the solutions, and qualifying the results. We hope these initiatives—and, even more, the recognition of the forces thwarting ambitious women and the thoughtful responses—will seed more innovative practices among all employers.

Educated women represent the vanguard of talent management. Just as emerging markets can bolster a company's bottom line, the lessons learned in attracting, sustaining, and retaining the best and brightest women in those markets can enhance and strengthen an organization's operations worldwide. For all companies, both multinational and local, a deeper understanding of the professional needs and aspirations of educated women in developing markets is the surest route to continued growth, now and in the future.

Part One

The Changing Face of Talent

For ambitious, educated women in emerging markets, the future has never looked brighter. New opportunities beckon, calling for and rewarding their skills and their determination to use them. Employers who cultivate their talent find their efforts reciprocated with impressive levels of loyalty. We'll explore the unprecedented advantages emerging markets women bring to the workplace in chapter 1.

But few companies can afford to be complacent about this rich lode of talent. We cannot emphasize enough the power of the societal forces tethering women's career aspirations, grounding their ambition and causing too many women to settle for a dead-end job or quit the workforce altogether. We'll describe the nature of these family-rooted "pulls" and cultural "pushes" in chapter 2.

1

Unprecedented Advantages

When Maria Pronina graduated from Nizhni Novgorod Linguistic University in 1995, she expected to follow the conventional career track and become an English language teacher. Disappointed with the low salary, however, she switched jobs and started to work as an interpreter, first for the regional government and then for a local company. She acquired a management degree and became a supervisor, and then she moved to a multinational technology company.

Pronina still remembers the moment when she realized that her career horizons had no limits. "I really did not believe that coming from a very low level I had a real chance to make it rapidly. But at my first annual performance assessment, I suddenly understood I could be recognized and could do well. That was the turning point for me."

Today, Pronina oversees fourteen direct reports and four hundred contractors as facilities and services team manager for Russia/CIS at Intel. Her ambition is to stay with her employer—and do even more. "My employer is doing a lot for my development and provides almost everything I would like to have. I would like to stay at this company but be responsible not only for Russia and CIS but also Europe."

Talented women in emerging markets are ahead of the curve in unexpected ways. Like Pronina, they see work not as a stopgap measure to fill the time between marriage and motherhood but as an opportunity to realize their ambitions.

This chapter explores the remarkable combination of advantages that talented women in emerging markets bring to the workplace: impressive qualifications, ambitious career visions, and great passion and commitment to their work.

EDUCATIONAL EXCELLENCE

The World Economic Forum's *2010 Annual Gender Gap Report* tracks gender parity for 134 countries along four dimensions: education, health, economic participation and opportunities, and political empowerment.[1] In the BRIC countries and the UAE, the overall gender gap has consistently narrowed, and this shift is most apparent in education.

Interestingly, the spark for many women was triggered by their parents, who recognized the value of an education in a changing world and encouraged their daughters to excel in their studies, either at home or abroad. For many families, like Hiroo Mirchandani's, educational achievement was expected of children of both sexes. "We were brought up measured on how we did in school," recalls Mirchandani, who grew up in New Delhi. "It didn't matter if you were a boy or a girl. What was expected was that you came at the top of the class."

Other parents pushed their daughters to overcome their own shortcomings through education. Woman after woman in our focus groups and interviews had a story similar to Lisandra Ambrozio's. When Ambrozio's mother was a girl, her dream was to learn English.

Her mother, however, wanted her daughter to learn to play the piano. Ambrozio's mother grudgingly studied piano for twelve years—"She hated it," Ambrozio recalls—until she married. "And she never played the piano again." But she never forgot her resentment at being denied the chance to learn another language, and as soon as Ambrozio could read, her mother asked whether she'd like to take English classes. When Ambrozio said yes, her mother was overjoyed. "Great!" Ambrozio remembers her exclaiming. "I'm going to pay for your English courses myself, because I think this will be good for your career and your personal life." As a result, Ambrozio was fluent in English before she went to Pontificia Universidade Catolica, Brazil's top private university, where she received her undergraduate degree and MBA.

Ambrozio's father also supported her educational aspirations. Ambrozio's dream was to take a year-long extension course at the University of California, Berkeley. "I was working and saving money for a couple of years," Ambrozio says, but when she finally accumulated enough money to pay for the course and her living expenses, Brazil suffered a massive currency devaluation. Half of her savings were wiped out. Ambrozio's father hadn't been happy about the prospect of his daughter's leaving the country, but he knew how much it meant to her. "He said, 'Okay, you pay for half of the course and I'll pay for the other.' *Greeeeat* father!" Ambrozio exclaims.

Today, Ambrozio is the human resources director for Pfizer, Brazil. Her brother is a civil engineer, and her sister is a lawyer. Ambrozio has never forgotten her father's action or what it represented. "This is one of the most admirable things that my father did," she muses. "He invested in our education."

This groundswell of expectation, encouragement, and support from both parents endorses one of our most striking findings: that women are flooding into university and graduate schools in record numbers. Just as in the United States, where women college graduates now outnumber men, there is an "achievement gap" in three of our target geographies: women represent 65 percent of college graduates in the UAE,

FIGURE 1-1

Percent of women in tertiary education

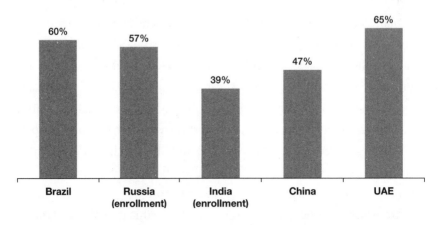

Source: World Bank Education Statistics Database.

60 percent in Brazil, and in China they are already 47 percent of this group (see figure 1-1).

It is no surprise that in Russia, where Communism promoted universal access to education, 86 percent of women aged eighteen to twenty-three are enrolled in tertiary education—compared with 64 percent of men the same age—and the numbers in the other BRIC markets are also impressive.[2] More than one-third of women in the appropriate age group in Brazil and the UAE are enrolled in tertiary education, a percentage notably larger than that of their male counterparts.

In China and India, with far larger and less urbanized populations, the overall percentage of women in this age group enrolled in colleges and universities is lower—23 percent and 10 percent, respectively—but the interesting story is who has the determination to go beyond the initial diploma. Half the Indian women in our sample hold graduate degrees, outstripping men by 10 percentage points, and the number of Chinese women with graduate degrees is virtually equal to the number of Chinese men. As one of the women we interviewed explained, "There was a time in India when people saved up money for their daughter's marriage or for their son's education, but the urban middle-class community in India doesn't do that anymore. Today, for a son or a daughter, the priority is education."

The BRIC/UAE education figures are impressive also in their sheer scale, because the actual number of university graduates in these countries has increased at a phenomenal rate. Thanks to the rapid expansion in the number of institutions of higher education, an area that has experienced reinvigorated government and private sector focus in recent years, higher education enrollment in China has more than tripled since 2000, and the number of doctoral degrees awarded annually rose sevenfold between 1996 and 2006.[3] In India, the number of universities has doubled since 1990, and the government has committed to boosting higher education spending ninefold, to $20 billion annually in the five-year period that began in 2007. This colossal investment will be directed toward seventy-two new postsecondary schools, including eight new Indian Institutes of Technology, seven new Indian Institutes of Management, five new Indian Institutes of Science, Education and Research, and twenty new Indian Institutes of Information Technology.[4]

The broadening access to higher education has been paralleled by vast improvements in the quality of education available in BRIC countries and the UAE. It's no secret that the quality of BRIC and UAE university graduates has been uneven, to say the least, with many degree holders unprepared to succeed in a competitive multinational environment. Each year, for instance, India produces as many young engineers as the United States, and Russia graduates ten times as many finance and accounting professionals as Germany; yet the McKinsey Global Institute estimates that a mere 25 percent of professionals in India and 20 percent in Russia are top-quality, "ready" talent; similarly, in China it is estimated that fewer than one in ten university graduates is prepared to succeed in a multinational environment.[5] Until very recently, the smartest students in developing economies sought entry to the most prestigious universities in the United States and Western Europe.

Today, though, emerging markets can boast about their own ivory towers. Six of China's universities are ranked among the top two hundred in the world, as are two each in India and Russia.[6] The shift in quality is even more pronounced at the graduate level, with the Indian School of Business (ISB) in Hyderabad and the China Europe International Business School (CEIBS) in Beijing recently included in the top twenty-five of the *Financial Times'* Global MBA rankings in 2010, taking their place alongside such storied institutions as Harvard Business School, Wharton, and the London Business School.[7] Notably, 26 percent of the students at ISB and 33 percent at CEIBS are women, a figure on par with representation at top MBA campuses in the developed world.[8]

Furthermore, many Western-based business schools are partnering with or opening their own campuses in emerging markets. France-based INSEAD, one of the world's top-ranked business schools, has offered full-time MBA degrees at its Singapore branch since 2000; it opened an executive education center in Abu Dhabi in 2007. This is no isolated trend: University of Chicago's Booth School of Business has had an executive MBA program based in Singapore since 2001, and Harvard Business School established a presence in Shanghai in 2010.[9] If the enrollment trends above are any guide, a significant percentage of the students will be women.

The good news for global companies: educated women in emerging markets are already important sources of skills and expertise. The rising demand for advanced education, the corresponding opportunities now available in their home countries, and the increasing number of women taking advantage of these opportunities will indelibly change the face of talent in the years ahead.

ASPIRATION AND AMBITION

"When I was growing up, I never thought I would be someone," confides Aisha al-Suwaidi. Both of her parents were uneducated: her father was a fisherman in Sharjah, her mother had gone to elementary school for only a few grades. As a result, after the UAE became independent in 1971, "both my parents pushed all of their children to get an education."

Al-Suwaidi's timing couldn't have been more fortuitous. The local economy was booming, foreign universities were establishing UAE satellites, and al-Suwaidi was in the thick of it, earning first a business degree and then switching her focus to career counseling.

Now the director general for Dubai Women Establishment, al-Suwaidi is passionate about improving opportunities for women in the UAE. "Political advocacy is one of the most important things I work on. I'm talking about being able to deliver something unique, which will impact a lot of people, for which you'll be remembered for generations."

Highly educated women the world over are ambitious, but the widespread nature of ambition and aspiration among women in the BRIC countries and the UAE is extraordinary (see figure 1-2). The majority of women surveyed consider themselves "very ambitious," compared with only 36 percent of their American counterparts. Aspiration levels are equally impressive (see figure 1-3).

Armed with their freshly minted diplomas, women in emerging markets are hungry to prove themselves, even more so than their male classmates. One HR leader for a global management consultancy that

FIGURE 1-2

Percentage of women with high level of ambition

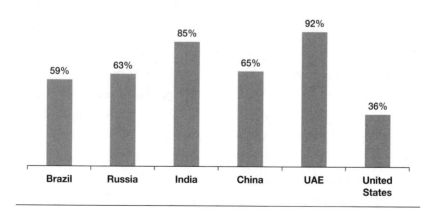

FIGURE 1-3

Women who aspire to a top job

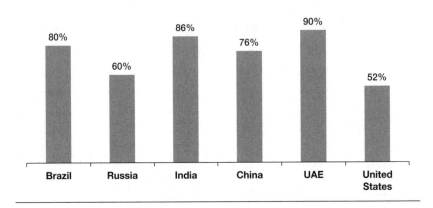

recently reentered the Chinese market says, "For the majority of college grads, career is a very important thing, but we often find female candidates to be as competitive, if not more so, than their male counterparts." So many highly qualified women are applying for jobs, in fact, that her boss jokingly remarked, "Finally, here's one place where we don't have to worry about equal opportunity."

These impressive levels of aspiration are no accident. The fast-evolving nature of the emerging market economies amplifies a sense of possibility and optimism. You only have to open your eyes and look around to see the proof that dreams can become concrete reality, says Alpna Khera, a senior commercial leader running a $30MM P&L at GE's transportation division in India. "People have created fortunes in this market, and it is encouraging to know that one can create opportunities for oneself and achieve great things," she says. Her own career trajectory is defined by an unambiguous desire for continued advancement within leadership ranks. Khera was the first woman in India to work in a gas-based power plant—at a time when there was no separate women's washroom—and aspires to eventually be the head of GE Energy in India.

Many of the women we spoke to were keenly aware of their role and participation at a significant point in the history of their countries, in essence being part of a huge national development project. ... adrenaline rush of being front and center in a tremendous transition fuels ambition in a big way. "In Europe, you would work on refining a company's business strategy. Here, you have the opportunity to be involved in high-impact projects that are reshaping countries and the region as a whole," explains Leila Hoteit, an Abu Dhabi-based principal at Booz & Company working with public sector entities.

Part of what propels the extraordinary ambition of women in emerging markets is a seismic shift in their family roles and social status. The regions' rapid economic growth has transformed gender roles in a way that the West tends to underestimate, not only by encouraging female participation in the workforce but also by enabling women to move into management positions in impressive numbers. They can aspire to high-flying careers because of another startling change on the home front: on average, women in BRIC countries have fewer than three children, and in China and Russia fewer than two—a huge decline from past generations.[10] (We discuss the details of this metamorphosis in the chapters focusing on specific countries.)

As women move into management positions, a startling number are earning salaries equal to or greater than their spouses. In Brazil, China, Russia, and the UAE, we found that nearly 20 percent or more of women working full time outearn their spouses. The power of the purse, even more than educational opportunities and career aspirations, is helping women break through the social traditions that held back many in their mothers' generation. After all, a mother-in-law is less likely to expect her son's wife to wait on her hand and foot when she's bringing home a big share of the family income.

With living costs escalating in emerging markets, especially in urban areas, women's contribution to household expenses is not only appreciated but also indispensable. Six of the thirty most expensive cities in the world are in Russia, China, and Brazil.[11] "Women have to work because the cost of living in Moscow and St. Petersburg is very expensive," says Veronika Bienert, a senior executive at Siemens Russia.

Similarly, a Beijing-based HR manager notes, "In China today, there is no way that only the husband can work and the wife stay home, because you need the income on both sides."

With financial need trumping cultural pressure, the majority of women in our sample do not experience social pressure to quit work after they marry or even upon the birth of their first child, with the exception of India, where traditional social norms adhere far more closely than elsewhere. Yet even there, change is imminent. One Indian executive explained that her entire family supported the choices she has made as a working mother: "My husband says, 'There's no way you are leaving your job. You're too driven, you're well qualified, and you have ambition.' My mother wanted to study and couldn't, so she pushed me to achieve things she was not able to. I would never consider leaving my job" for fear of disappointing her.

AN ENVIABLE WORK ETHIC

"I'm definitely happy being with GE," says Heather Wang, vice president of human resources of GE Global Growth & Operations, even though her job requires a crushing travel schedule. In one recent month, she circumnavigated the globe, spending two days at GE headquarters in Connecticut, flying back to her office in Brussels, visiting France, Germany, and London, and then heading off to Poland, Dubai, and China, where her husband and young daughter live. Despite the constant jet lag, she wouldn't have it any other way. "I feel inspired by helping people become successful. That's more important to me than my personal life."

The rich reservoir of ambition among educated women in the BRIC countries and the UAE represents a huge opportunity for employers, particularly because it is reinforced by an extraordinary degree of commitment and loyalty that these women bring to work.

Top talent in emerging markets has a reputation for being notoriously mercurial and hard to hold on to. A Towers Perrin survey found a mere 21 percent of global workers to be engaged in their work.[12] Turnover rates are high, with one-fifth of companies in developing countries reporting that they have to replace half their staff annually.[13] In Russia, recent university graduates with fluency in a couple of languages and a few years' experience at a multinational corporation "are constantly being pitched by headhunters, so people jump every few months for a minor raise in salary," reports Alexandra Shaforost, a management consultant advising foreign companies in Russia. India's business process outsourcing industry is particularly infamous for its churn. Before the financial crisis, software engineers employed by Wipro, Infosys, Tata Consultancy Services, and other Bangalore outsourcers were switching jobs as often as three times a year to boost their pay and scale up the management ladder, according to a recent article in *Bloomberg Businessweek*.[14] Although turnover rates froze during the recession, robust first-quarter 2010 results sent the industry's revolving door spinning furiously, with Wipro losing 17 percent of its employees, Infosys 19 percent, and HCL Technologies 22 percent in the January–March period.[15]

By contrast, our data on highly qualified women in the BRIC countries and the UAE counters the image of capricious job-hoppers, always on the lookout for a higher salary and willing to exploit the paucity of qualified talent to get it. Our analysis—which delves into actual intentions and career goals—reveals a surprisingly strong sense of commitment among women toward their employers. Nearly 90 percent express loyalty to their current employer, with 49 percent declaring a desire to continue working at their current company for three years or longer.

Furthermore, more than 80 percent of our respondents in Brazil, Russia, India, and the UAE report loving their work, and a similarly high percentage in Russia, India, and the UAE are "willing to go the extra mile" for their companies. Well-qualified BRIC and UAE women express a deep connection with and passion for their jobs, citing intellectual stimulation, a sense of personal growth, and the quality of colleagues as key motivators. A female professional services employee in China says, "My company has provided me with the platform to do things I really want to do," a message echoed by a senior manager at a multinational corporation in Brazil, who considers her company to be "like a university—you can learn so much here."

These factors mirror, in part, our earlier findings about what motivates top performers in the United States. As described in *Top Talent: Keeping Performance Up When Business Is Down*, a large majority of both men and women point to the challenge and stimulation of the work.[16] Compensation, recognition, status, "meaning and purpose," and flex options were also important drivers. Interestingly, money, though important, wasn't a dominating factor. Less than half (40 percent) of the respondents in our U.S. survey rated high levels of compensation as the main reason they loved their jobs.

Among female top talent in the United States, monetary rewards were trumped by four other factors. In focus groups, high-performing women repeatedly talked about the importance of respect and recognition—from bosses and companies—and the satisfaction they derived from working with a group of great colleagues.

Among women in emerging markets, compensation and job security are major motivators—no surprise in economies that have been marked by political, economic, and social volatility. But these women, too, like to feel good about their employers and to reaffirm that their efforts at work are part of a greater purpose, whether it's lifting up their country or finding opportunities that help their compatriots move forward. Booz's Leila Hoteit recalls, "One of my first projects was working on a huge cultural district being built here, with a multibillion-dollar budget and input from the Guggenheim and Louvre museums. One of the tasks we undertook on the project was to benchmark world-class museums and cities, such as Bilbao, that had been transformed by such cultural projects. So we went around the world benchmarking museums. The sense of satisfaction you get is different here."

THE LESSON FOR GLOBAL COMPANIES

The rich reservoir of loyalty and commitment among educated women in the BRIC countries and the UAE, however, cannot be taken for granted. Rather, the data need to be considered within the context of their high levels of ambition and aspiration. To fully realize the enormous potential of female talent in these countries, employers need to go the extra mile.

What can organizations do to keep these women stimulated, motivated, and committed? "I'm interested in having a very challenging position. That's something I'm always looking for," says Natasha, a senior executive in Russia. (Some names and affiliations have been changed. When only first names are used, they are pseudonyms.) Parvati, an Indian management consultant for an international company, is unambiguous about what she seeks from her work and employer: "I want the ability to solve interesting problems that are constantly different in scope and scale, problems that don't have a clearcut solution, so you have the intellectual freedom to figure things out." In short, employers must provide women with access to a meaningful range of opportunities to grow, develop, and advance.

The value proposition offered by educated women in emerging markets to employers is, in a word, compelling. In return for intellectually challenging work, good colleagues, respect and recognition, and competitive compensation—the mainstays highly qualified Western women want to underpin their careers—ambitious BRIC and UAE women respond with uncommon levels of hard work, loyalty, and commitment.

But there's a significant caveat intrinsic to this optimistic portrayal of women in emerging markets: as noted earlier, BRIC and UAE women are neither clones of their Western counterparts nor Western wannabes. To fully realize the potential of this rich reservoir of female talent, multinational employers must provide ways to break down barriers raised by culture and tradition.

Pitfalls and Trip Wires

When Subha Barry was the head of global diversity for Merrill Lynch, she noticed a curious phenomenon among career women in India. "You'd have women with the highest of qualifications, the most incredible talents, and yet, while in appearance and intellect and abilities at work they can hold their own with the best of Western women, you would find them doing surprising things, like saying, 'I had a baby. I need to stop working and go home.'" Barry adds, I'm not talking one or two. I'm talking droves."

Child care itself wasn't the primary issue. Although one of the most common career killers for women in the United States and Western Europe, it is a less serious problem for their counterparts in emerging markets. Instead, says Barry, who is herself Indian, it was being used as an excuse that masked the symptoms of a much more pernicious issue: family and social pressures pile on to women when they marry and ratchet up after they have children, and become almost crushing as their parents and in-laws age.

These family-rooted "pulls," together with cultural and social "pushes," can sabotage a woman's career aspirations, derailing her ambition and causing her to languish in a dead-end job or leave the workforce entirely. Subtle but intense, these pressures are so deeply and broadly woven into each culture's everyday fabric as to be almost invisible to an outsider. Yet unless multinational corporations understand these forces, they will never recognize the real reasons behind a high-performing woman's decision to drop out—or be able to craft solutions to keep her.

THE FORCE OF FAMILY

Anjali Hazarika, head of talent management and administration for Oil India, tells a common story: "I took a sabbatical for two years when I was earning my doctorate and having a baby. But after the two years were over, I had to go [back to work] and leave my son behind. We didn't have flextime. That's when my mother came to stay with me. I had gone through the guilt feelings most women have when they leave their young at home, completely dependent on domestic help. I was fortunate to have my mother, who said, 'I'm there for you. You go out and do what you want to do.' Because of her, I could go out and work." Hazarika continues, "And when my time came, I reciprocated." Hazarika's mother lived with her daughter's family for the last ten years of her life. Hazarika says, "I was happy I could do a little of what she did for me. Parent care—it's a part of Indian culture."

Working mothers in BRIC and the UAE are able to think big and aim high because they have multiple shoulders to lean on. Between grandparents, extended family, inexpensive and readily available domestic help, and an increasingly wide range of day care options, professional women in emerging markets are typically able to construct a support system without much difficulty.

Grandparents play a vital role in enabling working mothers to sustain a career, being involved in their grandchildren's care to a much greater extent than most grandparents in the United States and Western Europe. Many come from cultures where it was common to have children early; now that their children are having children of their own, they are still relatively young and in good health. Additionally, in many of these countries, the official retirement age remains lower than in the developed world, and expectations of retired life are very different. "My parents, in the Chinese tradition, are very willing to help," said a Chinese management consultant. "They don't want to relax and travel like parents in the Western world." Our research supports this, showing that more than 40 percent of women professionals working full time in Brazil and Russia—and a whopping 82 percent in China and 69 percent in India—have child care help from their parents or in-laws.

There are also fewer grandchildren to care for. Contrary to the prevalent view that all women in emerging markets have children, and lots of them, our data revealed that a significant proportion of educated women in emerging economies *do not* have children. Access to education and birth control—the same benefits that have lowered birthrates in the developed world—enables women in emerging markets to delay or decline motherhood. Among college-educated women aged twenty-one to sixty-four in our survey, more than half in Brazil, Russia, and India and almost half in the UAE did *not* have children.

Our earlier research in the United States showed maternal guilt to be a critical pull factor for women in high-pressure, demanding jobs, one that could override the gratification of and commitment to such work. Career women in emerging markets are no less immune to the maternal guilt suffered by their sisters in developed countries, despite the access to affordable child care and the propinquity of grandparents willing and able to take an active hand in their grandchildren's upbringing (see figure 2-1).

Patricia de Paula Braga's job managing product distribution for Latin America for Pfizer is so consuming that she can spend only two hours each day with her eight-year-old son during the week. "He asks me to stop working all the time," she says. "It makes me feel concerned. I really like my job; I know that he is very proud of my career and I also understand that my professional success will be reflected in his

FIGURE 2-1

Percentage of women working full-time who express maternal guilt

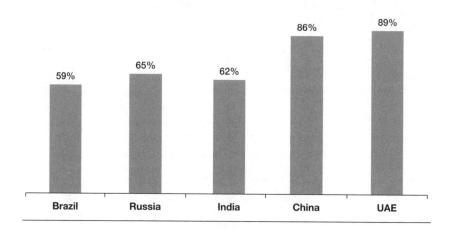

future—giving him the chance to study in a good school and having access to opportunities that would not be possible without my contribution to the domestic budget—but some days I wake up and think it would be great if I didn't have to go to work and if I could dedicate all my time to spend with my son."

The seeds of maternal guilt find fertile ground in traditional cultural mores in BRIC and the UAE. The majority of survey respondents say that it is socially acceptable for women with small children to pursue a career, but traditional voices in their family can be quick to criticize their choices. Many of the professional women we interviewed recall small sharp digs from family members. A principal with an international advisory firm recalls, "My mother-in-law visited when our daughter was one year old and said, 'I can't believe you're feeding her from boxes you bought in the supermarket rather than freshly cooked food. I guess that's the price of being a career woman.' That's the sort of comment you have to swallow." Her daughter turned three soon after she was made a principal. "I know my in-laws are proud that I got promoted, but there's always the feeling that if anything goes wrong with my daughter, it's because of me."

Such traditional views are persistent, even if in muted form. About one in five of the women we surveyed reported feeling pressured "to drop out" of the workforce when they married. The exceptions are Brazil—at 16 percent, it was the lowest percentage in the group—and India, which topped the charts at 51 percent of women expected to give up their career prospects after marriage. The pressure further ratcheted up after the birth of their first child, nearly doubling in some cases.

"My friends and I grew up in an era when you studied, did postgrad, worked for a year or two, and then got married," says Jayashri Ramamurti, an Indian woman now in her mid-thirties. Of the twenty women who graduated with her from a prestigious two-year graduate program in management, Ramamurti calculates that only four are working, most of them part-time. "They are intelligent women, but they are pretty much at home."

Ramamurti herself left her fast-paced HR job in a telecommunications company after the birth of her second child in 2001. Despite a robust support network—her father lived nearly full-time with her family, and she also had a nanny and a live-in maid—something wasn't working. "I wasn't happy with the quality of time I was spending with my children," especially her infant son, she says. In 2001 she quit, intending to take a couple of years off; instead, she stepped out of the workforce for more than five years. Ramamurti is now head of HR for Google India's engineering division and thrilled with her job, but she can't help taking an occasional backward glance: "Had I not had that break, would I have achieved a lot more?"

So strong is cultural pressure that some of the women expressed the realization that their maternal guilt was, to some extent, self-inflicted, with little or no bearing on the actual well-being or happiness of their children. "I feel guilty at times, but no one else makes me feel guilty," confessed an Indian working mother of two school-aged children. "My kids are actually proud of me."

When we probed deeper, we discovered a sophisticated awareness of the trade-offs of the costs of a high-powered career and an appreciation of its benefits. As one working mother in Brazil explained, "Sometimes I feel guilty, but I change my mind rapidly because without my job, I could not support education, health care, our house, vacations, et cetera."

Still, even without guilt and with multiple shoulders to lean on, it's not easy juggling career and children. Even as they are fulfilling the responsibilities of their demanding jobs, professional women still shoulder the lion's share of child care duties in Russia, the UAE, and, especially, Brazil, where, according to our research, the majority take on at least 75 percent of the load. "In [Brazil], women are the ones who concern themselves with the kids," notes Samara Braga, a financial markets leader for Ernst & Young in Brazil. "That's the way we're brought up—and that isn't changing."

The same is true in India. "No matter what you do, family—taking care of children or elderly relatives—is a woman's primary responsibility," says Anjali Hazarika. "She doesn't get exempted from family responsibilities just because she is a full-time working career person. There is an understanding with the family—sometimes explicit, sometimes unarticulated—that if you want to go outside the home to work, you will not neglect your family. Be ready for 24/7 and not only 9 to 5 five days a week. This can place additional demands on her, and that can lead to stress."

The close-knit nature of extended families in the BRIC countries and the UAE envelops its members in a circle of care. As daughters mature, its warm embrace provides support, and a source of strength. In interview after interview, high-achieving women affirmed that they couldn't have reached their level of professional success had it not been for their mother or father or an aunt or uncle pointing the way, encouraging their development and boosting them over the rough patches. In return, however, daughters are expected to shoulder their own share of family obligations, and that duty can undermine a career in surprising ways.

ELDER CARE: A TICKING TIME BOMB

When their mother fell seriously ill, Vasanti, an executive in the financial sector, and her sister, an equally highly qualified professional, were both working in the United States. "My sister quit her job and moved back to India with her family because one of us had to be there," says Vasanti. "Before that, we took turns going back and forth because my parents refused to move to the U.S. to live with either my sister or me. And the mere mention of the words 'nursing home' threw things into chaos. It was like we were the meanest daughters on the planet" for even thinking it. Like her sister, Vasanti also left her job to help tend to her mother. When talking about trying to balance elder care duties with a demanding career, she says, "It's a huge struggle."

The pull that *does* loom large in the lives of many women in emerging markets is elder care. Although many BRIC and UAE women in our survey did not have children, the vast majority—81 percent—care for their parents or aging relatives. Their responsibilities consume anywhere from eight hours a week in the UAE to a draining fourteen hours a week—that's two hours *every day*—in India. In the United States, in contrast, professional women dedicate about five hours a week to elder care.[1] Our study found overall consensus among adult children in BRIC and UAE that they would change their lives to take care of their parents and that, in fact, the obligation toward parents loomed even more important than that toward one's children. As Leila Hoteit explains, "It's seen that parents take care of you all their adult life, so when it's your time to pay back, you do it wholeheartedly."

Daughterly guilt is pervasive among professional women throughout emerging economies. It's especially strong in India, China, and the UAE, where despite massive demographic shifts and economic development, the traditional concept of filial piety remains powerful. In India and China, in fact, daughterly guilt exceeds maternal guilt among our survey participants (see figure 2-2).

FIGURE 2-2

Percentage of women who express daughterly guilt

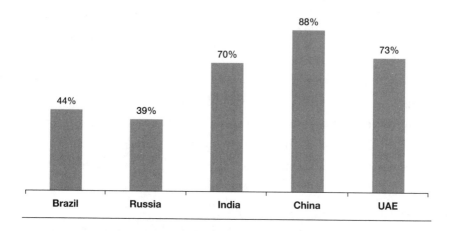

Daughterly guilt, like maternal guilt, finds fertile ground in the clash between tradition and modernity. May al-Dabbagh describes the family constellation in the UAE and the Gulf region: "In the past, people lived in extended families in a *Freej*—like a compound. Individuals in those families played different roles, so an aunt could take care of a young child, even if it wasn't her own daughter or son, and a cousin could take care of an elderly person. In terms of shared resources, this was very possible." Similar support networks, held together by duty and propinquity, were typical throughout the BRICs, too. Today, though, because of urbanization and the need to relocate for job opportunities, families are scattering to different cities and even different countries. The falling birthrate among educated women has left their adult children, now modern career women, with few siblings to share the responsibility. Although China's "one child" policy, launched in 1979, may give a grandchild four grandparents, it burdens the lone adult daughter with the care of her own parents and those of her in-laws. The circle of care has shrunk significantly throughout emerging economies, often leaving one woman standing alone in the spotlight.

"My brother has a family, and I'm responsible for our parents. I have always taken care of my parents," says Karine Kocharyan, a Russian division controller for a multinational engineering corporation. "My responsibility is every day, every evening. I'm responsible, 100 percent, and I value this connection. That's our way of life."

Kocharyan's mother lives with her. Again, this is typical of many women in emerging markets: our data reveal that more than half of career women in China and India have an elderly parent or in-law living with them. In the UAE and Brazil, the figure is nearly one in three, and in Russia, it's one of four. Our survey respondents accompany the elders to medical appointments, cook meals for them, and arrange transportation.

The alternatives that exist for child care, such as a nanny or day care, are rarely available for elder care. There are some glimmers of change; old age homes for the affluent are beginning to crop up in India and China.[2] Still, most of the time, options for delegating or outsourcing elder care don't exist, are socially unacceptable, or both. Although more than half of our respondents in Brazil, India, and China would consider using hired help for their parents or in-laws, placing them in a full-time care facility—the choice of more than half of adult children in the United States—is anathema in emerging markets.

When daughters aren't physically providing for their parents and in-laws, they're supporting them financially. More than half of women in China, India, Russia, and the UAE give monetary assistance; in Brazil, the figure is 33 percent. Financial aid from adult children is vital in countries where government benefits for the elderly are weak or non-existent. In Russia, for example, pensions average a paltry 2,000–4,000 rubles (less than $100) a month—less than 10 percent of the per capita income in 2009.[3] India entirely lacks a social security system that ensures income for the elderly, so informal family support is often their primary recourse. Our data show that the amount of money adult daughters contribute is significant: 18–23 percent of their annual income.

For women in emerging markets, elder care, far more than child care, has a significant potential to limit their professional ambitions or stall a high-flying career. Consider the question of mobility. "If a great job opportunity comes up that involves moving to a different city, even if the husband and wife agree from a career point of view, the question is what happens to the parents," notes Murali Kuppuswamy, senior human resources manager, drilling and production, GE Oil & Gas. "Child care is much easier. You can hire nannies."

Furthermore, women tend to off-ramp for child care at the time when their career trajectory has just taken off and has time to recover. In contrast, elder care responsibilities often hit at the peak of their profession, striking a blow to their career just as they are reaching the top.

The elder care burden on society in general and women in particular is a ticking time bomb. Although elders today represent a net benefit to the career woman in BRIC and the UAE, it is clear from the demographic projections that the situation is poised to shift dramatically in the near future. As a result of better health care and increased life expectancies, demographic projections for BRIC and the UAE point to a huge leap in the percentage of the population over sixty. Even in India's relatively youthful population, individuals over sixty are expected to constitute 20 percent of the population by 2050.[4] China's demographic outlook is even more dire: thanks to the double whammy of the one-child policy and rising longevity, by 2035 there will be two Chinese elders for every child, a social train wreck that no one knows how to prevent.[5]

Many high-achieving women in our study acknowledge these concerns, citing their own situations with parents and in-laws who are still healthy and active but whose care will become a top consideration in the near future. Few look forward to negotiating the balance between their careers and their elder care obligations. A female accounting professional in Beijing sums it up by saying, "It is a very heavy role."

EXTREME JOBS

It's 4:30 in the afternoon, and Claudia still has three teleconferences to go before she can head home for the day. As a Dubai-based executive for a multinational company whose headquarters are located nine time zones away, Claudia doesn't just *feel* that she works a 24/7 schedule—she is running a marathon that never ends.

She gets to the office at 6:45 in the morning and usually puts in a twelve-hour day at her desk. "I wish I could leave earlier, but New York [where the home office is] is starting their day when it's almost evening for us. All the telecons start in the evening here. Sometimes I get meeting invitations for 11 p.m."

Claudia would like to exercise after work, but instead she usually rushes home—she counts herself lucky to have only a thirty-minute commute—to spend time with her two children, having dinner with them, helping with their homework and putting them to bed. "Then I do a second round of e-mail between 9 and 11." During rush periods, she stays up even later.

Weekends don't offer much of a break. The Middle East takes its weekend on Friday and Saturday, so when Claudia fields the end-of-the-week crunch calls from New York, "it kills the weekend."

In our 2007 study, *Seduction and Risk: The Emergence of Extreme Jobs*, we identified a new challenge for top talent.[6] "Extreme jobs," as we dubbed this development, are characterized by extended workweeks, an always-on culture at work, and intense performance pressure. Our latest data adds to this scenario in the case of emerging markets.

In BRIC and the UAE, long workweeks are not limited to high-wage earners but are routine among college-educated employees. And although extreme jobs are the norm among highly qualified and ambitious women worldwide, the average workweek for employees of multinational corporations in developing economies is especially onerous. In Russia and China, the average workweek for multinational employees is well over sixty hours; in India and the UAE, it is more than fifty hours. "I think about seventy hours a week isn't uncommon," reports one Hong Kong-based manager for a consulting company.

No particular sector or industry stands out in our data as more extreme than others, and neither seasoned executives nor junior professionals are immune to these demands. "In India, people look at you if you leave early," observed a young finance professional. "It was only because people knew I was going to school that it was okay for me to leave at 5:30. You never do that unless it's only once a week or for a doctor's appointment."

Furthermore, the demands of work have intensified over the past few years: one-quarter or more of the women in our sample report working some eight to eighteen hours more per week than three years ago, a staggering one to two extra workdays.

The same factors identified in our original study—the global span of operations, modern communication technology, compensation structures, and leaner and meaner organizations that are increasingly demanding of an employee's time—are also driving the extended hours in emerging markets. But the fact that the sun never sets on a multinational company's operations has an inordinate impact on its offices in far-flung geographies. Professional women in BRIC and the UAE routinely suffer from teleconference schedules that favor U.S. and European time zones. We heard numerous examples of conference calls being scheduled during the middle of their night, on local public holidays, or on weekends (especially if weekends are taken on different days).

One underlying cause of resentment was a sense from our focus group participants that their bosses displayed greater sensitivity about after-hours calls to time zones in North America and Europe and that their schedules habitually got short shrift. "Thursday evenings (the start of the weekend here) are often destroyed by conference calls, as are Fridays," one UAE-based woman said. "They say, 'Sorry, sorry, but it's really important.' It often is, but essentially they make a joke out of it. There is no respect for boundaries."

The extended workdays and capriciously scheduled conference calls that come with a multinational job are reasons that public sector jobs look so attractive, with more than 80 percent of BRIC and UAE respondents applauding their benefits. The UAE labor laws, for example, restrict local companies to a maximum eight-hour day; employees in the public sector have an even shorter schedule, typically from 7:30 a.m. to 2:30 p.m.[7] That's half the amount of time that Claudia routinely puts in.

Exacerbating the pressures of the onerous day-to-day schedule are the protracted commutes endured by many of women in our research. Traffic jams are the bane of urban life in the cities where many of the women of our study live. IBM's 2010 *Global Commuter Pain Survey* ranked cities 1 to 100 for their commutes.[8] Based on factors such as traffic, road rage, and gridlock's effect on drivers' ability to get to work, São Paulo ranked 75, New Delhi 81, Moscow 84, and Beijing topped the charts at 99. More than 40 percent of the Moscow respondents have been stuck in traffic for at least three hours, and nearly 70 percent of Beijing commuters have experienced traffic so bad that they turned around and went home. Sizable percentages of commuters in the worst-affected cities said they would choose to work more if their commute time could be reduced.

Although many women bemoan the hours wasted in these extreme commutes, others note the toll on their ability to work. In the IBM survey, 95 percent of drivers in Beijing say the traffic has negatively affected their health. "It's just time-consuming and stressful ... *awful* roads and awful traffic," said an IT manager in India, adding, "I am so much more productive on work-from-home days. I work better and longer."

This was a common refrain, and one employers should note: avoiding traffic by working from a satellite or home office could enhance productivity and improve morale. Flexible work arrangements and work-from-home options are still a nascent idea in emerging markets. In some countries, such as Brazil, laptop computers are expensive and even when employers supply them, crime is so prevalent (as we discuss later in this chapter) that walking down the street with a laptop case is an invitation to be mugged. More significant, though, is the huge premium placed on face time in BRIC and the UAE. Women who are already dogged by the workplace biases described later simply can't afford to give their critics any more ammunition by not being at their desks when everyone else is.

BIAS AND STEREOTYPES

Since becoming the HR director for the Brazilian operations of a multinational pharmaceuticals firm, Andrea has become accustomed to feeling that she's always on trial.

> My male colleagues test me a lot. They ask questions or try to test your knowledge or how self-confident you are on the issue under discussion. It's different from the way they interact with their male peers. They try to go deeper and deeper into the details. I think it's not just because I'm the first woman to hold this job but a combination of being a woman and being younger than they are. There's a sense of "Let me test this little girl to see if she really deserves to be in this place."

> What I've learned from this is that I always have to be 150 percent prepared. Before having an interaction with them, I try to think about all of the questions and all of the resistance that might come up during the conversation. It's like I have to prove myself twice as much as if I were a man.

The subtle forms of discrimination faced by women in the workplace have been the topic of much scrutiny, particularly in the United States, and courses on "microtriggers" or "microinequities" are the cornerstone of cutting-edge corporate diversity curricula. On top of the unconscious biases that no doubt exist in workplaces the world over, professional women in the BRIC countries and the UAE face overt and explicit prejudice. In India and China, more than one-third of our respondents—both women *and* men—believe women are treated unfairly in the workplace owing to their gender. In India, the number is a whopping 45 percent for both sexes.

More than half of educated women in India, nearly half of their counterparts in China, and 40 percent of Brazilian women have encountered bias severe enough to make them consider scaling back their career goals or quitting altogether. Russia is the exception, in part owing to a Communist legacy that integrated women into the workplace better than elsewhere in emerging markets (see figure 2-3).

FIGURE 2-3

Percentage of women who say bias is strong enough to push them out of the workplace

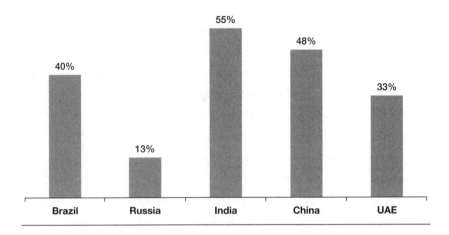

Workplace biases in emerging markets appear in a range of "flavors" that vary by cultural context. In China, for example, business discussions and decisions are often negotiated in informal settings—over drinks after work, during cigarette breaks in the course of the day, or at extra-curricular sports events—settings that are difficult for women to participate in as equals. An accounting professional based in Hong Kong laments, "It's hard for women to develop clients in China, because a lot of business involves drinking after hours," something working mothers typically avoid in order to cherish their scant hours of family time.

Similarly, vodka is a time-honored business lubricant in Russia, a key ingredient in nurturing the trusted partnerships that were the only way to do business under Communism. Even in today's open market, business relationships in traditionally male-dominated industries like manufacturing, engineering, and mining are still built in the *banya*, or sauna, and sealed with vigorous drinking. "That's where the decisions are made, in that close male community," says Galina, an executive whose multinational employer operates in those fields. She notes, "It's just not appropriate for a woman to go into the sauna with ten men."

In India and the Middle East, where traditional gender boundaries remain entrenched, women also need to exercise caution to maintain their reputations. Participating in activities such as smoking or social- izing in predominantly male environments, especially in the evening, is frowned upon. "I don't stay beyond 8:30 p.m. when the men go out," says one female executive in India.

Beyond general gender bias rooted in cultural and social practices, our survey results also reveal specific workplace biases confronted by BRIC and UAE women. More than 40 percent of our participants have faced bias associated with executive presence and communication style. This can take a number of forms, from demeaning or personal comments from male colleagues and clients about their appearance to assumptions about women's ability to be effective in a business setting (see figure 2-4).

Women also contend with conflicting social and professional expectations of proper behavior. In India and China, for example, women are often expected to be submissive and reticent, attributes that penal- ize high-performing women at work. Many women in our research felt crippled by this cultural bind, struggling to achieve self-confidence and the ability to demonstrate authority in the face of societal opprobrium. "As a woman brought up in India, you have to be likeable, you have to be liked. You have to be soft, you have to be polite, you have to listen to

FIGURE 2-4

Most commonly experienced biases in the workplace

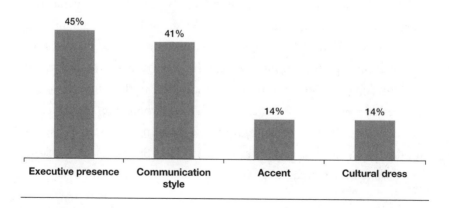

other people, you have to hold back a little," observed Padma, an Indian finance professional. "And none of this works in the corporate world." Others in her focus group agreed, with one participant noting, "We may be a square peg, but we will have to fit into that round hole."

This sense of not fitting in is pervasive among ambitious BRIC and UAE women. It's also pernicious. Several women in a focus group of Chinese managers felt a lack of confidence in their ability to be as convincing or have as much impact as their male colleagues.

Anjali Hazarika speaks for the majority of educated, ambitious BRIC and UAE women in our study when she describes her own experience in the push-me-pull-you quest to find a happy medium: "If I acted out of the stereotype, I was not a good woman, and if I colluded with the stereotype, I became invisible." Between the constant challenging and critiquing, whether subtle or explicit, perceived or self-inflicted, women are trapped in a no-win situation.

Workplace biases across the BRIC countries and the UAE escalate with motherhood. Working mothers find their commitment and potential under constant scrutiny. In India, women told us of returning from maternity leave to less-challenging projects or roles, or being given a lower performance rating. A Brazilian woman recounted the case of a colleague who was fired upon returning from maternity leave when she was overheard mentioning that she planned to have another child. In the UAE, female candidates in job interviews may be asked questions that would be considered illegal in developed countries: are you single or married? Are you planning to have children? "I've heard some real horror stories about women who were asked to take a pregnancy test when they were applying for a job, and if they were pregnant, they would only get a temporary contract," reports a woman in Dubai.

TRAVEL BARRIERS

Rana is a rising star in the fixed-income division of a multinational bank with offices located in the UAE. Her company regularly offers opportunities for professional development, but Rana had to decline an invitation to a recent training session in New York, because a single woman from the UAE can't board a plane or stay in a hotel unless a male relative is willing to tag along as her chaperone. Adding insult to injury, no video hookup was provided to allow Rana to participate from her home office.

There's an almost universal assumption that female professionals in emerging markets don't want to travel and are willing to curtail their prospects of advancement in order to stay home. However, more than 60 percent of the women in our sample express strong interest in an international assignment. Furthermore, when we asked married women whether their spouse would be willing to relocate, a majority said their spouses are open to such a move.

Although the BRIC and UAE women in our study are delighted that the economies they live and work in are becoming increasingly important to multinational organizations, they are keenly aware that professional advancement depends on gaining international experience. In China and India, in fact, nearly 80 percent of the women in our sample believe that international assignments are critical to their career progression, and there was no discernible difference in their preference for either short-term or long-term assignments.

However, the actual ability to land such assignments can be difficult for even the most highly credentialed women in emerging markets. Nationals of many developing countries are unable to travel outside their home countries without visas, especially to Europe or the United States, where post-9/11 visa applications require submitting reams of employment and personal documentation, paying hefty application fees, extended wait periods, and, even when the application is successful, limiting travel to specific durations. Sixty-two percent of respondents in India, 66 percent in China, and 54 percent in the UAE report difficulty in obtaining visas for international travel.

"We don't have the luxury of Western Europeans or Americans, who can get on a flight and go somewhere on short notice," explains an Indian national working for a multinational consulting firm. For a recent two-day trip to Germany to see a client, she was required to present copies of her round-trip airline ticket, proof of hotel confirmation for her entire stay, personal bank statements for the past three months, a letter from her employer stating the reason for the trip, a letter of invitation from the client, and proof that her travel and accident insurance covered medical evacuation. (For a previous trip to the U.K., she had to be fingerprinted.) She also had to appear for a personal interview and pay a fee. In addition to being time-consuming, the experience was "extremely demeaning," she says.

The issue of mobility becomes even more problematic when family is involved. "Mobility is a top obstacle for me, because I don't want to move to a city where my family can't relocate," said one ambitious Chinese professional. A Russian HR manager at an investment bank concurred. "It's important for me to get international experience if I aspire to a senior management role. But my priorities have changed since I have a small child." Even though her mother shares child care responsibilities, the manager acknowledged, "I am not so mobile now and really can't aspire to a senior management role at this point."

Although the majority of women claim that their spouse would support an international assignment, the reality is that it's often difficult for a "trailing spouse" to find a comparable position. Yet leaving a spouse behind is risky. As every participant in a long-distance marriage knows, living in a different city from one's spouse is rough on a relationship. The hardships multiply when partners are commuting to a different country.

Soon after Lisandra Ambrozio was married, her previous employer invited her to transfer from Brazil to Florida. "It was a really tough decision," she says. "My husband was not willing to quit his job in Brazil and go to Florida, but it was an amazing professional opportunity for me. We talked a lot about the situation." The upshot was that Ambrozio moved to Florida and her husband stayed in Brazil. "We saw each other every couple of weeks. Either he came to Florida or I went to Brazil. But after one and a half years, when I returned to Brazil and we started to have a normal married life again, it was very difficult. He had structured his own life, he was doing his own MBA course, he had several professional appointments here. The lack of day-to-day contact for a couple is very hard." Six months after returning to Brazil, Ambrozio and her husband divorced. She doesn't regret her decision to relocate but also acknowledges, "Maybe if I hadn't moved to the U.S., the story wouldn't have ended like this."

Within many emerging market countries there is also strong social disapproval of women traveling alone, with nearly three-quarters of Chinese and Indian respondents and more than half of UAE respondents citing difficulties. "It's not so much about prohibitions but how you would be perceived if you're traveling on your own," explains Vishakha Desai, president of the Asia Society. "I think about the people I know: my family wouldn't say, 'You can't travel,' but many of my relatives would have a problem if the wife is traveling because it would imply that she's not doing her duty as a mother and wife and daughter-in-law, she's too forward, and blah-blah-blah." In India, the concept of family is not limited to the nucleus but extends to a wide constellation of relatives and in-laws—"and everyone knows everything," says Desai. "That's a problem."

This disapproval places industries and corporate functions requiring significant travel at a disadvantage in attracting and retaining talented women. The pharmaceutical sector in India, for instance, struggles to attract women into sales roles that involve frequent trips to semiurban and rural locations, where women are uncomfortable venturing alone. The same applies to the industrial and infrastructure sectors. As a result, women gravitate more toward sectors such as finance or media, which are based in urban, modern environs and require minimal travel.

The surprisingly high number of Chinese women in our study reporting social disapproval of solo travel—74 percent—is unexpected, given the egalitarian legacy of Communism. Our analysis suggests that concerns about travel are driven by the pressure on women to stay close to home and fulfill their familial responsibilities, whether as a daughter, wife, or mother. Day-to-day work may be compatible with these values, but travel away from home—and given the vast geographic scale of China, trips can last several days—is considerably more difficult to integrate.

Women, expatriates and locals alike, have worked around these restrictions by concentrating in careers whose responsibilities are, by and large, local, for example, medicine, law, hotel administration, advertising, public relations, marketing, nursing, and education. But conventional career models that demand employee mobility for career advancement and assume that all employees will have the ability to travel freely are a poor fit for the context of emerging markets. BRIC and UAE women are well aware of the professional price they have paid for the limitations on their mobility. "It's much harder to make an impact and get exposure to global leaders from a remote site," explained an Indian focus group participant. "I'm not mobile in terms of working at different locations, and I know that's one of the things that has stopped me from getting promoted."

DAILY DANGERS AND SAFETY CONCERNS

The first time Samara Braga was robbed, she was eight months pregnant and sitting in her car, parked in front of her office building in downtown São Paulo, Brazil. "A guy with a gun broke the window, shouting, 'If you don't give me your watch, I'll kill you and your baby!' It happened right in front of the bank building in broad daylight, with everyone watching."

The second time, she was also in her car, on her way to work, and had stopped for a red light. A man bashed in the window and grabbed her bag. "You never expect this to happen at 11 o'clock on a rainy Monday morning."

The third time, she was attacked as she walked out of the bank building at the end of the day. After she complained to the company president, a system of bodyguards for women was established. "Every one of us who had to leave the office after 7 p.m. had the right to a bodyguard to take you to the bus, train, or parking lot. The president was a clever guy.

He knew the women were the ones working long hours because they were dedicated, so he said, 'I have to make you feel comfortable. I'll give you all bodyguards.' After that, I felt safe."

The combination of workplace pushes covered so far—extreme jobs, bias and stereotyping, and travel limitations—are akin to those we have analyzed for women in the developed world, although they affect BRIC and UAE women in different forms and to a different degree. Our latest research, however, reveals a push factor entirely unique to emerging markets: personal safety.

Safety concerns in connection with work-related travel are a harsh reality that professional women in emerging markets grapple with daily. One-third or more of women feel unsafe while commuting to and from work, a number that rises to more than 50 percent in countries with vast economic disparities such as India and Brazil.

In India, where mass culture remains tradition bound and male dominated, the rising tide of independent-minded and financially self-sufficient women threatens deeply rooted social conventions, with unfortunately predictable repercussions: between 2003 and 2007, rape cases in India rose more than 30 percent, and kidnapping or abduction cases rose more than 50 percent.[9] Most Indian professional women avoid public transportation and its gauntlet of verbal taunting, physical harassment, and other indignities. Many companies, especially IT firms, provide commuter vans to and from their campuses from train stations and other central points. Not surprisingly, telecommuting options, when offered, have a big uptake.

In Russia, hardest hit among the BRIC economies by the global financial downturn, crime is escalating, exacerbated by the fragility of a social safety net already shredded from the dissolution of the Soviet system. "Moscow is a very dangerous city," says Karine Kocharyan. "There are a lot of people in need, and they're ready to do anything. That's part of the everyday environment in such megacities."

São Paulo and Rio de Janeiro, similarly, are notorious for the high incidence of crime, and almost every Brazilian woman in our study has had firsthand experience with these daily dangers. One focus group participant had her cell phone stolen at gunpoint when she stopped her car at a traffic light; another, while traveling in a car with a friend from a wealthy family who was a kidnapping target, was followed and fired at on a major highway. White-collar professionals need to exercise constant vigilance, one woman explained, noting that if you wear a nice watch, use a BlackBerry or cell phone, or carry a laptop, "you're making yourself a target." Another matter-of-factly described the difference between crime in a small city versus a metropolis. "In a small city, they break your window and steal your radio. In São Paulo, they put a gun to your head and say, 'Let's go to the ATM.'"

These safety concerns strongly influence preferences about where to work, what position to take, and what type of career to pursue. And because women are mothers and caregivers, as well as vulnerable to a broader range of crimes, safety considerations factor in their work-life decisions to a far greater degree than do men. "I could make more money and have a more comfortable life in São Paulo," said Carolina, a Brazilian national and midlevel manager at a global financial services company, now based in corporate headquarters in the United States. "I would have a comfortable life and have great professional opportunities, but, frankly, the violence is too much."

THE LESSONS FOR GLOBAL COMPANIES

The overwhelming obstacles educated BRIC and UAE women face at home and at work—let alone *getting* to work—are demoralizing, frustrating, and, ultimately, deeply alienating. Compounded by the fact that promotions are often seen as based on an ability to fit in rather than an ability to produce results, many talented women feel stymied in their climb up the career ladder and even unwelcome in the workplace.

This sense is reinforced by the absence of senior female role models, mentors, and sponsors, as well as a lack of access to leadership training. Time and again, the women in our study mentioned how hungry they

What Do Women Want?
A Grope-Free, Leerless Commute

The millions of women who have poured into the workforce in emerging markets over the past decade have encountered every obstacle that tradition-bound, male-dominated cultures could throw at them, but few are more infuriating and demeaning than what they endure on their daily commute. Taunting, catcalls, pinching, groping, and other forms of harassment are so common and so persistent, our research found, that one-third or more of women in Russia, China, and the United Arab Emirates feel unsafe using public transportation to get to and from work. In India and Brazil, the number skyrockets to more than 50 percent. According to a study conducted by USAID in India, commuting concerns were a primary reason for women to consider quitting their jobs.[10]

As a result, an increasing number of cities in BRIC and the UAE are instituting an innovative alternative: single-sex transportation.

One option receiving a great deal of publicity is women-only cars on subways and commuter trains. "Ladies' Specials"—entire trains reserved exclusively for female passengers—were introduced in 2009 in India's four largest cities (New Delhi, Mumbai, Chennai, and Calcutta) to provide safe commutes during the morning and evening rush. Thanks to plenty of clean, padded seats and electric fans, compared with the conventional dirty, dark cars crowded with men, the service has been a hit from the start and added six more lines in 2010.[11]

Women-only cars also exist on the Rio de Janeiro subway, whose all-female cars circulate all day and not only during rush hours. Similarly, Dubai's metro offers a section reserved for women and children, in addition to its standard "silver" class and first-class "gold" sections.[12]

Single-sex buses are an increasingly popular option, especially in smaller cities. Whereas Mexico City made the news in 2007 for its inauguration of the Athena Program—pink-signed buses that board women only—Goiania, a city of 1.2 million people in central Brazil, had rolled out women-only buses a year earlier. "The beautiful women of Goiania are constantly being sexually harassed on our overcrowded buses by men who seem unable to control themselves," explained councilman Mauricio Beraldo, the bill's sponsor. "This is why I decided to introduce a bill calling for the introduction of buses that will carry only women."[13]

Finally, filling the gaps in public transportation are fleets of taxis driven by women for women. Moscow's Pink Taxi service was created in 2006 in response to an increase in taxi rape cases. Not only does the company guarantee a safe ride, but also all of the drivers of the fuchsia-colored fleet have gone to university and are encouraged to offer advice, share gossip, and make their passengers happy. "I don't know where to start," said Olga Kuznetsova, 34, a mother of three who travels with her kids in the taxis at least twice a week. "The male drivers smoke, spit, play loud music, and generally don't give a damn about the comfort of the passenger." As business has boomed, the company has diversified and now picks up children from schools and even makes grocery runs.[14]

Pink Taxi service has also been operating in Dubai for several years and recently spawned a sister organization in Abu Dhabi. The "Ladies' Taxis," as they're known, boast safety-enhancing features not offered by ordinary taxis. Video cameras linked to the communication center of the taxi regulatory authority monitor the driver at all times. Because speeding was a common complaint among women passengers in regular cabs, each car is equipped with a gauge to detect if the driver goes over the speed limit; if she does, she will be fined. A panic button is accessible to passengers if they feel threatened.

In a country in which, according to Islamic tradition, women do not talk to men other than those in their family, the service has been a triple win—not only for women passengers upset at being leered at by male drivers, but also for women drivers happy to have flexible work options and even for the transportation authorities. "Women are safer drivers statistically [than men] and are less likely to get into an accident," says Abdulla Sultan al Sabbagh, director of TransAd, the UAE taxi regulatory authority.[15]

are for more support from their employers and how much they would benefit from programs that would help them break out of their shells. Because this is the first generation of women to move into management roles in force, the networks of successful senior women, now common in the United States and becoming more so in Western Europe, are still in early phases in emerging economies.

Global companies know how to provide this kind of support: they've done it for female and minority talent in the United States and Europe. The challenge is to translate cutting-edge diversity initiatives to fit the contours of the culture of each country.

It's a challenge that can't be dismissed. These "soft" sentiments can have repercussions for employers. Our previous studies of highly quali-fied minority women in the United States found that more than 40 per-cent of Asians and African Americans, and nearly 50 percent of Latinas, in their prime childbearing and child-rearing years felt demoralized by workplace discrimination and seriously considered quitting.[16] In emerg-ing markets, where cultural and gender prejudices pulling women out of professional careers are far more pronounced, companies are at risk of losing their most qualified women at the peak of their professional powers. Worse, without the presence of those women acting as magnets for university graduates, employers will cut themselves off from the best prospects in their talent pipeline. In short, multinational organizations must move beyond Western notions of work-life pulls on women and craft solutions that help tackle this potent set of issues.

Part Two

The Markets

Despite the similar broad themes shared by talented women across BRIC/UAE markets, each country is characterized by its own idiosyncratic array of "pulls" and "pushes." The devil is in the details, as it were. The following five chapters unpack those details in depth and explore their manifestations in Brazil, Russia, India, China, and the UAE.

3

Brazil

In 1941, Austrian novelist and playwright Stefan Zweig traveled to Brazil and fell in love. His infatuation generated a book, *Brazil: Land of the Future*, in which he predicted that the country "was destined to become one of the most important factors in the development of our world."[1] Zweig may have been Brazil's most eloquent advocate, but he was not the first of a long line of foreign adventurers, entrepreneurs, investors, and seasoned businessmen to promote Brazil's potential, nor was he the last to watch dreams of wealth implode in a series of booms and inevitable busts: lumber, sugar, cotton, gold, coffee, rubber—so many that Zweig's book became the basis for a joke: "Brazil is the land of the future and always will be."

Today, though, the saying is that the future is finally here. Under the market-wise governments of Fernando Henrique Cardoso in the 1990s and his successor, Luiz Lula da Silva, Brazil managed to conquer triple-digit inflation, pay off foreign debt, and attain year after year of steady growth. Even the global financial crisis barely dented South America's largest economy. After contracting for six months, Brazil rebounded sooner and faster than most other economies and has since expanded at an average annualized rate of nearly 9 percent, "largely on the strength of domestic demand," according to an International Monetary Fund brief.[2]

Among the BRIC markets, Brazil presents the best conditions for sustained growth over the next few years, according to Goldman Sachs.[3] The surging economic growth, coupled with ambitious social welfare programs, catapulted 30 million people into the middle class and lifted another 21 million, almost half of those considered poor in 2003, out of poverty.[4] Despite the entrenched desperation of Brazil's infamous *favelas*, or slums, unemployment is at record lows.[5] Growth will be further fueled by events such as the 2014 Football World Cup and the 2016 Olympic Games, to be held in Rio de Janeiro. Rated the world's eighth-largest consumer market in 2007 by Ernst & Young, Brazil is predicted to leapfrog Germany, the United Kingdom, and France and settle into fifth place in the very near future.[6]

Brazil's women are among the biggest beneficiaries of this expansion—and one of its key engines.

The participation rate of women has grown from less than 40 percent of the nation's workforce in 1990 to more than 60 percent, an all-time high.[7] Among the one hundred companies listed in "Best Companies to Work For—Brazil," women account for 50 percent of total jobs.[8]

That's quite a change, considering that until the ratification of the 1988 Constitution, which confirmed Brazil's evolution from dictatorship to democracy, women had the same legal status as indigenous peoples and the mentally incompetent. Patriarchy came to Brazil with its Portuguese settlers, took root with subsequent waves of immigration from Spain, Italy, Japan, and Germany, and was nurtured by the Roman Catholic church, the de facto state religion. Women received the right to vote only in 1933, the right to divorce only in 1977, and full legal equality only in 1988.

"Without the formal and legal recognition of society, plus a sexist heritage, women were not welcome to have a professional career except for those related to education, which meant teaching, or health, which meant nursing," recalls Ieda Novais, corporate director of consulting firm BDO Brazil.

Now a woman is leading the country. Dilma Rousseff, a former cabinet minister and chief of staff to Lula da Silva, was inaugurated as Brazil's first female president on January 1, 2011. In her victory speech on election night, she vowed to focus on continued progress for Brazilian women. Since taking office, she has named at least eight women to cabinet posts—more than have ever held positions in a Brazilian government.[9]

Brazilian women are being hired for corporate senior management positions in far greater numbers than in the United States. In 2009, Brazilian women held about 40 percent of jobs, leading South America in share of female workers in the labor force, with 45 percent of managerial jobs and 30 percent of executive positions, compared to 20 percent in the United States.[10] Some 11 percent of companies in Brazil have female CEOs, the World Economic Forum's *2010 Corporate Gender Gap Report* found, making Brazil one of the top five of the thirty-four countries surveyed (after Finland, Norway, and Turkey, and tied with Italy).[11]

Some women executives, like Luiza Helena Trajano Inacio Rodrigues, head of a chain of upscale department stores, had something of an inside track to the corner office as heirs to family-run companies. Others worked their way up the career ladder of multinational corporations: Fatima Raimondi became the first Brazilian and the first woman to be appointed president of the Brazilian business unit of telecom giant Ericsson; Nadir Moreno, promoted to country manager of UPS Brazil in 2007, is the first female executive to lead the company's operations in the region; Regina Nunes heads up Standard & Poor's in Brazil.

Still others used their smarts and experience to start their own businesses. After a successful career in hotel management with Westin and with Caesar Park Hotels & Resorts, Chieko Aoki founded Blue Tree Hotels, now one of the largest hotel chains in Brazil. Ana Lucia Sierra launched Age with two (male) partners in 2000. Today, it's one of

Brazil's leading advertising agencies, twice winning the Owl Award—the Oscars of Brazilian advertising—and was recently bought by the British Aegis advertising group.

These are only the vanguard of a host of women on the verge of an inevitable career breakthrough.

Samara Braga remembers that when she began working in finance some twenty-five years ago, "financial markets were not a place for women in Brazil—not at all. Then, finance and insurance companies and banks were places for men to work." Today, the financial markets leader for Ernst & Young estimates that some 40 percent of the people working in the field are women. "Of course, these women are not yet at the same level as men," she acknowledges. "But in ten years they will be."

THE CHANGING FACE OF TALENT

Those whose concept of female Brazilian talent is based on stereotypes of bikini-clad bronzed beauties, are in for a surprise. Data show a widening disparity between the numbers of women and men getting tertiary degrees, with more than one-third of women ages eighteen through twenty-three enrolled in university compared with barely one-quarter of men, and 60 percent of tertiary degrees being granted to women.[12]

These women are flooding into the workplace. Between 2003 and 2008, the number of female workers in Brazil's six largest metropolitan regions doubled, from 21 percent to 45 percent.[13] This trend will only continue to gain momentum, driven as it is by an increasingly robust middle class and the effect of their wealth on the educational opportunities of their daughters.

It's impossible to overemphasize the impact of Brazil's burgeoning middle class in broadening horizons for smart and ambitious women, especially when it comes to education. The state education system suffers from a serious dichotomy: the public universities are generally rated as excellent, but the quality of education in the poorly funded and overcrowded primary and secondary schools is low. Brazilian parents who can afford the fees have long sent their children to private schools to give them a better chance of gaining entry to a (usually state-funded) university. Until recently, though, that number was restricted to a slim slice of the population. Now, however, with the economic rise of the middle class, especially the huge growth of the so-called Class C families making the significant leap from poverty to lower middle class, an increasing percentage of parents have the resources to invest in their daughters' education from the beginning. Reflecting the immense change reshaping Brazilian society, CWLP research shows that more than half (51 percent) of women under forty are the first in their immediate families to graduate from university.

Like most women in the BRIC countries and the UAE, female Brazilian university graduates report extraordinarily high levels of ambition. Some 80 percent of Brazilian women aspire to eventually hold a top job, compared to 52 percent of women in the United States.

Employers are noticing women's advances—and hiring accordingly. "When you look at the statistics, [women] are graduating at higher rates from some of the best schools and institutions, so they're among the best trained," observes Valentino Carlotti, who heads up Goldman Sachs Brazil. "These women are talented and well trained in their fields, it is important to our business and other businesses that we provide them with the opportunity and platform in order for them to be successful and help us be successful."

A COMPLEX WEB OF PULLS

"Women today are paving the road of the future," proclaims Cristina Adib, vice president of Value Team, a multinational consultancy, and the mother of a young daughter.[14] Maybe so, but it's a road peppered with potholes.

Even as Brazilian women are forging successful careers as the first generation to move into the workforce in significant numbers, they face a combination of challenges that conspire to move them offtrack. Social pressures weigh heavily on Brazilian women; much is expected of them in their roles as wives, mothers, and daughters. In Brazil's traditionally machismo culture, the home is seen as the woman's primary domain, and her career automatically takes second place. "It's okay to be a successful professional as long as you know your priorities," explains Yula Rocha, a New York-based news correspondent for Brazil's second-largest television network. "Career ambition is well regarded so long as you are perceived as being a good mother and good daughter, and capable of doing everything."

Trying to balance demands at work and responsibilities at home is a "complex game," fraught with the possibility of disappointment, says one executive. Notes a senior manager at a multinational bank, "Society judges success to the extent to which I manage my home and family, not by how well I do at work."

At the same time, as might be expected in a country that places a premium on physical attractiveness, professional women are expected to excel at their jobs without sacrificing their appearance or femininity. An Austrian financial analyst, who moved to São Paulo after postings around Europe, was surprised by the premium put on looking well polished. "It's hard to find time to get out of the office to get my nails done, but that's important in Brazil," she notes.

The tugs and pulls experienced by Brazil's career-minded women have parallels with those of their American counterparts of forty or fifty years ago. Fertility rates in Brazil are plummeting, with the average woman bearing fewer than two children, a 20 percent decrease from a decade ago.[15] Divorce rates have doubled since 1985.[16]

Whereas Americans have, for the most part, accepted the notion of seeking personal fulfillment outside the traditional boundaries of motherhood and marriage, Brazilians are only beginning to come to terms with the concept. Some of Brazil's most popular *telenovelas* now glorify small families and independent lifestyles, at the center of which are self-directed, strong women.[17] Still, family is generally seen to be of paramount importance, and social life often revolves around the *parentela*—the network of extended kin. Rooted in a background steeped in machismo, social shibboleths are that much more exaggerated, and women must work that much harder to neutralize them.

Marriage and Motherhood First

"A woman must never lose sight of the notion that her place is still the caretaker of the home, this is what the society of a country composed mainly by men reminds us (women) all the time" says Patricia Braga, a senior manager at Pfizer Brazil. She explains what that entails on top of a woman's professional demands: "She has to take care of the children's homework, participate in school meetings, drive them to the doctor, plan the vacations, take care of domestic problems, go to the supermarket to supply the refrigerator and pantry, keep on top of her husband's health, and take care of herself."

Our research finds that it is far more acceptable for Brazilian women with small children to pursue a career or place them in day care than it is for women in other emerging markets. As in all developing countries, women have plenty of shoulders to lean on. Within the close-knit *parentela*, parents and in-laws frequently live nearby and are willing to pitch in to help with their grandchildren. Domestic help is readily available and easily affordable. Some 70 percent of our respondents agree that it is socially acceptable for young children to be cared for by a family member other than the mother; 75 percent are happy to delegate to a babysitter. A São Paulo-based senior manager with a multinational pharmaceutical company describes her nanny and housekeeper as "my angel," saying, "I'm a very lucky person because I can count on Ida. She has worked in my home for ten years. She makes the difference" in the manager's being able to enjoy her child and her job.

"All of my friends have full-time nannies who sleep in the house five days a week. Then they have a second nanny for the weekend," says Yula Rocha. On a recent visit home, when she and her husband took their baby to the beach, "all of my friends brought their nannies."

Professional women in Brazil do indeed have multiple shoulders to lean on for child care. Among full-time working mothers, 47 percent rely on their parents or in-laws for child care, 25 percent use domestic help, and 37 percent use day care.

When Samara Braga decided to put her two young children into an all-day preschool, she encountered criticism from an unexpected source: her own family. "There were not many schools where kids could be all day long, but I found one that took them from 8 a.m. to 5 p.m. I was happy with the arrangement, and my husband was, too. But my two sisters were horrified. These are my sisters. Both have careers and are independent-minded women. But they were saying, 'It's too much for the babies being left all day long when they are young.' That's the Brazilian mentality." Braga got more help from the mothers of her kids' classmates. "They were taking my kids to the parties, for sleepovers. They were an informal network supporting me in my career."

One other element of Brazilian culture that makes life more difficult for working mothers is the hands-off philosophy of most Brazilian fathers. In an amped-up version of traditional family values, our research found that nearly 75 percent of full-time working mothers bear at least three-quarters of the child care responsibilities, the highest number in all the BRIC and UAE households surveyed. Among their U.S. counterparts, by comparison, 56 percent of full-time working mothers shoulder more than half of the child care duties.[18] "I talk to my friends in Brazil—their husbands have never changed a diaper," reports a Brazilian expatriate living in New York. "I don't think they even wash a glass."

According to a 2001 nationwide survey, 55 percent of women said they wanted to work more and devote less time to household chores, a number almost certain to have increased in sync with the number of women in the workforce.[19] Yet, in a sign of how career women are stuck in a ceaseless tug-of-war, the same survey found that 87 percent of women agreed that men and women should share housework equally, but 85 percent also agreed that when there are young children, women should stay home to care for them.

Our research findings also reflect deep shifts in gender roles and social expectations of women in contemporary Brazil. Among the BRIC and UAE, Brazilian women encounter the least social pressure to drop out of work upon marriage or having a child, in part owing to the economic necessities of urban life in Brazil. São Paulo and Rio de Janeiro, respectively, rank twenty-first and twenty-ninth on the list of the world's most expensive cities.[20] Nicknamed "the New York of Latin America," São Paulo actually takes a larger share of a paycheck than its namesake. Women's earnings traditionally were understood to be used for personal expenses, and not included in the family budget, a practice that gave career women at least the option of taking a break. That choice is no longer guaranteed. "Nowadays," says Lisandra Ambrozio, human resources director at Pfizer Brazil, "the salary of the woman is a very important component of the family income."

Beneath the perfectly polished exterior and in spite of seemingly successful balancing acts, Brazilian career women are dealing with a formidable workload. "It's not easy being an executive and a mother," acknowledges a partner at one of Rio de Janeiro's top corporate litigation firms who is also the mother of a ten-year-old daughter. "It's extremely rewarding, but it's a double shift—no, really, a quadruple shift because I still have the routines with the house and the husband."[21]

Elder Care: An Additional Load

Not only is the pressure to be a super-mom more acute in Brazil than in the United States, but also daughters bear a greater responsibility for their elders. Enhanced by tighter family ties, 69 percent of Brazilian women take care of their aging relatives, compared with 48 percent of Americans.

"My boys say, 'I want to be just like my mom.'"

Tania Mijas was born when her mother was sixteen. An illiterate migrant worker, her mother used to wake Tania at 3:30 in the morning to help wash clothes and prepare food for her three brothers before they all went out to the fields to pick cotton. At age seven, Tania began attending elementary school, thanks to a government program providing free tuition and two meals a day. She shone, winning school and teacher awards in English and Portuguese while holding down a part-time job at a local transportation company. A full-time job at a distillery followed as soon as she graduated from high school, and then, twenty-four years ago, she was offered a job at GE. "It was the best day of my life," she says.

Mijas oversees Latin America sourcing for GE Healthcare, although she's looking for a job at a different level; the 30 percent salary increase is important in her role as the family breadwinner. "My husband worked in manufacturing for twenty years, but lost his job during the financial crisis in 2005. He got another job, but at a salary that didn't even pay the monthly school tuition" for their two sons. "In January 2010, he was laid off because of the economy. He worked

Brazilians' definition of "family" extends beyond the immediate nucleus of spouse and spawn. Whether it's a relic of the patriarchal past or an indication that the cost of living is too high to manage on one salary, unmarried women live with their parents until much later in life than in many other countries. After they marry and establish their own households, it is not uncommon for aging parents to move in with them. Nearly half of women under forty in our survey (47 percent) live with their parents, a figure exceeded only in China and India.

Whether or not they share a household, one-third of the women in our survey provide regular financial support to their parents, contributing an average of 23 percent of their annual income. Such support part-time, but his salary was less than half of what I get." In November 2010 he got a full-time job with a little better salary as a manufacturing supervisor.

Mijas also supports her mother and her mother-in-law. "Imagine: it's only myself taking care of my two boys, my husband, and two households. It's very difficult but I am strong. But I'm very anxious to get this new job."

She is inspired by the thought of providing a better life for her children—and by Jack Welch. Mijas first encountered GE's legendary CEO at a training session and was astonished to discover that he stuttered. "He's a top leader, yet how many problems he must have faced to talk in public and do presentations," she marvels. "I thought, if he could do that, I can do it, too."

Even as Mijas hopes that an MBA degree, which GE is subsidizing, will propel her still higher, she doesn't forget how far she has traveled. "When I was little, we didn't have electricity." And now she lives in a nice house, drives a company car, sends her two sons to private school, and makes twice as much money as her husband. When her boys visit her at work, they admire her office, her latest-generation laptop, her many awards. "They say, 'I want to be just like my mom.'"

is not only appreciated but also necessary; an aging population and a longer life span are stretching a social security system already under strain.

"There is an expectation here that the daughter will take care of the parents," says Renata, a business operation director for a multinational corporation. "That is much more the case for women than it is for men. There is no obligation for them."

That assumption, too, though, is beginning to change. "I see women asking more and more from their brothers and husbands," says Samara Braga. "They say, 'I'm taking care of my mother, yes, but I'm asking my brother to share this.' Now in the office, I hear many men complaining that they're sharing duties with their wives."

PUSH FACTORS AT WORK

Two years ago, a multinational consumer-products company hired consultants specializing in gender diversity to assess the issue of bias in its Brazil operations and find out why women weren't getting promoted into the higher levels of the organization. The company held focus groups and personal interviews with approximately two hundred employees, both men and women.

When one of its human resources directors saw the results, she recalls, "My first reaction was, 'Wow! We have two different companies here.' There is one company where men are working, and then there's a different company where our women are working."

When the men were asked for their perception of career development, they overwhelmingly answered, "It's great. We have great career opportunities. There is no difference between men and women." When the women were asked the same questions, their responses were the opposite: "You need to be twice as good as a man to get a better position. Managers don't understand that we have to balance our personal and professional life, so it's harder to get promoted."

"The perceptions of career development, career opportunity and work-life balance were so different between men and women," the HR director notes. "It was incredible."

Bias and discrimination are severe enough to make 40 percent of CWLP survey respondents consider quitting. Stereotypical assumptions about women's abilities manifest across a spectrum of indignities, from curtailed assignments to smaller salaries to penalties for taking maternity leave (see "The Maternity Penalty").

Exacerbating this dilemma, Brazilian professional women are confronted with a deep-seated cultural ambivalence about their right to be ambitious. According to a 2008 survey of values and attitudes toward women in Argentina, Brazil, Colombia, and Mexico, being ambitious is considered the most important individual value in every country *except* Brazil. In Brazil, being ambitious rates as the *least* important individual value. The most important is being polite, making it all the more difficult to fight back.[22]

PROFILE

The Maternity Penalty

When Brazil's 1988 Constitution guaranteed, among other far-reaching new rights for women, the extension of maternity leave from three to four months, the backlash was swift and fierce. Women job candidates were unblushingly asked by prospective employers to prove that they had had their tubes tied.[23]

In July 2010, Brazil's legislature extended paid maternity leave to six months for public and private sector employees. Rather than help professional women, however, the new law may actually stymie their career advancement. Women are still asked to discuss their plans for having children in job interviews.[24] "When we have two candidates and one is pregnant, I would probably choose the other one," says one female executive. "I know it is horrible, but it's because of the period the pregnant woman would be out of the company."

According to the Brazilian labor code, a mother on leave cannot work part-time for her regular employer. A woman who opts to take the full six months may find when she returns that her substitute may have supplanted her, her position may have lost importance, or her responsibilities been diminished. "The risk of being dismissed is high, because the law does not guarantee that she will keep the job," warns Ieda Novais of BDO Brazil.

Sonia ran head-on into the maternity penalty when her annual contract with her employer came up for renewal one month into her maternity leave. Her new contract stipulated that her employer could fire her at any time without paying severance. When she objected, she was told that everyone was being asked to sign similarly open-ended contracts. "I was in a vulnerable position, because I had a one-month-old baby and needed the money," Sonia says. "I couldn't leave."

After she signed, she discovered that none of her male colleagues had received that kind of contract. "I felt really discriminated against. Because I was a new mother, they took advantage of my vulnerability to give me something that in a regular position I would never have signed." Her baby is now almost a year old, and "so far, so good—they haven't revoked my contract," Sonia says. "But every month I wonder, am I going to keep working for them or will I be fired tomorrow?"

Bias and Discrimination

Despite Brazil's many advances, gender bias is deeply entrenched. It is rooted in the country's patriarchal culture, strengthened by Latin American machismo. Male chauvinism isn't flaunted in Brazil, as it is in, say, Mexico or some other Latin American countries. Instead, the issue of bias is more *sub rosa*. Yula Rocha compares it to the topic of race in the United States. "We know it's a big deal, but there's a kind of 'let's not talk about it' feeling. And I think the same applies to Brazilian women and discrimination. It's the kind of subject that no one acknowledges." Renata, a business operations director at an MNC in Brazil, agrees. "No man would ever say, 'You can't do *this* because you are a woman,' but women in general need to prove themselves every day."

Despite the inroads made by Brazilian women managers, the key players in many Brazilian companies and multinationals are still men— "and old men," notes one female manager with wide global experience. "In Europe and the U.S., it's okay to test your manager in a productive way or take an idea and make it better. Here, people are promoted on their ability to say yes to their manager."

When asked to rate the very important aspects of their work, 87 percent of Brazilian women in our survey checked off "being able to be myself," outstripping having high-quality colleagues (77 percent), high compensation (75 percent), or a powerful position (40 percent). Yet as a participant in a CWLP focus group notes, "It's a challenge to reconcile being feminine and being a leader, especially when the leadership [paradigm] is driven by the other gender."

To fit in to the "boys' club," the first generation of Brazilian women to breach the barriers of senior management often find themselves forced to change their personalities. "Women who get into senior positions are women who act in a male way and have male leadership characteristics," observes an expatriate working for a multinational. "They have to be very tough, very aggressive in their style."

As the first female director at her MNC, Renata agrees. "Throughout my career, I needed to fight every day. It's a horrible thing to hear, but it's a reality. When you are growing in a company, you need to prove your competence, your intelligence, and a woman needs to be much harder at this to have the same results as a man." She continues, "I don't want to be hard, but I need to be. If I enter into a discussion with my colleagues on the board of directors and I am not firm, they don't respect me. And that is not good."

The difficulties of trying to conform to existing leadership styles can be a barrier to women's advancement. "I don't think it's a lack of ambition or talent that's stopping women," says Vanessa Bateson, a Brazil-based head of Diversity and Engagement for HSBC Latin America. "It's that you have to change your personality. Many women think, 'I don't want to be someone I'm not.'"

Women also must fight cultural stereotypes that bar them from coveted assignments or plum job opportunities. More than half of the women in our survey (53 percent) see an international assignment as critical to their career advancement. Yet because it's assumed that a woman's responsibilities to her home, husband, and children take precedence over her commitment to her career, she is often passed over in favor of a man. Conversely, men are seen as being able to devote more attention to work, to be available to travel and stay late at the office because they have a wife supporting them at home.

Lisandra Ambrozio ran into this barrier at a previous employer when she and a male colleague applied for a posting in the United States:

> The feedback I had from my manager was, "You know, Lisandra, you were a great, great candidate for this position, but we were afraid of sending you to the U.S. because you are a woman, and you're very young, and you might miss your family. There's also the risk that when you come back to Brazil, you might more easily decide to leave this company for another opportunity. So we prefer to send the other candidate because he's male and he's going to move with his family, so we believe they're going to adapt more easily. And since he's older than you, we believe our investment in him is better, because when he returns to Brazil, he will think much more than two or three times before leaving the company."

As it turned out, the company was wrong on all counts about the male candidate. "His family didn't like living abroad, so six months later they returned to Brazil. He stayed [in the U.S.] and when he came back to Brazil after his appointment was up, he left the company." So did Ambrozio.

Yet another driver of gender bias is age. Fabiana became the office manager for a multinational news organization when she was twenty-five. "I would sit down at a meeting and a fifty-year-old man would look at me and say, 'Who are you? *You're* representing this company?' When I'd negotiate over the phone, I'd get the respect. But when I'd meet them in person, they'd all ask, 'How old are you?' Every one, without exception."

Age discrimination will continue as long as senior leadership continues to be composed of older men imbued with a "father knows best" mentality. "There is very limited promotion based solely on people's capability," says a British expatriate working in her company's São Paulo office. Citing the appointment of a thirty-five-year-old director in the firm's U.K. division, she notes, "That would not happen in this country."

When all of these manifestations of discrimination are added up, it's not surprising that the result is a sizable wage gap. Brazilian women may have achieved legal equality with men, but when it comes to pay parity, they're still second-class citizens. On average, women earn only 71 percent of men's wages. For women with a university degree, the gap is even wider: 40 percent less than men with an equivalent level of education.[25] A 2009 study by the Inter-American Development Bank found that, despite its powerhouse economy, Brazil sits at the bottom of a list of eighteen countries in Latin America when comparing how much women and minorities are paid for the same job done by a white man.[26]

The gap is so high, says Hugo Nopo, an IADB economist and the lead author of the study, because women are absent from the highest levels of corporate hierarchies. Adriana Paz, a sociologist at Brazil's Federal University of Rio Grande do Sul (UFRGS), confirms that the greater the number of professional women in a given field, the smaller the pay gaps.

"The lower presence of women ensures greater wage disparity," she says in an interview in *Exame*, Brazil's equivalent of *Fortune*.[27]

Wage inequality exists even in multinational corporations that have a policy of gender pay parity, a function not so much of selective ignorance as an indication of persistent bias on the part of male bosses who simply don't see why a woman should earn as much as a man. "Every year, my annual evaluation is excellent, but I've never received a merit increase," says Beatriz, who has worked at a multinational U.S. corporation for nearly twenty-five years and has been in charge of its Latin American sourcing operations since 2006. "My responsibilities and the volume of work have increased, but I am at the same wage as 2006."

Recently, her boss—a Mexican man—hired a man in a lesser position. "In six months, he had a higher salary than me and was given two direct reports, where I have only one report. These things make you frustrated. Even if you meet your goals and objectives, you still don't receive a salary increase." Beatriz isn't alone. "This is happening to other women too, in other departments. They have a lot of responsibilities, but they don't receive a salary increase. Most of them are frustrated, too."

Safety Concerns

Educated women have always put up with a lot in order to have a career: overt bias in the workplace, wage inequality, penalties for taking the full amount of maternity leave allowed by law. But few face the threats to their safety that Brazilian women routinely experience; 62 percent of our survey participants—the highest among all respondents—report feeling unsafe while commuting to work.

When one of our focus group participants relocated from Brazil to New York, she recalls that the most striking difference was that she felt safe on the city streets. "I could walk by myself at night and not feel terrified. I would never do that in São Paulo. You're always looking to see if someone is coming."

With *favelas*, Brazil's desperately poor urban slums, sprawling literally in the shadows of glittering high-rise condominiums, it's not surprising that São Paulo and Rio are notorious for the high incidence of crime; according to a recent U.S. State Department report, "Assaults and burglaries continue to be a part of normal everyday life."[28]

Armed hold-ups of pedestrians and motorists by "motoboys"— young men on motorcycles—are a common occurrence. As a result, in Rio de Janeiro, motorists are allowed to treat stoplights as stop signs between the hours of 10 p.m. and 6 a.m. to protect against attacks at intersections.[29] "Most of my friends drive low-key cars with darkened windows so you can't see who's inside," says an equity analyst for a multinational financial firm in São Paulo. She doesn't own a car and so must rely on taxis, most of which don't have tinted windows. "What happens is you're using a cell phone or a BlackBerry and you get caught in a traffic jam. People on motorbikes see you and do a quick robbery. If they have a gun, you open the door. When I'm in a cab, I take care to keep my bag on the floor and to not be seen on a mobile phone."

Robberies on the street are also common, with laptop computers and cell phones the first choice. "I'd never use a BlackBerry or cell phone on the street, to avoid calling attention to it," notes the analyst. Despite the presence of armed security guards around the building, she and her colleagues must exercise constant vigilance. Knowing that "there could be someone hiding and watching—it's become part of the reality," she says.

THE LURE OF THE PUBLIC SECTOR

More than in any of the other emerging markets in our study, Brazil's public sector offers stiff competition to multinational and locally head-quartered companies. Some 65 percent of educated Brazilian women describe the public sector as "very desirable" to work for, significantly more than in China (57 percent), India (51 percent), and even the UAE (48 percent) and far ahead of those who want to work at a U.S.- or European-based multinational (39 and 50 percent, respectively) or a local company (49 percent).

Their reasons have little to do with power, prestige, interesting projects, or advancement and everything to do with benefits, job security, and work-life balance. When asked to rate very important aspects of their work, 86 percent of female respondents opted for job security and 75 percent pinpointed high compensation; these results are not surprising in an economy that not long ago experienced triple-digit inflation and has a history of booms and busts. The public sector provides both of those in abundance. Job tenure is assured virtually as long as the employee is breathing; regardless of performance evaluations, employees may not be fired except for willful misconduct. Salaries are hefty at the entrance level, and thanks to one of the world's most generous pension systems, employees can retire at full salary and continue to receive the same pay-scale increases as their successors.

Working wives and mothers struggling with social expectations of their roles at home or who just want to spend more time with their families appreciate the civil service's legal maximum workweek of forty-four hours—plus overtime pay of 150 percent of base salary—something that's barely given lip service in private companies.[30] The public sector mandated a six-month maternity leave two years before it was implemented in the private sector. Time off for vacation and medical reasons is generous. Retirees from the public sector receive pensions equal to their last paycheck plus increases in the same amount as employees still working. Most attractive, however, is job tenure; regardless of performance evaluations, a public service employee may not be fired except for willful misconduct.[31]

Until recently, Brazilians used to talk about "asking" for a job in the civil service, rather than "applying" for one, a legacy of the days when the government doled out positions as political favors. Today, all candidates are screened through a rigorous entrance exam, the *concurso publico*. But even though the public sector may no longer be quite the sinecure it once was, few people view it as offering great career development, interesting assignments, or professional recognition. One of our focus group participants went so far as to say that it "stains resumes." Still, public employment offers a comfortable safety net that supports women weary of deflecting the pushes and pulls of a traditional society in transition.

CONCLUSION

Brazil's first widespread generation of career women is witnessing an evolution in the work environment that is familiar to their U.S. counterparts. Brazilians are finding a path to career satisfaction in a society that has long restricted female ambition to motherhood and marriage. They have had to fight for their place in the management hierarchy, sometimes even adopting a male model of behavior that directly contradicts their cultural definition of femininity.

As they forge new roles, they expect their employers to be partners, offering the opportunity for women to grow professionally without penalizing their personal lives. This is their vision of the future. Of all of Brazil's dreams, this one has the most power to become reality.

4

Russia

When post-Soviet billionaires appear in the news, they are inevitably men who have made their fortunes in the rough-and-tumble world of oil drilling or metal mining—and the women on their arms appear to be little more than the spoils of their success. Consider a recent profile of Mikhail Prokhorov, Russia's second-richest man and now principal owner of the New Jersey Nets basketball team. A reporter followed him one evening in December 2009 to a Moscow nightclub, where he reserved a balcony section for a group of male friends and long-haired, slim women whose high heels and equally high hemlines on their close-fitting black dresses screamed "aspiring model." Prokhorov joked with his guests, his hand lightly resting on the women's waists, before sitting down to watch a bevy of female dancers in white corsets, panties, and Cossack-style white fur hats. Pointing to the floor show, he confided to the reporter, "That's where the energy is."[1]

As Russia explores the new world of an open-market economy, Prokhorov might be right about the female energy surrounding him, though not in the way he presumably meant. Our research found dozens of examples of successful Russian women whose ambition and determination have enabled them to survive the messy metamorphosis from Communism to capitalism—persevere and triumph.

One example is Nadezhda Kopytina, founder and president of Ledovo Group, a frozen seafood company. According to various news accounts, she came from a poor Siberian village and, in the early 1980s, when she was sixteen, went to Lvov, now in Ukraine, looking for a job. A group of men gave her a place to stay and then took her identity card and demanded sex. She has since spoken out about the experience, saying, "I know that if you go through all these humiliations, anything is possible."[2]

With the advent of *perestroika*, the restructuring and reform of the Soviet economic and political system initiated in the mid-1980s, Kopytina plunged into a series of entrepreneurial ventures before starting Ledovo in 1994. She has also hosted a talk show and is a member of Russia's Committee of 20, a group of high-powered businesswomen modeled after the Committee of 200 in the United States. The Russian group includes a number of names that are well known in their homeland: Tatyana Zrelova, who was a cofounder of the first U.S.-Russian information technologies joint venture; Olga Dergunova, who became country manager of Microsoft at the age of thirty; Anna Belova, who headed Booz Allen Hamilton at a time when no other Western company in Russia had a woman in charge; and Yelena Yatsura, Russia's leading film producer.

A 2006 article in the *Irish Times* about the committee described a certain ruggedness among these women; they have had to be tough in a country where in certain circles, most men automatically equate the term *businesswoman* with *prostitute*. "They see themselves as pioneers," the article said, "trying to build Russia into a business superpower, breaking its reliance on oil and gas."[3]

Since moving from central planning to *perestroika*, Russia's economy has resembled a roller-coaster in its booms and busts, largely because of its subjection to the price swings of oil and other raw commodities. Russia has the world's eighth largest reserves of oil, the world's largest reserves of natural gas, 25 percent of the world's timber reserves, and substantial reserves of metals, especially nickel and gold. The last major swing in world commodity prices came with the collapse of the entire global economy in late 2008; after a decade of extreme growth, Russia's economy, which depended on oil and gas for two-thirds of its exports, shrank by nearly 8 percent in 2009, according to widely published government figures. Although oil and gas prices have swung back up since then, Russia is still reeling from the downturn and the massive unemployment it caused as local and multinational companies slashed their budgets.

Economic diversification away from what some pundits call Russia's "oil welfare" is important to women in that new investment is likely to be channeled to more women-friendly industries: retail, consumer products, property, IT, telecommunications, and service sector businesses such as banking, accounting, consulting, law, and hospitality. By most estimates, women make up only 10 percent of top management jobs, but women are already making significant inroads and the glass ceiling has begun to crack: 73 percent of businesses now have at least one woman in senior management.[4]

As in Western countries, there tends to be a gender-based clustering in work management roles, according to a study from Boston College. The study found that women represent 54 percent of managers in housing and social services; 5 percent in transport; 7 percent in construction; and 11 percent in science fields.[5] A 2010 survey by PricewaterhouseCoopers and the Russian Association of Managers found that as many as 93 percent of chief accountants, 70 percent of personnel directors, and 47 percent of finance directors are women.[6]

In the Russian business environment corruption remains endemic and a major hazard for anyone, male or female, thinking about starting a company or working for a company in Russia. In Transparency International's rankings of corruption levels around the world, Russia is among the worst in the index, ranking 154 out of 178. But with women like Kopytina and others bravely exposing the problems and lobbying for reform, much of the country's integral power is indeed coming not from its remote oil fields but from its unstoppable women.

THE CHANGING FACE OF TALENT

The Soviet Union, for all its flaws, indoctrinated the country with the idea that women should work. For the seventy years of the Soviet system's existence, "it was considered bourgeois for a woman not to work," recalls a management consultant who grew up under Communism. That explains why in the CWLP survey Russian respondents had the highest percentage of mothers who had worked: 94 percent of women under forty, and 97 percent of women forty and over, said their mothers had worked—even more than China, at 79 percent and 88 percent, respectively. Sixty-nine percent of women age 15–64 were in the paid labor force, one of the highest in the BRIC and UAE.[7]

Under Communism, girls were given the same educational opportunities as boys, and the precedent continues—although women take greater advantage of those opportunities. Russian women led the pack among the BRIC countries and the UAE in university attendance; 86 percent of Russian women aged eighteen to twenty-three were enrolled in tertiary schools, as opposed to only 64 percent of the men.[8]

Russians have always been proud of their intellectual prowess, but now they have a chance to see how their educational institutions stack up against global competition. There's good news and bad news. According to World University Rankings 2009, two of Russia's universities are ranked among the top two hundred in the world: Lomonosov Moscow State University (number 101) and Saint-Petersburg State University (number 168); this, compared with six of China's universities and two of India's.[9] Still, there's plenty of room for improvement. Russia has ten times as many finance and accounting professionals as Germany, and yet top-quality, "ready" talent is estimated to be a mere 10 percent and 25 percent, respectively, of the total.[10]

Russian parents do not generally pressure their daughters, or even their sons, to pursue advanced degrees in the way that upwardly mobile Chinese and Indian parents do, and that difference shows. In spite of the high numbers of university-educated women in Russia, in our sampling only 6 percent of the women were graduate degree holders, as were only 6 percent of the men.

That may change, though, especially now that MBA programs are springing up in Russia to satisfy the needs of multinational corporations and the desire of the growing number of local companies that want to operate with the same level of professionalism. And even though advanced business degrees were nonexistent until 1999, our interviews included a number of women who studied economics or finance as undergraduates. "In the 1990s, we [saw] the Soviet rule going down and everyone started to want to be a professional in economics, finance, or law," explains Julia Repryntseva, who works in HR as the compensation and benefits and talent director at Alcoa Russia. She was no exception, although she wasn't sure at first what she would do with her economics degree. HR was so unfamiliar in Russia that she had never heard of it until after graduation. But from her first job in HR at Coca-Cola, she was happy with what she was doing, particularly because it was a learning experience. "I started from scratch," says Repryntseva. "Every day I learned something new."

Just before the collapse of the Soviet Union, worker productivity was abysmal and motivation was barely a concept. As in most collective systems, individual ambition and assertiveness were frowned upon. That ingrained "see no evil, hear no evil, speak no evil" culture persists to a certain extent. "One of the biggest challenges I've heard about from foreign colleagues is that no one wants to take responsibility for anything," says a Russian woman with an MBA from INSEAD who has worked for many multinational corporations. The Russian stereotype, she says, is that "they're attuned to following orders, so it's difficult to push them to open their minds."

Today's Russian women, however—often more than their male counterparts—are responding to the open-market economy with enthusiasm and ambition. Part of the reason is that their foreign language skills, especially their proficiency in English, are stronger. "Twenty years ago, women who graduated from the educational institutes as English teachers were almost the only ones who knew English," explains Ludmila Petryahina, who works at Alcoa Russia as the HR director in charge of learning and development and people shared services. At the time, women were overwhelmingly drawn to teaching English because the hours were easier; men avoided it because the pay wasn't good. Although Petryahina avers, "We've got lots of men speaking English," women of her generation—she's thirty-eight—got a linguistic head start, which in turn gives them a leg up in the hallmark industries of the new economy: finance, marketing, and consumer goods and services.

Many Russian women credit their strong-minded mothers with having nurtured their sense of aspiration. "What dreams was I allowed to have as a girl? Anything," says Petryahina. Her energetic mother, a retired shop-floor manager for a major Russian chocolate factory, brought her up to consider ambition normal and even laudatory. "I was 200 percent sure that whatever I wanted to do, my parents would support me and I would have success."

There's a definite sense of widening horizons and expanding possibilities among Russian professional women. Although only 60 percent of the Russian women we surveyed said they aspire to the top job—the lowest among the BRIC and UAE statistics—almost two-thirds described themselves as "very ambitious." Eighty-one percent claim they are willing to "go the extra mile" for their employers, on par with the U.S. figure of 85 percent.

And whereas women in the Soviet Union worked because it was "bourgeois" not to, today in the Russian Federation, careers have cachet. "A woman wants to have a career because otherwise she wouldn't be interesting enough," says Inga, a senior executive at a Russian-based company. "Even the women who are married to the guys with money need to show that they are doing something."

Ambition as a career motivator is closely matched by the rewards that come from reaching the top. Life in contemporary Russia is expensive, especially in Moscow, and fraught with uncertainties, and these conditions might help explain why high compensation was very important to Russian women responding to the CWLP survey. The vast majority—87 percent—rated high compensation as more important than job security, a powerful position, high-quality colleagues, or "being able to be myself." That was much higher than in any of the other BRIC nations and the UAE and more than twice as high as in the United States.

A COMPLEX WEB OF PULLS

During Soviet times, almost every Russian city erected monumental sculptures glorifying women's contributions to building the state—as farmers, factory workers, tractor drivers, soldiers, cosmonauts, and, of course, as mothers. Most followed the same school of heroic Socialist Realism, with the statue set on a massive pedestal, striding forward into a bright future. Many of these statues still exist, a concrete reminder to today's working women of the differences between past promises and present realities.

The Perils and Perks of Motherhood

It's impossible to overestimate the myriad ways in which World War II shaped and scarred both the landscape and the psyche of the Soviet Union. "The Great Patriotic War," as it's known, took more than 20 million lives, literally decimating the population. Repopulating the Motherland was considered a national duty, with rewards for excelling at one's duty. "The Hero Mother Order," rendered in gold and enamel, was conferred upon women who had raised ten or more children. Lesser medals, called "The Glory Motherhood Order" and "The Motherhood Medal," were awarded to women who had raised between five and nine children. More than 18 million of these medals were issued.[11]

The program worked, and the country's population peaked at 148 million in 1991, aided by social pressure for women to marry and begin childbearing at a young age and a state-sponsored safety net of almost universal child care that enabled mothers to return to the workforce as soon as they were physically able.

Even if a working mother didn't take advantage of institutionalized nurseries and kindergartens, child care was still easier under the Soviet system. "When I was growing up, parents didn't need to look out the window, because the whole apartment compound knew everyone," recalls Alexandra Shaforost, who grew up in Ukraine in the 1980s and has worked as a senior manager at several top 100 companies. "You didn't even need a babysitter."

With the breakup of the Soviet Union, the push to encourage motherhood fizzled and the national birth rate plummeted. In part, it is because educated urban women have benefited from the advances that have lowered birthrates in the United States and Europe. They've also taken advantage of the easier access to Western contraceptives; Soviet ones were notoriously unreliable, one reason that until very recently, abortion was the most common form of birth control.[12] But the greatest change—and probably the most salient reason that in our sample of college-educated women between the ages of twenty-one and sixty-four, fewer than half in Russia were mothers—is the cost of rearing children.

There are notable economic obstacles to becoming a parent, according to data from the Russian Information Services, which cites as the main problems a high cost of living—Moscow and St. Petersburg are among the world's most expensive cities to live in—inadequate child allowances from the government, and a shortage of preschools. Russia has public kindergartens that are free to parents, but there is often a long waiting list. Private kindergartens have spots available but are expensive.

"It's common to have education cost $50,000 to $70,000 a year for private elementary school," reports Inga. "The schools are organized on the club model: There's a membership fee—you become a member for life—and every year you need to provide a certain amount of money."

Nearly 50 percent of the women surveyed put their children in day care, and some kind of day care is essential, because many of the women we interviewed put in a full day at work, made even longer by commutes that can easily take ninety minutes each way. "We wake up at half-past six and start off for the kindergarten at half-past seven," says Natalia, who works in IT for a multinational corporation's Moscow office. "I drop my daughter at the kindergarten at 8, then leave for the office. In the best case, I'm in the office by half-past 9 and I stay until 6. I'm home at half-past 7. My grandparents—my daughter's great-grandparents—pick her up from kindergarten, so she is already home."

Having relatives to pitch in makes Natalia something of an anomaly. Russian families tend to be close knit, but, paradoxically, they often lack the web of relatives to provide child support because the grandparents are still working. "If my parents have time, they help us with pleasure. But they are both working people and can't help us very often," says Anna Michailowa, a controller at Siemens Russia. We heard this refrain over and over: "My mother is an engineer—full-time." "My mother is a doctor." Having had their own children at a young age, the grandparents are still working full-time when their grandchildren are young; much as they might like to lend a hand, they can't. For that reason, only 44 percent of Russian women in our survey counted on their parents or in-laws to help with child care, the lowest figure of any full-time working women in the BRIC countries.

The solution? "Without our nanny, it's not possible to do anything," says Michailowa. "She started with my first son and has been with my family for ten years." Yet nannies and babysitters, too, are expensive—between $1,000 and $3,000 per month, according to Inga. Not surprisingly, given the cost, nannies are the exception rather than the rule in Russia. Only 4 percent of the women had a nanny on a daily basis, and only 24 percent felt that it is socially acceptable for small children to be cared for by a nanny or babysitter.

Without a babysitter, Russian women have a heavy load to shoulder. By and large, the women are saddled with the child care; 59 percent of Russian women respondents who worked full-time said they carried at least three-quarters of the child care responsibilities, as opposed to only *4 percent* of men working full-time.

"Most women work and take care of house and children, while the man just works," says Shaforost. "It's exceptional when men get equally involved in house errands. The men who are successful work twenty-four hours a day. It's a woman's responsibility to manage the house."

Inga doubtless speaks for many of her peers when she says, "Men? It's absolutely normal that the man doesn't do anything. But on the other hand, he does need to provide [money]."

Although maternal guilt afflicts 65 percent of full-time Russian professionals, it's not enough to derail them professionally. More than 80 percent said they felt it was socially acceptable both to pursue a career and raise small children. However, with a cornucopia of new careers to choose from and cognizant of the high costs of child rearing, educated women are delaying marriage to concentrate on their careers and are putting off motherhood until they can afford it. "When I was growing up, if you were twenty and not married, you were considered a wasted woman. It was as if you were past your prime for a man," recalls Shaforost. "Now people delay having children, because they understand it will cost tremendously more to hire a nanny or child care. You first need the money and then you have children."

For women who can afford to have children, Russia's maternity leave policy is extraordinarily generous—too much so, in the view of many employers. It is illegal for an employer to fire or even lay off a woman for three years after she has had a baby. During the first four months, the mother is paid her full salary by the regional government. After that and up to eighteen months, she receives a governmental subsidy, followed by a smaller subsidy for the last eighteen months. During that time, she has the right to return to her same position at the same salary at any time, without any notice. If she does return, she also has the right to take a leave of absence at any time during that three-year period, although without her salary.

"That's a big problem," says Alcoa's Repryntseva. "I see a lot of examples where a woman on maternity one day decides, 'Oh, I'm tired of sitting at home. I need to go to work.' She comes to the office and says, 'Hi, I'm here, and I want to continue my role. Where is my desk?' And the employer has to offer her the same job and the same salary. If she doesn't like working, she can go to her employer and say, 'I'm tired, I'm going back to my maternity leave.' And her employer can do nothing but say, 'Okay, we'll wait for you to come back.' During those three years, the woman can repeat this scenario as many times as she wants, and the employer must provide her with her job."

A co-worker at Alcoa, Ludmila Petryahina, has a ten-year-old daughter, so she has experienced the law's repercussions from both sides. She herself took only three months off when her child was born. "I'm a woman and understand how difficult it is to come back to work after three months," says Petryahina. "But if I were to have stayed at home longer, it would have been almost impossible for me to switch back to work. After three months of absence, it was like being out for three years. If I were to stay out three years, I would have had to start from zero. You lose the whole idea of the business, because things are changing so fast."

The bottom line seems to be "the higher the level of the position, the less time the woman wants to spend at home," she adds, "If the woman wants to work and is career oriented, she will come back as soon as she could afford to."

Like Repryntseva, Petryahina knows of less-ambitious women who game the system; as an HR director, she finds it infuriating. "If you choose a career, then three years is too much [time to take off]." Katia, a manager at another multinational firm, scoffs about women who take advantage of this well-known situation, "Work is some kind of enter-tainment for them."

Both women are well aware that the laws can backfire by caus-ing bias against hiring young married women. Promotion seems to be unaffected, says Repryntseva, especially if the woman has already dem-onstrated her abilities and commitment. But hiring is another matter. "Everyone keeps in mind that this woman could take maternity leave."

Elders on the Edge

Julia Repryntseva's parents are independent—her mother is retired but her father is still working—but already she helps them from time to time with money. She is accustomed to the idea that she will provide continuous financial support when her father stops working. "If everything is at same level where I am now, the career path, the level of the jobs, I do not expect any big changes," she says. She has it all worked out. "I have a master in economics, so I am good with financial planning."

When the Soviet Union dissolved, so did the social safety net for its senior citizens. It was left to their adult children—and *their* children, now entering the workforce—to step in and help out.

A large number of women in Russia have elder care responsibilities—78 percent, according to the CWLP survey. Around half of those said they provide monetary support to their parents—some 21 percent of their annual income, with men and women shouldering similar loads. "Most parents live on full-time support. If your mother is in Russia, financial support is expected, since you're the breadwinner and the pension is not enough even to cover the basics," says Shaforost.

The current generation of aging parents, working as they did for Soviet-owned businesses where the salaries were generally low, has come into the capitalist system cash-poor, albeit with their housing and medical care still provided by the state. All housing was free until the mid-1990s, and many older Russians have been able to remain in the state-subsidized homes they had then. Privatized housing, on the other hand, is so expensive that young married couples often live with their parents—and may delay having children until they can afford their own homes.

Then when the parents become elderly, it falls to the children to take care of them. Although hired help is not expensive, few of the Russian women in our survey were comfortable with outsourcing elder care. Only 24 percent said they would consider using hired help. A devoted daughter would think twice about putting her parents into an institution considering the frequent incidence of deadly fires in nursing homes. Many nursing homes have lost their funding since the Soviet collapse;

the alarm systems are faulty, and the homes are located in remote spots with no nearby firefighting units, according to a recent news account from Radio Free Europe.[13] Not surprisingly, only 5 percent of our survey respondents said they would consider placing parents or in-laws in a senior care facility.

Tolstoy Said It Best

No one knows better than the Russians that, as Tolstoy wrote in *Anna Karenina*, "each unhappy family is unhappy in its own way."

Divorce is very common in Russia. In 2008, there were 8.3 marriages and 5.0 divorces per 1,000 people (up from 7.8 and 4.5, respectively, in 2006).[14] The reasons for a high divorce rate are many: a passionate culture, a high rate of alcoholism, a nation of husbands who don't help with housework and wives who work long hours, as well as Amnesty International findings that three in four married women are the subjects of domestic violence, with a woman battered to death by her husband every forty minutes.[15]

It continues to be a woman's job to take care of the house and children if she gets a divorce. There are laws that mandate child support, but divorced women in Russia, like women all over the world, often find themselves struggling financially. "Divorce laws are murky," notes Shaforost; there's no guarantee that a woman will automatically receive half of the estate or even will receive alimony.

The median length of marriage ended by divorce is slightly less than ten years.[16] However, the chances of a divorced thirty-something Russian woman finding another partner are slim and virtually disappear as she gets older. Although there are slightly more males than females at birth, by age fifteen, the ratio begins to reverse and plummets with each succeeding year. According to the *CIA World Factbook*, there are currently eighty-five men to every one hundred women in the total Russian population.[17] And considering that in our survey only 19 percent of the women working full-time in Russia earned more than their spouses—whereas 74 percent of the men said they earned more—it is not surprising that the average divorced woman is under tremendous pressure to keep her job and strive to earn more.

PUSH FACTORS

After nearly a century of women being entrenched in the workplace, there is little bias against women in entry-level or middle-management positions, although, as mentioned earlier, there's a great deal of bias against women in senior roles. "Women have equal opportunities and equal chances to grow and develop a career path," maintains a male HR manager who has worked for two multinational corporations and one Russian energy giant. "In the majority of cases, women with potential who are not in a management role means only one thing: these women don't want to be there."

But even though ovent gender bias may not derail educated women, plenty of other forces test their ability to stay on their career track.

Extreme Job Demands

Long hours are the norm for any ambitious woman, but Russians put in average workweeks that are longer than almost any others in the BRIC countries and the UAE. The average workweek at a local corporation is an onerous sixty-three hours, higher than both local and multinational corporation demands in Brazil, India, and the UAE. Russian women working at multinational corporations log in seventy-three hours a week. Nearly a third are working an average of twelve more hours per week than they did three years ago—the equivalent of more than an additional working day.

The pressures of long days are exacerbated by protracted commutes. Russia's crumbling highway infrastructure long ago lost the race to keep up with its expanding economy. Two- or three-hour commutes each way are commonplace, not only in Moscow and St. Petersburg but also in secondary cities like Nizhni Novgorod and Samara. In focus groups and individual interviews, women routinely bemoaned the hours wasted in these extreme commutes.

In Moscow, a city with traffic so appalling that the *New Yorker* recently devoted an entire article to the topic, a risk manager in Siemens's Moscow office drives ninety minutes each way—"and that's the best case."[18] She knows people whose commutes are even worse. "I once met a colleague at 6 a.m. in the office because he said, 'If I leave home half an hour later, it will take three hours to get to work. If I leave now, it will only take one hour and a half.' People try to find the optimal time management scheme, so to speak."

Moscow's perennial bottlenecks are so notorious that they drive people away. Ludmila Petryahina, who works at a multinational corporation's satellite office in Samara, a city in Russia's industrial heartland, has turned down job offers from Moscow-based companies. Traffic is not "the most important reason," she concedes, but it's a potential dealbreaker. "I cannot afford to live in the traffic."

Perhaps one reason a high salary is important to Russian women is that an expensive car can be a protective suit of armor. The *New Yorker* article described an element of socioeconomic warfare in the way drivers of luxury cars get away with tyrannizing drivers of smaller cars. In February 2010, two women doctors, the driver and her daughter-in-law, were killed when, according to witnesses, a luxury Mercedes S-500 belonging to a vice-president of Lukoil crossed over into the central emergency lane and then into oncoming traffic, crushing their modest Citroën. The Mercedes driver was not prosecuted.

Flextime and telecommuting are relatively new concepts in Russia—under Communism, face time trumped productivity—but seem to be warmly welcomed, with 68 percent of survey participants saying they would prefer a flexible or part-time work arrangement. Siemens is in the vanguard; its new building in Moscow has an open-office design with desk-sharing. The structure allows employees to be more or less unbound, so that everyone becomes used to the idea of having people work both inside and outside the office. Anna Michailowa is enthusiastic about trying out the desk-sharing program. "It's important for the employer because they will save some on overhead," she says. "But it's important for employees, too, because they see the company trusts them, and they can organize their lives better."

They may also feel safer if they can control when they're on the streets. As in other BRIC countries where there is huge economic disparity, crime escalated in Moscow after the global downturn; in one month in 2009, the city's murder rate rose by 16 percent and its fatal assaults by 44 percent.[19] More often, though, a woman's main concern on city streets is purse snatchings and other kinds of robbery. Women we interviewed talked about being perpetually aware and on the defensive.

Petryahina travels frequently between Samara, Moscow, and other Russian cities. "Traveling in Russia could be unsafe, but it's not directed against women," she says. "Handbag stealing can happen to anybody in any country. You have to know and follow the rules. Using public transportation or taxis to and from airports, that could be unsafe. It's preferred that someone is assigned to meet you at the airport and take you to the hotel."

The Lure of Multinational Corporations

Despite the long hours and vexing commutes, multinational corporations are a powerful magnet for ambitious, educated Russian women.

At the top of the list is a predictable and professional code of conduct backed up by decades of best practices, and a results-oriented work environment reinforced by plenty of training and career development. "The difference is huge," says Inga. "You will get less money working for an international corporation, but you'll get a better work environment, more transparency, a clear career path, and not much corruption. And if you're thinking long-term, it's easier to sell the experience of a multinational corporation. Saying 'I've worked for Siemens or for GE' means something on your CV." Repryntseva agrees. "You earn much more money in some Russian companies than in multinationals. But many people prefer to work for less money in a more transparent environment."

To be sure, some women like the fluidity and anything-goes spirit that prevails in Russian entrepreneurial enterprises. Shaforost explains:

> If you're smart enough, it can be easier to implement your idea. You're freer to experiment if you're at a high level. Russian companies can be more creative. You have dinner with a senior official, and he spells out a certain process for a future merger, and you explain why it's not going to work, and then two weeks later you see that they've completely changed their strategy. They're more fluid in making major shifts.

> When I first moved to Moscow and wanted to work for a Russian company, I made a few calls to friends and I was offered a job at a dinner, even though no one ever asked about my qualifications. The CEO's decision is often based on intuition. It's not as rigorous as in the U.S.

The absence of formal processes or standard business practices can be good or bad. "You can be promoted very quickly or even made a partner," Inga notes, but she warns, "Or you can be laid off very quickly. It depends on your relationship with the owners. You can start working on the promise of a multimillion-dollar contract, then one month, no salary, two months, no salary, and when you ask, the answer is, 'You're not poor, you can wait for three months.' You wait another month, and suddenly the project is stuck and your position isn't needed anymore. And if you try to claim your money, they'll claim you're incompetent." Caveat emptor, she advises. "If you work for oligarch companies, you need to be aware of the hazardous character of the business. The guy can change his mind for no reason." Repryntseva concurs: many more Russian companies than multinationals approach business with a "firefighting style, which adds more stress."

Government jobs were not thought to be attractive by educated Russian women: only 32 percent of the women in our survey say they

"The more challenge there is, the more fun I have."

Marta loves using both her PhD-level knowledge of computer science, her communication skills, and her understanding of the business to analyze financial and compliance risks for her company's projects. "The more challenge there is, the more fun I have," she says about her job in the compliance department of the Moscow office of a diversified multinational engineering firm.

Marta's parents were both engineers, so studying technology, she says, "was kind of pre-set." There was never a question that she would have a career. It is only now, with a working husband and a daughter in kindergarten, that Marta has the luxury of thinking about the importance of work-life balance. She was in graduate school when her child was born, and the experience was instructive. "When you're studying at the university, you have a flexible schedule and you can work at home," she says of maternity leave. "If I'd had a nonuniversity position at the time, it would have been hard to manage both."

Marta's daughter, like many Moscow children, often stays in her public kindergarten from about 8:00 a.m. to 7:00 p.m. Marta drops her off on the way to work; her grandparents—Marta's parents continue to work full-time—pick up the child and bring her home three days a week, and Marta and her husband switch off on the other two days.

are "very desirable" to work for, the lowest of all the BRIC and UAE respondents, and even then the benefits outweigh the job security, the power and prestige, and a female-friendly work environment. "Government jobs are very stable," concedes Katia. "You'll never lose one, never. But it's very low-paid and, in most cases, not very interesting, and a big level of corruption is there, for sure."

Child care is a subject that has come up in the initial meetings of a newly formed affinity group at Marta's office. She is actively involved in a women's global leadership initiative within the group, which is looking at a subject of great importance to her: how to make young parents happy. Also, she and her colleagues think it would be nice if companies would subsidize kindergarten fees or ease the daily commuting and child care logistics with day care centers or kindergartens near the office.

Her employer has begun to offer telecommuting and flextime, options that Marta takes advantage of from time to time. However, even though flextime might help employees achieve work-life balance, it is not a solution for those who have a long commute in Moscow traffic because the bottlenecks begin as early as 7:00 a.m. and continue all day and into the night. Marta's commute ordinarily takes about ninety minutes each way. "Once or twice I came into the office at six in the morning because I had work to finish," she says. "Then it took me only twenty-five minutes to get there."

Marta's job is one that is crucial to a company's success in Russia. She looks at any potential partners, customers, or contractors in the project, scrutinizing their financial statements along with their transparency in addressing questions, their integrity, and their reliability—as well as the corruption risks associated with the partners and the project. "I like my work," she says. "It's fun, and it's also a tough challenge, creating a culture of integrity." But for the future, Marta says, she wants to be sure her work allows her to have quality time with her family. "Otherwise, I would quit."

Petryahina, Shaforost, and Inga all point out that the government is trying to change its image by becoming more transparent and putting smart, credible women like Tatyana Golikova, minister of health and social development, and Elvira Nabiullina, minister of economic development, in key positions. "Something is happening and the situation will change, but that is a long, long, *long* story and will take years," says

Petryahina. Meanwhile, Shaforost concludes, "there's relatively little pride and no money for the amount of work you do there, so it's almost ridiculous to go there."

CONCLUSION

Western-based multinational corporations often mistakenly assume that because Russia is Europe's next-door neighbor and its citizens *look* European, implementing their business models is a simple matter of translation. But even if contemporary Russia may have dropped some of the secrecy that led Winston Churchill to famously describe the Communist state as "a riddle wrapped in a mystery inside an enigma," the potential for cultural misunderstandings is great.

Particularly frustrating to MNCs, says Andrey Donets, CEO of Alcoa Russia, are the problems they might encounter in building trust in a country where people are understandably suspicious of any authority and in getting Russians to show initiative.

This is where Russian women show their strength. Ambitious and determined to succeed, a generation of Russian women now in their twenties and thirties has grown up in a forward-thinking, survival-of-the-fittest society. In their schools and homes they grew up hearing that opportunities were opening up all around them—opportunities to make money, to travel, to compete in a world where something new was happening daily. Although they may not have studied business abroad in the numbers that their Chinese and Indian counterparts have, they've acquired street smarts. Those who are pursuing careers are confident and resolute.

"The young women today have excellent communication skills," says Veronika Bienert, who works in the regional Cluster Russia Central Asia for Siemens. "They are straightforward, and they know what they want. They are less frightened about conventions. They have their plan, they inform themselves what their options are, what skills they need, their preconditions for the next step, and they do it much more diligently than the generation before."

And they look to their employers to satisfy those preconditions: from compensation to job security to high-quality colleagues and the ability "to be myself." When those conditions are met, they are more than willing to go the extra mile and show their employers that Russia's educated, ambitious women are indeed, as Mikhail Prokhorov noted, "where the energy is."

5

India

Chanda Kochhar is a superstar in the Indian business world. Since taking the helm of ICICI Bank in May 2009, Kochhar has been credited with turning around India's largest private bank, transforming it into a retail banking powerhouse. She now oversees a financial firm with assets of $100 billion and counts as one of most powerful women in business, both in India and on the global front.[1]

It is often assumed that Kochhar and other highly successful Indian women who are making their mark on the global stage—women like Indra Nooyi of PepsiCo, Inc., Sara Mathew of Dun & Bradstreet, and Kiran Mazumdar-Shaw of Biocon—are isolated exceptions. Many Westerners continue to view India as tradition-bound and poverty-ridden, a place where women are disempowered and marginalized. There is much truth to this portrait: in 2010, India was ranked an unimpressive 112th of the 134 countries by the World Economic Forum's Gender Gap Index Report.[2] Fewer than 40 percent of Indian women work, and a mere 10 percent between the ages of eighteen and twenty-three are enrolled in tertiary education.[3]

So it may come as some surprise that in 2009, women represented 11 percent of CEOs—nearly four times the 3 percent figure for the *Fortune* 500 in the United States and the FTSE 100 in the United Kingdom—and 15 percent of senior executives in India. These numbers are only the tip of the iceberg; in the words of one commentator, "For every Indian woman who makes headlines, there is a legion of middle-class Indian women in the workplace."[4]

As these statistics illustrate, India is defined by vast contradictions. One of the world's youngest countries, it is governed by the world's oldest cabinet; the world's largest democracy with some of the highest voter participation rates in the world, it continues to elect dynasties.[5] And while the ranks of dollar millionaires swell to more than 100,000, one-quarter of all Indians live below the poverty line on less than a dollar a day.[6] In fact, it is often noted that there are "two Indias" separated by a deep socioeconomic divide.

Our focus is on the modern, thriving India, the India that has been variously described as the "New India" or "India Inc." Since its economy was liberalized in 1991, India has experienced unprecedented growth and change. The eleventh largest economy in the world, it has been the second fastest-growing major economy over the past three years, aptly referred to with increasing frequency as a rising superpower. This is the India to which multinationals are flocking in search of growth and innovation. It is also the India in which educated, highly skilled women are staking their claims and making their presence felt: they've moved into the labor force in unprecedented numbers, steadily scaled the corporate ladder, and, in cases like Chanda Kochhar and her peers, taken on the mantle of leadership in arenas from business to politics.

Why is female talent in India important to multinationals? With the third-largest university system in the world (after the United States and China), India generates 14 percent of the global talent pool, and managing, developing, and advancing Indian professionals will be on the agenda of any global corporation. Significantly, of the roughly 14 million students enrolled in tertiary education in India annually, 40 percent are women; this percentage has grown steadily over the past two decades and is only expected to rise.[7] In terms of quality, India is home to top-notch technology and management schools, including the highly competitive Indian Institutes of Technology (IITs), Institutes of Management (IIMs), and the Indian School of Business (ISB) in Hyderabad, the latter counted among the *Financial Times* Top 20 Global MBAs. A 2009 analysis found that half the CEOs of India's largest two hundred companies had obtained their degrees from one of the IITs or IIMs.[8] This figure speaks to the caliber of graduates of these homegrown institutes and their profound economic impact on India Inc. The demand for top-caliber "ready talent" in India, however, significantly outpaces supply. A recent BCG study anticipates, for instance, a shortfall of 600,000 graduates over the next five years.[9] Moreover, Goldman Sachs points to the scarcity of top talent as the number 1 constraint in sustaining the momentum of growth.

The solution to India's talent crunch? The millions of educated, ambitious women entering the workforce each year. These women have entered en masse into professions long out of reach to females—from technology to sales, finance to management. At the same time, they have had to negotiate a complex terrain of age-old social and cultural restrictions.

THE CHANGING FACE OF TALENT

Scholars of ancient India claim that women had equal status with men in many spheres of life during the Vedic period (second and first millennia BCE). Passages from the earliest Indian texts, the Rig-Veda and the Upanishads, contain references to female sages and seers, providing evidence that Indian women in that period married at a mature age and freely chose their partners.

Following this early era, however, women's status went through a period of steady decline, influenced in part by the Mughal invasion in the twelfth century and the advent of Islam and Christianity. Nonetheless, female icons continued to be held in high esteem: Mirabai, a Rajput princess turned poet-saint and a central figure in the influential Bhakti religious movement, is revered to this day. Other examples include Razia Sultana, the Mughal princess who ruled Delhi in 1236, and Nur Jehan, the wife of the Mughal emperor Jahangir, who was widely known to be the real power behind the throne.

More recently in the twentieth century, female leaders such as Sarojini Naidu, the first female president of the Indian National Congress and subsequently a freedom fighter in India's independence struggle, have played a critical role in paving the way for Indian women in the political arena. Indira Gandhi, India's prime minister from 1966 to 1984 and the longest-serving female premier in history, is the best known of these powerful women leaders; others include Sheila Dikshit, Delhi's chief minister since 1998, and J. Jayalalitha former chief minister of Tamil Nadu, elected to numerous high offices between 1991 and 2006, now leading the state's opposition party. High-profile executives like Kochhar are forging paths to power for women in business.

An Accomplished and Valued Talent Pool

Indian women excel in a range of disciplines, relatively unfettered by cultural preconceptions that can steer women in the West away from hard sciences and mathematics. In our sample, for instance, 41 percent of women held undergraduate degrees in the sciences and another 27 percent in business administration, management, or commerce. Indian women are also getting ahead in terms of graduate degrees: 50 percent of women held graduate degrees in our sample, versus 40 percent of men. These trends have not escaped the notice of employers. "If you look at the number of top graduates from any Indian school," noted one HR manager, "a disproportionate number are women. Whether management or engineering, the numbers are growing."

Despite a society characterized by stark gender divides—from the way girls are socialized to the tremendous weight of the cultural expectation of married women to be the keepers of the home and family—women in

India are valued for the different and distinctive attributes they bring to the workplace. From a business perspective, they are seen in comparison with their male peers to be more empathetic and sensitive to others' needs and more adept at multitasking and managing relationships—competencies that drive success in the workplace. One pharmaceutical executive found women to have a competitive advantage based on their strong communication skills and their ability to persuade doctors and decision makers at medical institutions to choose their product over others. Others felt that women were relatively more efficient in the workplace, doing a "better job of getting more out of something" or even "more productive because it means more to them."

Given these vital roles, it is no wonder that educated Indian women are among the most highly motivated and ambitious in the world. Our survey respondents consistently and overwhelmingly demonstrate positive attitudes toward work and aspiration: more than 80 percent report, respectively, that they love their jobs, feel highly engaged ("are willing to go the extra mile at work"), consider themselves highly ambitious, and aspire to a top job. Interestingly, there is little difference in enthusiasm for work between older and younger women: no matter what their age, Indian women show levels of ambition far higher than their U.S. counterparts.

What drives the tremendous levels of professional motivation for the vast majority of the female talent pool? The zeal to achieve starts early, during their student days. Many of the successful professionals in our study have exemplary academic track records, spurred on by a competitive system that prizes academic achievement for men and women alike. Hiroo Mirchandani, business unit director for Pfizer India and the seniormost woman in the company's India operations, observes that girls in India often outperform their male peers in academics, and this fosters a sense of equality and ongoing drive for achievement that continue as they begin to participate in the fast-growing Indian economy.

The good times in India have been particularly good to highly qualified individuals. For this group the economic boom has brought vast increases in salary; India has seen the highest year-on-year salary increase in the Asia-Pacific region, and annual increases of 20 percent are not uncommon even in the wake of the global recession.[10] In so dynamic an environment, there is plenty of room for far-reaching career aspirations, and dramatic social shifts have followed the economic boom. "Women no longer have to apologize for their ambition," observes Vishakha Desai, president of the Asia Society, a leading expert on the region.

Commitment and Loyalty

A common assumption about ambitious and highly sought-after talent in emerging markets is that they are prone to job-hopping, lured from one company to another by ever more lucrative paychecks. Our data reveals a different reality in the case of Indian women: contrary to common perceptions, they express considerable commitment to their employers.

More than two-thirds (68 percent) of our respondents consider themselves very or extremely loyal to their employers, and 81 percent value job security as a top work priority. Both figures are notably higher for women than men.

Smart companies in India have long recognized the immense value of appealing to women's sense of loyalty. Building on a deep, nuanced understanding of the priorities and needs of Indian women, companies such as ICICI, Wipro, Genpact, and Biocon have developed an alluring and differentiated value proposition that enables them to retain the best and the brightest. Incidentally, both ICICI and Biocon are headed by women, but what really sets these companies apart is their ability to offer opportunities for highly motivated women in the context of the realities of Indian culture and society.

A senior HR manager for a US-based multinational shared how he discovered what matters most to this talent pool. "When I tried hiring women leaders from companies that got it right, I just couldn't do it," he said. "At the end of one of those meetings, one candidate said to me, 'You can offer us better salary and benefits, but as a woman in India, a lot of other things matter. How do I know your company's culture, your language, and how it will be perceived if I leave at 3 to take care of my kids? Why would I give up the familiarity and flexibility I have here for a 20 percent pay hike?' There has to be a certain understanding of their reality."

Rather than take for granted the rich reservoir of loyalty among Indian women, employers of choice for women in India recognize and cultivate their commitment. "Women employees want to give their full commitment," noted one of the employers in our study. "They make a conscious decision to work, and it means more to them."

Yet in many cases, women's ambition still outstrips what is generally accepted. Onerous demands at home and outright bias at work together can stifle even the most promising careers.

A COMPLEX WEB OF PULLS

Indian society is in transition between tradition and modernity, a picture complicated infinitely by the diversity within India's billion-plus population. To a great extent, the experiences and career paths of educated women are shaped by their families and class backgrounds and, upon marriage, those of their spouses.

Duty is central to the Indian ethos; as one expert on the region observes, white-collar women in India are caught in the bind of trying to fulfill an expanded set of both professional and social pressures. "Many working women come up against these social obligations: not simply to be a wife or a daughter-in-law, but to be the keeper of the family traditions," she notes. "When people are sick you go to visit. That's still a woman's domain in India." She adds, "The 'social' thing is different from in the West, and you really need to pay attention to that."

The strength of family ties in India cannot be overestimated. These bonds are social, cultural, and economic. Even among urban, college-educated professionals, tradition holds sway, and the persistence of traditional family structures and relations in India has a disproportionate impact on women: our data shows, for instance, that 85 percent of college-educated men and women over thirty in India are married, 57 percent live in multigenerational households with their parents, and 53 percent have a senior or elder living in their household.[11] Some 57 percent of the women in our sample report providing monetary support to their parents, on average, 23 percent of their annual income.

Traditional family structures and relationships in India have a disproportionate effect on women. Any measure of equality young women experience in their lives and careers quickly disappears upon marriage; this is when an intense range of pressures definitive of traditional Indian society kicks in full force. Married Indian women are pulled by family demands from a constellation of relatives: in-laws, parents, uncles, aunts, cousins, and beyond. We heard numerous accounts of highly educated, successful women who struggle daily to conform to the paradigm of the "ideal wife," "ideal daughter-in-law," and "ideal daughter" in their personal lives. Because a high-performing woman is used to being an overachiever—and because there may be resentment and suspicion about her decision to have a career—the bar is set extra high. It wasn't at all rare to hear of a successful and ambitious professional who wakes up at 4:30 a.m. to make breakfast and lunch for her children and parents-in-law, goes to work, and returns home to clean up after her family and prepare dinner.

Although most white-collar female professionals in India have shoulders to lean on—domestic workers and extended family members—for child care and general household tasks, the double shift they shoulder is of a sort quite different from that of their Western peers. "The day-to-day details are done by women, even when both spouses are working: the wife looks after the house and relationships, and men go to work, working longer," explained one professional. "Men don't get involved on a day-to-day basis. In spite of education and progress, it all seems to revert to what their parents did."

In some respects, educated women in India have forged ahead in terms of their identities and education but society has by and large remained tradition bound. The burden of the extreme double shift can derail women's careers. "Social factors are an immediate reality, and typically, a married woman has to take care of her husband's parents," explained one executive. "For a couple aged thirty to thirty-five, just at the time both careers are about to take off, if a decision has to be made about whose career takes precedence so the family responsibilities—such as elder care—can be dealt with, it's the woman's career that takes a backseat."

Faced with the extreme double shift of married working women, a number of female professionals in India choose to remain single. In our sample, 100 percent of men over forty-five were married; the figure for women in the same group was 78 percent. "There was never a man more compelling than my career," joked one highly successful single executive. A senior sales professional went so far as to say that remaining single had helped her advance in her job. "When women are making calls at night, one issue is the family, especially if you are married and have responsibilities at home."

The picture for working women in India is further complicated by the growing necessity of two incomes in urban areas. In years past, families were typically headed by a male breadwinner, but in the new India dual-career families are becoming the norm. In our sample, 74 percent of the men and 98 percent of the women have spouses who are either employed or seeking employment. With the rapid escalation of living costs in cities such as Bangalore, New Delhi, and Mumbai and a steady rise in consumption patterns, women's choices in relation to work are dictated by both need and desire.[12]

Our data also shows that it is not uncommon for Indian women to outearn their spouses, as reported by 34 percent of the men among our survey respondents. This disparity is bound to present difficulties on the elder care front. As parents age and require care, it may no longer be feasible for the daughter or daughter-in-law to give up her career if she brings in the bulk of the household income.

Elder care throws an enormous shadow over the bright prospects of ambitious women. As a result of better health care and increased life expectancies, demographic projections point to a huge leap in the percentage of the population over sixty. Even in India's relatively youthful population, people over sixty are expected to constitute 20 percent of the population by 2050.[13]

"Daughterly guilt"—and its alternative, daughterly responsibility—can be an even greater burden than maternal guilt: in fact, more Indian career women experience daughterly guilt (70 percent) than maternal guilt (62 percent). In bearing the double brunt of guilt, Indian women are similar to their Chinese counterparts, who also find themselves pulled by the care needs of elders and children. Although Indian women readily avail themselves of multiple shoulders to lean on for their child care needs, they are far less open to delegating or outsourcing care arrangements for their parents and in-laws. Barely half (51 percent) are willing to use hired help, and only about one-quarter (27 percent) would consider assisted living or a nursing home. An Indian woman in one of our focus groups spoke for everyone when she said, "In the Western world, outsourcing elder care is perfectly acceptable. People plan for it in advance, like they do for college education. In India, there's a huge stigma attached to using professional help or complete outsourcing, like sending them to a home."

Yet as we learned from our interviews and focus groups, regardless of income or position, for most Indian women traditional pulls remain unabated, and for working women, family priorities are expected to prevail over work demands. This view can leave highly ambitious women feeling judged for their commitment to work, pitied for having to take calls after hours, urged by family and friends to "not work so hard." Anuradha Mathur, a highly successful entrepreneur in Delhi, dreams of a time when Indian women are not universally expected to prioritize their personal lives. "I await the day when how working women allocate their time between 'home' and 'work' is not prejudged," she says.

PUSHES AT WORK

Bias in the Workplace

Educated women in India grapple with the forces of tradition both at home and at work. In our survey, Indian women reported workplace biases to a much higher degree than their counterparts in other emerging markets: 82 percent have experienced style bias, and 45 percent feel that women are treated unfairly in the workplace because of their gender. Although most societies retain disparate expectations of men and women, the model for women in India is unique in its complexity, tenacity, and pervasiveness. Our respondents shared an acute consciousness of being constantly observed and measured against an exacting set of ideals for women, of being expected to act in a "modest, humble" manner, and "being conditioned to fit into roles defined by age-old expectations."

In certain professional contexts, women can be taken less seriously and viewed as having less potential purely on account of their gender. "There's a sense that a woman is just working until she gets married, i.e., she is not a long-term resource," said a senior finance professional.

The struggle to counter negative preconceptions about their commitment or competence can drive many Indian women to overcompensate, putting in extra work to be noticed or rewarded to the same degree as men. "They question my strategic skills, my thinking skills, my business acumen, my ability to understand their business," said Chitra Sood of Microsoft India.[14] Over the years she has felt that she has always had to go the extra mile to prove herself.

These biases appear to impact women regardless of seniority and track record. "Despite having proven your competence, when you get a new assignment you have to start all over again. This doesn't happen in the case of men," a senior professional in the oil industry observed. Institutional memory in India, it seems, can be unreliable when it comes to women's successes and competencies.

We also heard disheartening examples of women being penalized or discriminated against at work after returning from maternity leave. It was not uncommon for women after their leave, however brief, to be assigned to less-challenging projects or roles or to be given a lower performance rating. Although such conduct is in flagrant violation of written company policies, these explicitly discriminatory behaviors were widely observed and experienced in practice. Rather than having access to formal on-ramping options, many working mothers in India battle against preconceived notions and biases regarding their commitment and potential.

How do these biases impact women's attitudes toward work? More than half (55 percent) of our respondents felt that problems of style and persona can make them scale back at work and reduce their ambition and engagement, feeding into the very biases they grapple with. The biases and stigmas associated with career breaks and non-traditional work situations—part-time work, telecommuting, staggered hours, project-based seasonal roles—also need to be tackled in the Indian business context, a tall order in a labor market that supplies hundreds of candidates, albeit of questionable quality, for each job. "Firms need to be more accommodating and understanding that if, after having a family, a woman is opting for flexible work, it doesn't mean her career has taken a backseat," said an accounting professional, calling for a broader shift in mind-set within companies. Her view is endorsed by Bharati Jacob, a partner with a Bangalore-based venture capital firm, who took a three-year break after her daughter was born and has worked from home for the past ten years. "I know a lot of men and women look at me and think, 'This is a part-time thing she's doing.' But even though I work out of my home, my commitment is absolute."

Safety and Travel

The vast economic and social disparities in India translate into safety concerns related to commuting to and traveling for work; according to our research, more than 50 percent of women feel unsafe on a regular basis. After-hours commutes are a growing issue with the rise in extreme jobs that keep people in their offices until 7 or 8 p.m. "If you have to work late hours, personal security is a major issue, particularly if you rely on public transport," said an Indian executive. "You cannot work late hours in India if you don't have your own transport." This means that large numbers of ambitious young women will be blocked in their ascent up the career ladder because they aren't yet able to afford to buy a car.

The harsh reality underlying these concerns is borne out by recent statistics on the escalation of violence in the giant cities that most professional Indian women call home. Between 2003 and 2007, rape cases in India rose by more than 30 percent, kidnapping or abduction increased by more than 50 percent, and torture and molestation also jumped sharply.[15] According to a study conducted by USAID in India, commuting concerns are a primary factor for women when they consider quitting their jobs.[16]

Several women in our discussion sessions commented on the indignities women risk in taking public transport in India. Such factors have led to a range of creative and distinctive solutions in India. In 2009, the ministry of railways, headed by a woman, Mamata Banarjee, introduced eight "Ladies' Special" commuter trains in four of India's largest cities—New Delhi, Mumbai, Chennai, and Calcutta. These single-sex trains provide a safe haven for working women, away from the taunting harassment (referred to in India by the term "eve-teasing") they risk when using mixed-gender public transportation. Another similar phenomenon is that of taxi services catering to women with female chauffeurs, for example, Priyadarshani Taxi Service has operated in Mumbai since 2007.

To make matters worse, there is also widespread cultural disapproval of women in India traveling alone, especially in semiurban and rural areas. Although there are no formal prohibitions against women's mobility as there might be in the Middle East, these attitudes are influential enough to make it difficult to hire women into jobs that require

PROFILE

"I've become a role model for myself."

Shrishti grew up in a small town in central India. The second of three children, she was raised in an upper-middle-class family in which both parents were professionals and placed great emphasis on educating their son and daughters alike. Shrishti studied biology at a university and received a degree in human pathology, going on to do graduate work in organic chemistry. Upon completing her postgraduate work, she went into teaching and then worked at a pharmaceutical company. Pursuing an education and a career had always been on Shrishti's list of goals, but like many girls in her socioeconomic milieu, she also dreamed of finding a "good and loving" husband. In her mid-twenties, she entered into an arranged marriage to a graduate student in neurology. Her husband had lived abroad for eleven years and came from an educated family similar in background to her own.

The marriage marked a turning point in Shrishti's life, her first experience of adversity. "My husband and in-laws expected me to say yes to everything and not have any opinions or individual aspirations," she recalled. "I tried to make things work, but then he started hitting me." After struggling in the relationship for two and a half years, Shrishti divorced her husband, at a time when such a move was taboo in India. Luckily, Shrishti's family was supportive and broad minded; they welcomed her back and helped her get back on her feet. "My mother was very strong in standing up for me. She told me never ever become weak in front of any other person. I'm thankful that I have such a progressive family."

By this point, Shrishti had lost a great deal of self-confidence. With her family's encouragement, however, she enrolled in management school and after graduating landed a job in Delhi. The move to Delhi was no small feat for a single woman from a small town; Indian society remains traditional, and few unmarried women live alone. But Shrishti was determined to be independent and prove herself. "When you are shattered, the company around you makes or breaks you," she says, speaking of how critical her network of family and friends had been in helping her rebound from the low point of her unhappy marriage and divorce.

Today at age thirty-six, Shrishti is an altogether different person. After six years of living alone in a major city, she is self-confident and optimistic, very much on a path of success. She has reestablished herself financially and bought her own house. On the professional front, she has worked for the past two years at the senior managerial level in a multinational corporation. "I've tasted life and built myself completely up," she says. "Now I'm confident that even if life presents something negative, I have the guts to take it on."

Shrishti finds the environment at her company woman friendly. Although many women continue to quit in the face of work-life pressures, her office has few female senior leaders heading business lines and is making a concerted effort to get more women to the top. The professional women's network in her location recently launched a mentoring program and a working mothers' network. "In the mentoring initiative, we talk a lot about what women should do to advance their careers," she explains. One area of focus is helping women be more assertive in the workplace, especially in asking for things and calling more attention to their accomplishments. "Women work very hard, but when we ask for rewards, we minimize our efforts. And, of course, male colleagues and top management need to broaden their horizons and encourage women to reach the top."

In spite of the bumps in her journey, Shrishti is passionate about her career and highly ambitious—she aspires to a leadership position at a large company like the one she is currently working in or in a business of her own. And she would like to use her experience to help other women. "I think India has progressed a lot, but there are still even highly educated professional families where females are brought down. There are cases where women are physically assaulted. When I see a person like that, I tell her about the emotional and foolish person I was. I used to be afraid to go through a dark room alone; I'd hold my sister's hand and ask her to accompany me. And now, just imagine, I've lived alone in a major city for six years. I've had some strong female role models, like my aunt and my mother, but I think I've become a role model for myself."

significant travel. The pharmaceutical sector, for instance—one of the fastest-growing markets in the world—faces an uphill battle in attracting women into sales roles that involve frequent business trips outside urban areas. The same applies in the industrial and infrastructure sectors.

The sectors that women do gravitate toward, such as finance or media, are based primarily in urban, modern environs and require minimal travel. "Women will go into sectors where traveling on their own is not a big part of their job, "said Vishakha Desai. "Part of it has to do with social issues, how you would be perceived if you travel alone all the time. For a married woman, this becomes, 'My God, how can she travel so much when she has kids at home?'" Frequent travel demands at work can be a minefield for women in India: not only are they perceived to be too independent or "forward," but also they are seen as neglecting their "primary" duties as a mother, wife, and daughter-in-law.

The Lure of the Public Sector

How do successful Indian women manage the complex balancing act between work and life? In part, they do so by choosing sectors that allow them to more easily reconcile their aspirations with heavy demands on the home front. The public sector ranks high among preferred career paths, with more than 50 percent of the women in our sample viewing these jobs as highly desirable.

In the West, private sector companies have long been uncontested in their ability to offer the best and the brightest a distinctive—and often superior—value proposition in comparison with the public sector. Typically, these advantages are assumed to consist of higher pay scales, performance-based compensation opportunities, accelerated advancement paths, and a richer range of experience, to name a few. The public sector, in contrast, has often been viewed as a stronghold of bureaucracy, characterized by poor pay, unchallenging roles, and slow career advancement.

In India, however, the public sector is an attractive alternative for the highly educated, particularly for women. As recently as 1995, the public sector in India accounted for 70 percent of jobs.[17] Top students vied for entry into civil service career tracks such as the prestigious Indian Administrative Service (IAS) or the Foreign Service. Although the private sector has expanded immensely in the past two decades, even in 2005, 58 percent of women in India's labor force held public sector jobs.[18]

The 2008 global financial downturn has also had some impact, and the notion of having a *sarkari naukri*, or government job, has once again become attractive. This was the unexpected finding of a recent survey of seventy-five hundred university students in Gujarat, in which 60 percent of respondents expressed a preference for government jobs over private sector ones, largely because of job security.[19] "The public sector is very desirable on account of the stability it offers during recession," said an Indian working mother who herself is in the private sector but whose husband is a public sector employee.

Encouraging these attitudes, the Indian government is taking steps to create more public sector jobs, at the very moment when many multinationals and private sector companies in India have scaled back. The public sector in India is also busy cleaning up its act and image in an effort to move beyond decades of stagnation and corruption, to prepare India to be the global economic giant it aspires to be.

CONCLUSION

With its demographically youthful population, over the next decade India will account for the largest contribution to the global labor force, an estimated 110 million workers. This talent pool will be characterized, according to a study by Goldman Sachs, by urbanization and the greater presence of women.[20]

Urban, middle- and upper-middle-class women in India have already made great strides toward equality in education and in the workplace. India's embrace of modern media has accelerated these changes as younger generations plug in to online networks such as Facebook or Twitter, gaining comfort in gender-neutral environments. At the same time, Bollywood movies and television series broadcast portrayals of confident and empowered women in India and beyond.

Educated Indian women represent tremendous potential for the global companies, and yet they continue to grapple with a set of distinctive pulls and pushes when it comes to work and career decisions. Attention to the complexities of Indian society—which is and will continue to be in great flux—will require companies to adopt a nuanced and tailored approach to tapping into this talent pool.

6

China

"**W**hen I was growing up in China, I couldn't imagine that I could ever work for a foreign company," says Heather Wang. "At that time, we were not even allowed to speak with foreigners." At about the time Wang was starting college, Chinese leader Deng Xiaoping's open-door policy changed everything. Rather than follow her father's career path in the military, Wang decided to major in English, a move that aroused her curiosity about the outside world.

Wang joined GE China sixteen years ago and then was accepted in the company's Global Human Resources Leadership Program, where she was identified as someone with talent and a great deal of potential. Now forty-seven, she is vice president of Human Resources for GE Global Growth & Operations, overseeing not only all of Asia but also Latin America, the Middle East, Africa, Russia, and Europe.

"Working here has helped me see my potential in ways I never dreamed I could," she says. "I want to stay in this role and help other people become global leaders. I feel inspired by helping people become successful."

The Communist revolution in China gave women equal rights with men, at least officially. Mao Zedong's famous pronouncement that "women hold up half of the sky" was a battle cry for women to serve the revolution as soldiers and iron welders, farmers and bureaucrats. Women's rights were pushed to the foreground, not only because their labor was needed to forge a new order but also because their inferior status was a hallmark of the old, traditional ways.

When Deng Xiaoping, who became premier in 1980, instituted market reform and declared that "to get rich is glorious," he urged China's men and women to help the country grow strong and wealthy by going into business and making money themselves. Women now in their forties and fifties came into adulthood at a time when working hard in the private sector was seen as a way to serve a higher calling rather than purely satisfying their personal ambitions. Today, China has the highest female labor force participation rate of all BRIC nations, with 75 percent of women ages fifteen through sixty-four in the workforce.[1]

Their energy helped propel one of the most rapid industrializations in modern history, transforming China from economic desolation to a global powerhouse. China suffered in the recent global recession, but only in relative terms. The gross domestic product (GDP) grew at a rate of 9 percent in 2008 and 2009—a slowdown compared to the previous five years, when GDP growth was a blistering 10-plus percent, but way ahead of the United States and Europe, where growth was at a standstill. In 2010, China's economy was back again to double-digit expansion.[2]

As China's economy has boomed, so has personal wealth. According to a recent Goldman Sachs report, in 1990, 1 percent of the Chinese population could be considered middle class. In 2008, that number was 35 percent, and Goldman predicts it will be almost 70 percent by 2020.[3] Within the ranks of the new middle class are an increasing number of women leaving rural areas and small villages to go to college, enter the business world, and follow a well-beaten path to wealth and success.

Role models are plentiful. Evidence abounds of what Chinese women in business can do: in *Forbes* magazine's 2010 list of global billionaires, half of the fourteen self-made female billionaires were from mainland China.[4] Other notable examples of Chinese women in top positions include Wei Sun Christianson, CEO of Morgan Stanley China; Mei Yan, CEO of Viacom China, whose father built the censorship system for China; Mary Ma, former CFO of Lenovo, who recently started her own investment fund; and Wu Yi, former vice premier of China, whom *Forbes* three times named the second most powerful woman in the world.

Backing them up are legions of ambitious and qualified women. According to figures released in 2007 in the Grant Thornton International Business Report, 91 percent of Chinese businesses have women in senior leadership, the second highest percentage in the world (after the Philippines). Further, 32 percent of senior management is composed of women—a figure greater than that in the United States (23 percent) or the United Kingdom (19 percent).[5]

In politics, too, 21 percent of seats in the national parliament were held by women (637 of 2,987 seats) as of 2009.[6] However, although this is a significant accomplishment (and higher than the equivalent U.S. figure), the real power is not held within the national parliament but rather within the Politburo Standing Committee, which has only male members.[7]

Even as professional opportunities abound, educated women are struggling to find their personal identity, caught between a world evolving as quickly as the Shanghai skyline and a resurgent past. Communism never fully eradicated deeply ingrained cultural beliefs, such as obligations to one's elders. The one-child policy is leaving young professional women with a heavy burden of elder care, one that threatens to stifle their career aspirations. Traditions that value men over women, officially stamped out by Communist support for women's rights, have resurfaced with the loosening of sociopolitical restrictions. Despite a 2005 amendment to the landmark 1992 Law on the Protection of Women's Rights and Interests, known as the Women's Constitution, that makes gender equality an explicit state policy and outlaws sexual harassment, discrimination is widespread, especially in Chinese-operated companies. Employers commonly specify gender, age, and physical appearance in job offers. In private life, concubinage, outlawed by the Communists after they took power in 1949, has reemerged.

"The main issue we face is confusion, about who we are and what we should be," Qin Liwen, a magazine columnist, was quoted as saying in a recent newspaper interview.[8] "Should I be a 'strong woman' and make money and have a career, maybe grow rich but risk not finding a husband or having a child? Or should I marry and be a stay-at-home housewife, support my husband, and educate my child? Or should I be a 'fox'—the kind of woman who marries a rich man, drives around in a BMW, but has to put up with his concubines?"

At once forward looking and rooted in tradition, ambitious Chinese women confront a tough balancing act. Even as they adapt to and profit from market forces, they face pressures strong enough to derail successful and fulfilling careers.

THE CHANGING FACE OF TALENT

The teachings of the sixth-century BCE philosopher Confucius infused Chinese culture with a regard for elite education that borders on worship—and while the Confucian belief system placed scholars at the top of society and was openly contemptuous of businesspeople, present-day China has come to see a university education as the key to business success.

In 1998, when then-president Jiang Zemin announced plans to bolster higher education, Chinese universities and colleges produced 830,000 graduates a year.[9] By 2010, the number was more than six million and rising. As of 2008, the date for the latest available statistics, women constituted 48 percent of all college graduates in China, a huge pool of talent potential, and were pouring into advanced degree programs.[10]

There's a frustrating paradox at work, though. Multinational companies in China are clamoring for qualified candidates; according to a recent survey, 37 percent of U.S.-owned enterprises said that finding talent was their biggest operational problem.[11] Yet a study by McKinsey found that fewer than 10 percent of Chinese college graduates are prepared to succeed in a multinational environment.[12]

The reason: an educational environment that places an inordinately high value on test scores rather than problem solving and creative thinking. China's invention of the *keju* system, which used tests to select government officials, was a great development, because it enabled talented individuals to join the ruling class regardless of family background. But the discipline that promoted a meritocracy evolved over time into a nightmare as the system changed into one that rewarded memorization of Confucian classics.

Although *keju* is now dead, its spirit lives on in the *gaokao*, the nationwide college entrance exam. This mandatory exam determines whether students can attend university and which one they are eligible for. Often dubbed the "baton" that conducts the whole education orchestra, the *gaokao* wields such influence that students, parents, teachers, school leaders, and even local government officials all work together to produce high scores. It's impossible to overstate the significance of the *gaokao*. With a limited number of university slots available, "your life is made or broken by how well you do," says Pamela Berns, a global leadership consultant and a visiting professor at the Beijing International MBA program at Peking University (BiMBA). "If you make it into one the top tier universities, you're set for life. If you don't, you may be stuck forever."

But if, as some employers complain, the *gaokao* shapes students into top-notch test takers but underdeveloped individual thinkers, it also forges diamond-hard ambition at an early age. China's primary and secondary schools are competitive crucibles. Joan Wang, a venture capitalist with SIG Asia Investment, describes how, when she was in school, an intense spirit of competition was instilled by the Chinese education system from first grade on. "Everyone's name and score for each subject was placed on the wall in the classroom. Even before we knew the score, there was Parents' Day. All the parents saw your score before you did." As a result, she says, the thinking went, "Oh my God. It is shameful to be the tenth highest in the class. I've got to work hard and be on the top of the list in the next term."

Until recently, Chinese universities followed a traditional system of pedagogy: exams involved "a lot of regurgitating what teachers tell you, and the more precisely you regurgitate, the higher the test scores," explains Edward Tse, Booz & Company's chairman for Greater China and author of *The China Strategy*. The result is what Tse calls "a disconnect between readiness and alignment for jobs" in Western companies. But this is now changing, he observes. "The changes are slow, but they have been able to accelerate through arrangements with foreign universities"—such as the increasing number of joint MBA programs between Chinese and foreign business schools.

As a result, even though those women whose MBAs are earned at elite foreign schools are still seen as the crème de la crème back home in China, credentials from homegrown business schools are rapidly gaining in prestige. Six of China's universities are ranked among the top two hundred in the world. The China Europe International Business School (CEIBS) in Beijing—where some 33 percent of the students are women, a figure on a par with representation at top MBA campuses in the developed world—was included in the top twenty-five of the *Financial Times'* 2010 global MBA rankings.[13] Women accounted for only 18 percent of the country's business school graduates in 2005, but by 2009 the number had climbed to 32 percent.[14]

The drive that pushes Chinese women to ace the *gaokao* fuels the motivation to succeed in their careers. Another force propelling them: China's one-child policy, instituted in 1979, focuses an entire family's aspirations on the only child. "My generation had a lot of pressure growing up, because they were the one hope in the family" for the future, says Julia Zhu, national operations director, Corporate Clients, for Sodexo

China. So many urban parents ascribed to the belief that music lessons enhance a child's intelligence that Zhu jokes that all her peers in Shanghai can play the piano.

Then there are the considerable rewards of success. "Today's women are more exposed to possibilities," says Berns. "Through the Internet, through working in multinational corporations, they learn about how other people live and that inspires them to want a new lifestyle." The perquisites of that lifestyle—a spacious apartment or maybe even a suburban villa, a comfortable car, and money for sumptuous vacations, nice clothes, and dining out—exert an irresistible attraction, especially compared with the spare surroundings that most of these women grew up in.

Marilyn, an executive in a pharmaceutical firm, scored the third highest ranking in biology in all of China when she took the *gaokao*, but she decided against a career in academia. China's economy was opening to Western companies as she entered university, and in her third year, she was awarded an internship at a large German firm. "I made $3,000 a month. My parents worked in the Chinese science academy, and I think they made $600 a month."

With the combined force of those pulls and pushes, it's no wonder that educated Chinese women show high levels of ambition: three-quarters (76 percent) of the women we surveyed aspire to a top job, more than twice the proportion in the United States. They display impressive levels of commitment; 88 percent are loyal to their current employer, 76 percent are willing to go the extra mile, and only 15 percent say they have "one foot out the door," one of the lowest numbers in the BRIC and UAE.

Recently, Marilyn's employer asked her to take a personality questionnaire. The first question: "Do you think you're ambitious?" Marilyn asked her HR director whether *ambition* in English had a negative connotation. No, no, the HR director reassured her; it's a neutral word that means that you're eager to be successful. "In that case," Marilyn immediately replied, "I'm that kind of person."

But whether Marilyn and her peers can, in fact, fulfill all their potential depends on how well they navigate a complex web of traditional pulls, work-related pushes, and cultural pitfalls that threatens to hobble their high-flying ambition.

A COMPLEX WEB OF PULLS

The view of what an ideal Chinese woman is—speaking only when spoken to, always obedient to her husband and his family—dates back at least as far as the Confucian era. In his writings, Confucius advocated an ideal society, which he saw as a harmonious place in which a wife obeyed her husband just as a subject obeyed the ruler. Harmony was maintained by a rigid adherence to hierarchy: everyone knew his or her place. The chaos of the Cultural Revolution and the loosening influence of market reform may have relaxed strictures in Chinese society at large, but within the intimate circle of the immediate family, traditional expectations still persist—and possess surprising force.

The Good Daughter

Every woman in China, as in many emerging markets, knows that her primary responsibility is to be a good daughter or daughter-in-law. Fulfilling family obligations trumps satisfying personal career ambitions, no matter how successful that career may be. There are no exceptions. "Under our culture, we take care of our parents," says one executive in the financial sector. "When they get older, they will expect us to be around them and spend time with them. And that is something we're prepared to do. Whenever they need me, I will be there"—whether that means relocating to be near them, as this executive plans to do, or leaving the workforce entirely.

Every woman we interviewed knows someone—a colleague, a boss, or a friend—who put her career on hold to care for an aging relative. A few years ago, when her mother and her aunt fell ill, Adeline Wong, who is in her late thirties, responded to the crisis like a model Chinese daughter. "I left my former job in Taiwan, where I was working with one of the top venture capital firms," says Wong, who joined Booz Greater

China in 2005 and is now the Head of HR. "It was a very good career, but I had to stop because both my mom and her sister fell ill. I quit and spent several months taking care of them."

Many Chinese women, including Wong, also provide financial support to their parents or in-laws. The CWLP data shows that 58 percent of Chinese women lend a monetary helping hand to the tune of some 18 percent of their annual income. One professional woman we interviewed contributes 30 percent of her paycheck—and that's not unusual. In a country like China, where state support for the elderly can't keep up with the soaring cost of living and the social security net is uncertain, contributions from adult children are not only appreciated but are necessary. An American expatriate lawyer based in Hong Kong, who has a Chinese wife with a similarly high-powered career, succinctly explained the allocation of their income: "My job is to earn money to take care of her, and her job is to earn money to take care of her parents."

Heather Wang is a financial mainstay for her husband's parents, who, like many in-laws, live with her. "My mother-in-law had two heart surgeries already, and we paid for all of it," she says. "We put her in the best hospital, with the best doctors, and that wasn't covered by insurance. I think that's part of our responsibility, and I'm glad we can do something for them."

The pressure of being a good daughter or daughter-in-law can produce more guilt than the pressure to be a good mother or wife. The statement "I feel guilty about the trade-off between work and my elder care responsibilities" in the CWLP survey elicited an "agree" response from 88 percent of Chinese women who were working full-time. The only other country that came close to that figure was the UAE, at 73 percent.

Adding to a high-achieving woman's burden, the one-child policy means that many women have no siblings to share the obligations of elder care. Of the Chinese women surveyed by CWLP, 95 percent already have elder care responsibilities. Putting elders in institutional care is rarely an option; few nursing homes or assisted living facilities exist, and, in any case, placing a parent in one is viewed as tantamount to abandonment, a grave sin in a society that prizes filial duty. Although reliance on hired help is part of the solution—70 percent are willing to bring in a housekeeper or *ayi*—more and more women will inevitably be in the position of Adeline Wong, forced to leave their careers at the peak of fulfilling their potential.

The Good Mother

For the present, though, the imbalance in the number of elders favors working mothers: 82 percent of full-time working mothers receive regular child care help from their parents or in-laws. Every child has two sets of grandparents to help out, and they do to a degree almost inconceivable to Americans and Europeans.

"If you have to work and are the only child in your family, the best solution is to have your parents-in-law or parents help out," says Julia Zhu. Every Sunday evening, she and her husband drop off their two-year-old daughter with his parents. Zhu travels frequently for business; when she is home, it takes an hour to drive to her in-laws, so Zhu doesn't see her daughter again until Friday. "Of course, I miss the chance to be with my daughter from Monday to Friday, but working mothers have to focus more on work," she says. "Besides, when the child is very small, you only focus on how she eats and how she sleeps. When she is older, especially when she goes to primary school, I'll need to spend more time with her—to teach her how to do math, how to pronounce English. But my daughter is only two years old now. She has a long way to go."

The social opprobrium or raised eyebrows that accompany the notion, in the West, of separating mothers and children, often for years at a time, doesn't exist in China. There's a long tradition of sending one's child away, and, notes Rosalind Hudnell, chief diversity officer for Intel Corporation, "There's just not the same level of guilt associated with that." During the Cultural Revolution, urban parents sent to work in the countryside regularly left their children with their own parents, where they would have an easier lifestyle; later, as China's economy began to expand, parents went where the work was and didn't have the wherewithal to care for a child. Many of the women we interviewed spoke of being sent to live with their grandparents in cities in order to take advantage of better educational opportunities. Although their heartache is very real, today's Chinese female professionals don't hesitate to make the same choice.

For Marilyn, the decision to relocate her thirteen-month-old son from their home in Shanghai to live with her in-laws in Beijing wasn't easy, but it solved a variety of problems. Marilyn's father died only two days after she returned to work from maternity leave; she felt so guilty about her mother living alone that she seriously considered quitting the job she loves in Shanghai and relocating to Beijing, where her mother lived. Instead, she and her husband came up with a complicated solution: for four of every six months, Marilyn's mother lives with them in Shanghai, where, Marilyn says, "my mom feels better because she is busy taking care of my little boy." The other two months, the grandmother returns to her home in Beijing. In the winter, Marilyn's son and nanny also move to Beijing, where they stay with her husband's parents. Because the country's public utility system provides heat only to the northern half of the country, Beijing's apartments are heated and Shanghai's are not. "He's warmer and more comfortable in Beijing," says Marilyn. "We plan to visit him every two weeks. Meanwhile, we call him every day, and we can see him through an Internet camera. This arrangement will last until he goes to kindergarten."

Because Communism bred an expectation that all women should work, only 35 percent of women surveyed reported pressure to quit their jobs upon the birth of their child, one of the lowest numbers among the BRIC countries and the UAE. When grandparents can't help out, good institutional child care is generally widely available and accepted, with 60 percent of our respondents using day care. Nannies are inexpensive, providing another option.

Still, despite the pragmatism they expressed, even very ambitious women in our interviews acknowledged feeling torn between their career and their child. Some 86 percent of Chinese women in our survey expressed maternal guilt, the second highest among their BRIC and UAE counterparts; many speak wistfully of quitting their jobs to be full-time mothers. Tradition still has the power to trump ambition. As a senior woman for a multinational pharmaceutical company quips, "We hold up half the sky, but there are five thousand years of history behind us."

PUSH FACTORS AT WORK

A variety of forces—from tradition-based bias to clashes between Chinese culture and the expectations of multinational corporate work environments to the crushing demands of what it takes to succeed in that world—causes many high-performing Chinese women to question whether they want to stay on the fast track, detour to a more scenic route, or abandon the journey entirely.

Bias and Discrimination

An old Chinese aphorism says that a woman in a leadership position is "like a donkey taking the place of a horse, which can only lead to trouble."[15] Since the 1980s, there have been many documented cases of sex discrimination limiting women's careers in both local and global companies.

Paradoxically, even though the market economy opened opportunities for women to succeed in the private sector, it also gave them the "right" to consume makeup and fashion, to the point that the consumer culture fueled a kind of sexism familiar in the West—the use of images of idealized women to sell products, along with pornography and the return of prostitution. By the early 1990s, China was so rife with complaints about gender bias that the government passed a law forbidding discrimination in employment, housing, politics, education, and other areas. Nearly every year since, the government has announced newly vigilant programs to promote women's rights. Still, even though women have full equality on the books, enforcement is imperfect.

It is not uncommon for employers to specify "men only" in job postings or, if they are considering women, especially recent college graduates, to cite demands for height, weight, and an attractive appearance. Problems of bias have been severe enough to make some 48 percent of the women responding to CWLP's survey disengage or consider quitting their jobs.

One of the most common causes of discrimination is maternity leave. By law, women in China are granted ninety days for maternity leave. Women who give birth after age twenty-five receive an additional month off at full salary. Furthermore, employers must grant one "feeding hour" per day for the baby's first year, also paid. Most companies give new mothers the choice of coming in one hour later or leaving one hour earlier; some offer the option of an additional month's leave.

But women's jobs are not always waiting for them when they return. "I have some female friends who had children while they were working, then came back to a crisis," says Ginny Luo, twenty-nine, an MBA candidate at BiMBA, who is married but does not yet have children. "Sometimes they find their position is occupied by someone else and they have nothing to do, though they still can get their salary. They are psychologically discarded. In this situation they normally quit their job, albeit reluctantly, even though they get financial compensation."

From the employer's perspective the maternity laws can be something of a burden. A Hong Kong-based partner in a Wall Street law firm says the best lawyers in Asia are women—"for sheer raw talent and verbal capability"—but the firm takes a chance when hiring them. "We have had 100 percent pregnancy rate among female associates, and where offices range from five to fifteen people, it wreaks total havoc."

Although it is illegal to fire a woman for getting pregnant, it's not illegal for employers to ask whether she plans to get married or have a child—and not hire her if they think she will. "The law doesn't achieve protection as much as limit opportunity" for young women with high potential, notes venture capitalist Joan Wang, although she recalls that when layoff rumors arose at a former employer, "suddenly the office was full of pregnant women."

That puts at risk women in their childbearing years who have not yet had a child, especially if they are still making their way up the career ladder. "You have to demonstrate a much stronger drive to prove that you can accomplish as much if not more than your male counterpart," says Joan Wang. "It's tougher, but it's doable."

The flip side is that a woman who has a child becomes more desirable to potential employers. "If you already have a child, they know you won't have a second child. And if you can handle the load with one child, you can keep handling it," says a pharmaceutical executive. Joan Wang agrees. The CEO of one of her portfolio companies explained his choice of a female candidate for comptroller by saying, "Her child is already in kindergarten, so there's nothing to worry about. She can focus on the job all the time."

Style Sabotage

Ironically, it's not only male bias that can get in the way of women's advancement. When it comes to projecting the management style, communication abilities, and executive presence required to succeed at multinational corporations, Chinese women can be their own worst enemies. "The key challenge we have with women associates in China comes when we expect them to develop into franchise builders," says the Hong Kong law partner. "That requires them to be assertive, make cold calls, forge bonds and relationships with male clients"—something many Chinese women aren't comfortable with.

The reasons aren't surprising. Women in their mid-thirties and older grew up with a double lesson in the value of making themselves invisible: Confucian tradition dictated that a woman should be silent and submissive, coupled with plenty of examples under Communism of the folly of standing out. The result: "There's a high level of humility, self-deprecation, of apologies," says Joni Bessler, a Shanghai-based partner at Booz & Company. "Men have the same characteristics, but it's worse for women and it hurts them more. I tell female staff, 'Speak up!' But it's a struggle to get them to behave that way, because it's so counter to everything they've been taught."

Heather Wang had to learn how to "unlearn" these traits. "When I came to the U.S. in 1996, I was very shy," she says. "I wasn't aggressive about communicating my deliverables. A few years later I managed a team of ten people, and while other team leaders always shared great stories about what their people were doing, I thought our team results would speak for themselves. My team got upset with me for not letting everyone know about all the important things they were doing." She credits GE's management training program with helping her change her approach.

This behavior pattern is changing among the younger generation, but, according to a Chinese accounting professional who participated in a CWLP Virtual Strategy Session, "There's still a perception that women don't want to be aggressive, and if clients have to choose between a man and a woman, they will opt for the man." Others believe that women don't dare to act "aggressive" because such behavior is "too male" and will scare off potential husbands. That's no small threat in a culture where a spouse shares the burden of supporting aging relatives and provides the crucial second income necessary to enjoy urban China's materialistic lifestyle.

These entrenched stereotypes of Chinese women, portraying them as docile and deferential, are clearly at odds with what it takes to get ahead in a multinational environment. Yet a shift in communication and management style in the opposite direction can be risky, steering women toward yet another negative stereotype, that of the the authoritarian dragon lady. In effect, professional women in China face a complicated balancing act when it comes to style, somewhere between the extremes of too submissive and too aggressive.

These two deeply ingrained models—dragon lady and deferential employee—continue to resonate in hierarchical situations, such as in the workplace. China's long authoritarian tradition helps explain why a

Chinese woman in a management position might adopt an authoritarian tone with subordinates. It also explains why foreign managers of multinational corporations in China are often frustrated in their efforts to get their female Chinese staff to express personal viewpoints that might be perceived as questioning the boss.

And it explains why it is difficult for many Chinese women to master that enigmatic quality called "style compliance." The CWLP survey found that among Chinese women, 70 percent of respondents had experienced style compliance issues, the top three of which were a too-quiet speaking style (34 percent), a too-loud speaking style (23 percent), and overly emotional behavior (23 percent). "For men, 'executive presence' is the presence of power," explains Pamela Berns. "For women, it's a delicate dance between power and femininity. In my classes, I see women struggling with this all the time." One exception to the reticent stereotype: an influx of Chinese women who came to business school from careers in TV journalism. "These women are models of female executive presence," says Berns. "They could teach Western women a thing or two about how to leverage femininity in their expression of power."

Berns has also met older women in senior government ministry positions who might qualify as dragon ladies. "These women are tough— very vocal, and their subordinates are terrified of them."

Too much authoritarian fire-breathing in a corporate setting can result in a suspicious rate of staff turnover and problematic performance reviews. But some dragon lady characteristics aren't necessarily a bad thing, Berns says. "When women in corporate settings look for mentors, there is something to be learned from the more aggressive style," says Berns. "Their tough fight to the top, their perseverance. For a young woman, there's a bit of a sense of 'Wow, could I be that way? If I could act that way, I could also act in a thousand other ways.'"

Ginny Luo, who is a former student of Berns's, has given a lot of thought to how a woman should handle the role of boss. Although she initially considered a female former boss too "soft," Luo changed her mind after learning in her MBA class that a woman boss with men on her team might do well to play the submissive female angle. "Most Chinese men will not like it if a woman gives them orders," she says. "So I find it works to give men their assignments in a very polite way, pretending you need their help to get this job done."

Training can help, both in toning down a domineering management style and helping a reticent person come out of her shell. But whereas an MNC employer offering business school attendance or executive training will see this as a way to recruit or retain talent, a Chinese employee might take offense, depending on the way the opportunity is presented. "This has traditionally been a culture of punishment, not reward," says Berns. "In a traditional Chinese company, training is seen not as a perk but as a message that you're a bad worker and we want to fix it." One good way to entice Chinese women into a training forum, she says, is to bring a group of them together. "That," she says, "will give them an environment of safety, where they can share their personal challenges away from the company of their male colleagues."

Extreme Hours

Inevitably, among those with high aspirations are a great many women working in extreme jobs. Highly qualified women working for global companies average seventy-one work hours per week in China.

As a senior manager for a multinational company with a wide presence in China, Jeannette packs her suitcase and kisses her five-year-old son goodbye for a few days almost every week. Her husband works long hours and often doesn't get home until after the boy's bedtime. "I have a nanny," Jeannette says. "She can take care of my kid in terms of making dinner and sending him to bed and reading stories, but she can't replace a mother or father." Jeannette worries that her frequent absence may drive a wedge between her and her child. "You only have a certain amount of time with your kid, and if you keep traveling, you don't get

PROFILE

"I still question myself—is this the right decision?"

After nearly two decades of high-flying achievement abroad, Booz principal Jessica Zhang returned home to Beijing, her impressive career now complicated by work-life pressures. She's squeezed from all sides, often wondering how she'll cope.

Her work remains a top priority, and her hours are marathon, with clients across China. Her husband is still in Tokyo, where he works for a high-tech Japanese company, making Zhang a de facto single mother to their two-year-old son. And even though her octogenarian parents in Beijing are healthy for now, Zhang returned to her hometown from Japan in 2009 to be closer to them, preparing for the day when they may need her care.

"One day if one or both of my parents cannot live on their own, they will need help. That's one of the reasons I decided to come back to Beijing," says Zhang. But with her husband unable to join her for now, the transition has been difficult. "I still question myself—is this the right decision? It's extra pressure on myself."

Like many professional women of her generation, Zhang expected to pursue a secure career in government. Her parents worked all their lives for the State Planning Commission, which managed China's centrally planned economy beginning in the early 1950s. Zhang majored in chemistry in college, hoping to follow in her parent's footsteps and work for the government, specifically for the Ministry of Metallurgy.

But by the time she graduated from college in 1988, the nation was in transition. Most graduates at the time had no say in where they worked, but

that time and the kind of relationship that belongs with your children. I often feel guilty," she acknowledges, so much so that she fears her concern could compromise her career. "This may actually distract me from what I'm doing."

there were glimmers of flexibility and choice in careers. Taking advantage of the slow loosening of the state system, Zhang did two years of graduate work in international relations in Japan and then stayed on for four years, working in marketing for Mitsubishi Oil (now part of Nippon Oil Corp.).

Following an MBA from Yale and short stints with Booz in Hong Kong and a Beijing start-up, Zhang spent most of the past decade with Booz in Tokyo. She gained valuable consulting experience, first in energy markets and later in automotive and consumer goods markets. Travel was minimal, because most of her clients were based in Tokyo, a boon for a first-time mother.

Back in Beijing, however, she faces an array of heightened professional and personal challenges. Her parents live across town in Beijing, next door to her brother and his wife. But Zhang's brother and wife also care for his wife's parents, so future elder care worries are on Zhang's mind. Her new clients are spread across China. Her son attends a half-day nursery school and she has a full-time live-in nanny, and yet she knows that her child care arrangements may not last. "It's all luck," she says of finding—and keeping—the right nanny. "You try the one you like and see what happens."

Perhaps the greatest sticking point for Zhang as a dedicated mother and devoted professional is the long hours—a challenge no less arduous for its predictability in the consulting industry. Although she appreciates the flexibility offered by Booz, Zhang knows that she can't compete in this sector without putting in ten- to twelve-hour days. She's seen numerous working mothers in her industry leave over this issue.

"If you do this job, it requires long hours. You cannot change it. That's the difficulty. If I decide to stay in this job, that's the life," says Zhang. But after a thoughtful pause, she adds, "As a mother, I would like to spend more time with my son."

Travel and Safety

In June 2010, China notched a new milestone: IBM's *Global Commuter Pain Study* ranked Beijing traffic as tied with Mexico City for the world's worst.[16] The study depicts commuters in many cities struggling to get to and from work each day, but Beijing workers reside in a special circle of commuter hell: 95 percent say that roadway traffic has negatively affected their health, and 84 percent blame the congestion, incessant honking, and nerve-shredding gauntlet of automotive chicken for adverse work performance.

"It's very, very bad," says Joan Wang. "There's no such thing as peak hour any more. From 8 in the morning to 9 at night, it's peak hour every hour." Public transportation isn't any better. "My colleagues who take the subway say five trains have to pass before they can get on. The bus is even worse, because it's limited by the traffic. You see hundreds of people standing at the bus station, just waiting for the bus to come."

Traffic was snarled for more than sixty *miles* on stretches of two highways outside Beijing in August 2010; the jam took more than nine days to clear. Inside Beijing, according to the IBM study, congestion can be so frustrating that nearly 70 percent of respondents turn around and go home. Jeannette knows exactly how they feel. "The traffic is a huge waste of time," she complains. "I don't think it's necessary for me to physically be in the office all the time. A lot of internal work can be done by video-conferencing. If I had flexible work, I could gain two hours a day. And if people produce results, what's the big deal?"

Although commuting and traveling within China aren't as perilous as, say, in India or Brazil, they're hazardous enough to cause nearly one-third (31 percent) of women in the CWLP survey to feel unsafe. Julia Zhu isn't concerned in Shanghai, but visiting Sodexo clients in less-developed sites is another matter. "When you're a woman and young and alone and in a rough area, you feel threatened," she says. "On a business trip, you have to wear good clothes and everyone assumes that you are rich. Taxi drivers will take you to a remote area and demand money. Two years ago, I saw the people in a taxi behind me threatened with a knife." In Shanghai, Zhu pays for everything with a credit card, but plastic still is rare in the countryside. "If you're held up and you don't have money, they think you're lying," Zhu says. As a result, whenever she travels, she always asks her husband to stuff her wallet with $50 in cash.

The Competition: The Public Sector and Chinese Companies

When China opened its doors to foreign companies and private ownership, almost anyone with a spark of adventure was eager to leave the old Communist "cradle to grave" care of state-owned enterprises for a chance to travel, get rich, and innovate.

Marilyn graduated from university in the mid-1990s, a time when multinational corporations were the obvious choice for a smart woman with ambition. "MNCs paid more. And the MNCs are located in the most beautiful buildings in Beijing. You feel good that you're working in that atmosphere."

Like most recent graduates, Marilyn hadn't given much consideration to career development; she was happy with a monthly salary that was five times what her parents earned in the state science academy. Then in her first year, her employer sent her for training to its headquarters in Germany. "I would never have been able to afford to travel by myself to Europe. It was very, very exciting and opened my eyes to see the world. And it gave me lots of motivation—of course, you choose to stay" with that employer.

Actually, Marilyn left two years later—to take a job with her current employer, another foreign firm. There's no question in her mind that she will continue to work for MNCs. "High-quality talent and people who are ambitious want to work with international talent. They want to see the world and the business management systems of the U.S. and Europe. I talk a lot with people working in government-owned companies, and there's a head-and-shoulders difference."

"It's a different game" working at a state-owned enterprise (SOE), agrees Joan Wang. "What wins you big applause at a multinational corporation won't work there. You have to know whether you'd like to play that kind of game and whether you're good at it."

Furthermore, "the public sector has historically been and largely still is dominated by males," notes Jeannette. Women can achieve a high-ranking senior management position, but, Joan Wang says, "for someone who wants to be a CEO, doing it in a state-owned enterprise is more difficult."

But tough competition has a way of changing one's perspective. In 2010, more than 6.4 million university graduates entered the job market, up from one million in 1999.[17] The number of high-skilled, high-paying jobs has not kept pace. As a result, the "iron rice bowl" is looking increasingly attractive: China's news services reported that in 2009 a record 1 million people took the national civil service exam, up from 775,000 in 2008 and 500,000 in 2005.[18] Fifty-seven percent of CWLP female survey respondents rated the public sector as an attractive option.

Government jobs generally offer shorter hours and more security than the corporate world, along with a supportive environment where a work unit is like a family, and even provide subsidized housing and education. The latter are serious factors in cities like Beijing and Shanghai, where skyrocketing living costs strain even a two-salary family budget. Nor are government agencies automatically peopled by uncreative, obstructionist drones. Some, at least on the local and provincial levels, are trying to overcome a reputation for stagnation and corruption, and a significant amount of China's green technology and scientific research is conducted within the public sector. Another attraction: "The Chinese in general have a good sense of nationalism, so being part of the public sector addresses the Chinese desire to continue to help their country be more successful," says Edward Tse.

"Most of my female friends prefer to work for the government because the workload is not heavy and they have enough time to spend with their families," was the view of one focus group participant. But that's not always the case, warns an executive in the private sector. "Some sectors are very demanding. You don't have weekends. When your boss wants to have a meeting, you have it. There's no annual leave—you're entitled to it, but you're not supposed to take it." She concludes, "For me, it's a trade-off. You can have a more relaxed life but under a certain framework, and that framework may have more constraints. It's a one-sided benefit, for sure."

If state-owned enterprises and multinational corporations represent opposite ends of the employment spectrum, educated women are finding fertile ground for their ambition in between. (An increasing number are becoming entrepreneurs, as described in the following sidebar, "A Business of One's Own.") Global giants like Huawei, Haier, and Lenovo, to name only a few homegrown companies that have muscled into leading roles in the world economy, exert a magnetic force. In his recent book, *Billions of Entrepreneurs: How China and India Are Reshaping Their Futures and Yours*, Tarun Khanna describes a visit to Huawei's facilities in Shenzen, in the southernmost tip of China. He was met by a young woman, a college graduate from Hubei province, far away in the center of the country. She had applied for a job on the Web without ever having visited the facility or talked with its managers. Khanna asked why she had not sought a job closer to home. "'Why?' Her look told me she thought the answer totally obvious. 'Because it is one of China's best companies.'"[19]

"There's a certain amount of celebrity associated with a reputable company," says Pamela Berns. "If a company is a well-known organization, Chinese people use the English phrase 'famous company.' And there's something about being associated with something that's famous. Ambition is driven by that."

Once applied almost exclusively to multinational corporations, now the phrase "famous company" gilds Chinese firms, too. When Berns began to teach at BiMBA in 2001, China had just entered the World Trade Organization. "My students used to eat out of my hand to know how we do it in the West. Now there's more of a nationalistic perspective. They say, 'That might work in the West but it would never work in a Chinese company.'"

A Business of One's Own

An increasing number of women are being lured away from multinational corporations, not by Chinese companies or state-owned enterprises but by the prospect of running their own show. A recent report by *China Entrepreneur* magazine found that there are currently more than 29 million female entrepreneurs in China, accounting for more than 20 percent of the total number of entrepreneurs in the country.[20]

"Entrepreneurialism is in the Chinese blood," says Edward Tse, Booz & Company's chairman for Greater China and author of *The China Strategy*. For many years, though, starting one's own business wasn't a respectable occupation for women. But with fewer social inhibitors today and greater opportunities, women no longer fear that they will be seen as lesser businesspeople if they eschew a government or corporate job. And, Tse adds, as witnessed by the overwhelming Chinese presence on lists of the world's wealthiest women, "you can hit the jackpot."

Many would-be entrepreneurs start their careers with a multinational company before striking out on their own, says Joan Wang, a Beijing-based venture capitalist with SIG Asia Investment. "I have a friend who got her MBA at University of Chicago and worked for McKinsey for a few years before starting her own Internet advertising company two years ago." It is, she says, an increasingly typical strategy, especially for women looking to succeed on their own terms. "They think they can achieve better by doing their own thing, rather than going through a career path designed by men or foreigners."

So attractive is that possibility that entrepreneurship is one of the most popular courses in Peking University's prestigious BiMBA program, observes Pamela Berns, a visiting professor for a number of years. "Women are really eager to get the lowdown in that class," she says. Entrepreneurship "seems to be the way of the future."

CONCLUSION

The generation of women now in their twenties and thirties has grown up in a China where skyscrapers rise up almost overnight and the outside world is clamoring to be a part of their country's development. They saw their parents work hard to create a comfortable life for them. Many came from one-child families, and even if they weren't treated like the spoiled "little emperors" (or empresses) that have become another stereotype, they have grown up with the luxury of putting their own interests first.

"The Chinese women I see entering the workforce now feel they can control the whole world," says Heather Wang, who has met many young women through HR interviews. "When my generation of women was young, we knew we'd sacrifice for the future. The new generation seems to take things for granted. They are much braver about being aggressive in asking for things."

For example, the concept of work-life balance—once foreign, not to mention proscribed—is an increasingly popular topic of conversation. Julia Jia, thirty, a former student at BiMBA who is now working for Louis Vuitton China's retail department, speaks for many when she says, "Of course, I want to be in top management. But if there were a conflict with taking care of my children or elders, I would give up my career."

One reason many women keep working, despite the arduous hours, is that, much as they might like to take a break to care for their children or elders, they can't afford the financial hit. China's cities are becoming increasingly expensive, and many women work because the best way they can take care of their families is by adding to the household income. Another reason is that on-ramping opportunities are virtually nonexistent. Women sadly joke that the chance of getting a job after dropping out of the market is even smaller than finding a wealthy husband.

But the increasing discussion of such topics speaks to a desire among women to find a middle way, between the pushes and pulls of their career and care obligations and fulfilling their professional aspirations without shortchanging their personal lives. As of now, women have few options when their towering ambition becomes unsustainable. Pamela Berns warns, "If they have to trade off something, it might very well be their upward mobility." That's not good for either women or their employers.

Companies have an unprecedented opportunity to help women—and help their own bottom lines. By offering flexible work arrangements, creating on-ramping programs, and recognizing and addressing the unique issues confronting high-performing Chinese women, employers will gain a powerful competitive advantage: not only will they unleash the power of an impressive army of talent but also, in developing a reputation as a "famous company" for women, they will attract and retain the best women warriors for years to come.

7

United Arab Emirates

For many global multinationals, the oil-rich global crossroads of the United Arab Emirates is the commercial point of entry to the Middle East. This federation of seven states on the Persian Gulf—Abu Dhabi, Dubai, Sharjah, Ajman, Umm al-Quwain, Ras al-Khaimah, and Fujairah—controls the world's seventh-largest oil reserves and has gained prominence on the global stage far in excess of its size and population. In little more than a generation, the formerly sleepy British colony transformed itself into an economic heavyweight: its GDP is the fourteenth largest in the world, and its per capita income is comparable to those of the United States and Western Europe.[1] With Dubai as its financial hub and Abu Dhabi as its cultural, industrial, and political center, the UAE is a magnet for businesses, investors, and expatriates from around the globe.

Rapid economic development has resulted in an explosion in the number of jobs and an influx of foreigners, highly skilled professionals as well as unskilled laborers and domestic workers. As a result, the UAE's population has more than doubled over the past two decades, and of its 5.6 million inhabitants, a mere 20 percent are Emiratis. As much of the world is aware, Dubai's fortunes took a nosedive in 2009, and, even after a bailout by Abu Dhabi, Dubai remains deeply in debt. Nonetheless, the specter of a massive exodus of capital and expatriate talent never materialized, certainly not to the extent that had been feared. Six months later, Dubai was on the path to recovery, and the UAE's position as a dynamic economic hub and the gateway to the Middle East remains largely uncontested.

As in many other parts of the Middle East, the UAE is a land of striking social, economic, and political paradoxes, providing a complicated backdrop for women's advancement. Emirati women have benefited from the expanded access to higher education that has accompanied the economic boom; 35 percent of college-age women are enrolled in tertiary education, and 65 percent of university graduates in the UAE are female.[2] Emirati women are also putting their credentials to use, entering careers out of reach for prior generations. Pioneers in the region—such as Sheikha Lubna al-Qasimi, a tech expert and the UAE's first female economics minister, and Hessa Al-Jaber, who helped form ictQatar (the country's Supreme Council of Information and Communication Technology) and currently serves as its secretary general—provide role models for ambitious young women. In fact, with 42 percent of women active in the labor force, the UAE has one of the highest rates of female labor force participation in the region.[3]

Yet in a society where tradition and modernity collide daily, women face tremendous obstacles in pursuing their professional aspirations. The combined weight of cultural constraints, workplace marginalization, and a legal double standard shapes the realities not only of educated Emirati women but also of their expatriate sisters.

In the course of our research, we were frequently asked to clarify whether our focus was *educated Emirati women* or *educated women in the UAE*. Global companies in the UAE draw primarily upon the latter—a hybrid and cosmopolitan female talent pool that is a mix of educated Emiratis and expatriates of Western, Middle Eastern, and Asian extraction. Although we highlight the particular challenges faced by expatriate women (see "Expatriate Women: An Uneasy Compromise" later in this chapter), our scope is the broader pool of educated women in the UAE.

THE CHANGING FACE OF TALENT

Karim Sabbagh, a partner in Booz & Company's Middle East operations, has the following words of advice for global employers in the region: "Put aside all the stereotypes about women in this part of the world! There are way too many urban legends. Take the time to really understand what this talent group is."

For the outsider, Arab women are typically perceived as disempowered and oppressed. Our research reveals a much more sophisticated and progressive reality, the result of the rapid transformation of attitudes and expectations in recent decades. With a broadening range of educational and professional opportunities available, a significant proportion of women in the UAE have become highly skilled, motivated, and ambitious, while at the same time remaining deeply respectful of their cultural and religious traditions.

What makes the experiences of Emirati women distinct from those in other emerging markets is the role played by the centralized government. The UAE government has embraced as its mission, making the UAE a leader in women's rights in the Arab world. In 2010, the UAE was the ranked first among 134 countries in secondary and tertiary education for women in the World Economic Forum's Gender Gap Index.[4] A big part of the government's message is that women can and need to play a vital role in the UAE's development.

To walk the talk, the government has taken action on multiple fronts. Entities such as the Dubai Women Establishment have been created to take on the task of promoting women's roles across the region, and reports such as *Women in the United Arab Emirates: A Portrait of Progress* are regularly commissioned.[5] A *National Strategy for the Advancement of Women* was developed jointly with the United Nations Development Fund for Women in 2006, and in the past few years the UAE has hosted women's leadership conferences of global and regional scope, such as the Women's Global Economic Forum in 2007 and the Arab Women's Leadership Conference in 2009 and 2010.

How real is the impact of what some have called "state-sanctioned feminism"?[6] The UAE can certainly pride itself on the strides made on the education front. Women outnumber men two to one at the university level. This remarkable situation is due in part to universal access to publicly funded higher education. It's also shaped by the fact that academic achievement is not viewed as counter to religious or traditional dictates; even in traditional families, women can pursue their studies in a segregated setting, in adherence to the Islamic tradition of *qiwama*, or patriarchal protection of women and family. In our sample of college graduates, 19 percent of women also held postgraduate degrees and 61 percent of female graduates are actively employed or seeking employment in the workforce.

One factor driving these trends is "Emiratization," a national program to decrease the UAE's reliance on expatriates. Launched in 2006, Emiratization encourages private sector companies to hire Emirati nationals through quotas and metrics. With women dominating the educated Emirati talent pool, this has meant an influx of women into the workforce. Private sector players are contributing to the further development of the Emirati talent pool by establishing in-house training and leadership programs that bridge skills gaps. Emiratization, however, has not been without its problems: it has engendered resentment among expatriate professionals, some of whom view it as unfairly favoring Emiratis with weaker skills over better qualified expatriates. Nonetheless, one positive consequence is the elevation of women's participation in the UAE workforce.

Our data shows that the UAE government's focus on women's advancement has had a definitive impact on the attitudes and aspirations of female talent. Of our sample of college-educated women, 61 percent are employed and 19 percent are looking for work. These numbers mirror other studies on the career aspirations of female graduates in the

UAE, that even though the male talent pool is largely tapped out, the female talent pool still has considerable capacity.[7]

The vast majority of the women in our interviews felt work to be integral to their identities, and our UAE survey respondents had the highest positive responses—85 percent and greater—to questions about passion, engagement, and ambition relating to work. "Every day you learn something new," says Aisha al-Suwaidi of her job as the director general of Dubai Women Establishment. "You are challenged every day. And you get the opportunity to network with fantastic people who always have something to share with you. I think it's a blessing to get to know people who know more than you do and are willing to support you with their knowledge and their expertise."

Many of the women we spoke with shared al-Suwaidi's enthusiasm about contributing to the blank slate environment of the UAE.[8] The need for institution-building and hunger for new ideas provide a sense of purpose for highly skilled professionals, both local and expatriate. Many of our focus group participants cited the motivation and satisfaction of working on high-impact projects having the potential to reshape the region.

One unexpected finding about women's attitudes toward work in the UAE is their intense loyalty to their employers. A staggering 97 percent, the highest percentage in our sample, view themselves as loyal, and 46 percent intend to stay at their current employer for three years or more, a number that is similar in range to other emerging markets. Delving deeper, the top motivators at work for women in the UAE are also not so different from women elsewhere. Beyond job security and compensation, "being able to be myself" was a leading motivator for 98 percent of our female respondents, together with the caliber of colleagues (96 percent). These figures hint at the role work plays in women's identities in the region.

First, work opens up the opportunity for Arab women to take on pioneering roles and to challenge negative stereotypes. The current generation of highly educated Arab women are keenly aware of their status as role models within their societies and to the rest of the world.

"One of my main goals is to convey a positive image of Arab women," said Noha, a regional manager for a multinational in Dubai in one of our focus groups. "I want to show the world what Arab women can accomplish." Having broken the mold of their secluded, family-bound mothers, young Arab women push to prove their mettle. "I want to prove that I am equally smart, just as competitive, better than the standard image of an Arab woman," said another focus group participant.

Implicit in these remarks is a deep pride in Middle Eastern culture and tradition. Contrary to Western preconceptions, few educated Arab women felt the dictates of their culture to be constraining or limiting. Consider the issue of Islamic clothing: in the UAE, although women are not required by law to cover themselves as in neighboring Saudi Arabia or Iran, many women choose to wear the *sheila*, a traditional black headscarf, and the *abaya*, a robe that covers the entire body. Far from being viewed as oppressive or disempowering, as is often assumed in the West, such Muslim attire is worn with pride, a symbol of their faith, modesty, and heritage.[9]

A second common thread is the striking influence of the immediate family. Some women spoke of strong female role models—mothers or grandmothers who had gained an education and pursued careers at a time when few Arab women ventured out of the home. Others pointed to a supportive parent who celebrated their daughter's intelligence and encouraged her—often in the face of reservations from other family members—to follow her dreams. Nesrine, for example, says, "My family placed a strong emphasis on education and my grandmother attended several universities." When Nesrine wanted to move to London alone to continue her postgraduate education, "my grandmother's influence overrode my father's reservations."

Against the conservative backdrop of the Middle East, these women felt immensely grateful for having a family member ready to defy convention in support of their goals. This is especially true for working mothers, for whom the role models are few and far between. Joanne

Alam, a communications manager based in Abu Dhabi, recalls how few professional women there were in her mother's generation. "Now you see more and more women devoted to careers, more working moms," she observes, "and there is an appreciation and respect for it.

The overwhelmingly positive attitude toward work is fueled by the rapid development of the country. "Emirati women have run a marathon in the last twenty-five to thirty years," said Erin Walsh, a senior adviser in the U.S. State Department's Office of Near Eastern Affairs who heads up programs to empower Middle Eastern women. Many of the breakthroughs for women are concentrated in the past decade: the first female minister, Sheikha Lubna al-Qasimi, was appointed in 2004, and the nation's first female judge, Kholoud Ahmed Jouan Al Dhaheri, was sworn in 2008, the same year women were first appointed to ambassadorial posts. That firsts of this nature still make headlines is at once a sign of progress and an indication of how much remains to be done.

PROFILE

"We're looking for a certain type of individual."

Fatima is a young woman from Qatar who has lived in the UAE for several years, where she works in the pharmaceutical sector. Fatima holds two undergraduate degrees—one in business and another in science—from U.S. universities. Education and achievement were always very important to her family, and she credits them for encouraging her aspirations. In Qatar, Fatima also benefited from the support of a number of outside organizations, such as Rotary and the British Council, which recognized her ability and her promise and provided access to scholarships and professional guidance.

Over the years, however, Fatima has faced her share of challenges. Although her nuclear family has been there for her, her extended family and the broader community looked less favorably upon her aspirations. "They said, 'You're a girl.

You should be married,'" she recalled. Her decision to go to university in the United States was also problematic given that Europe, where more of her relatives reside, was seen as a more acceptable choice. After graduating in 2001, Fatima returned to Qatar, where she worked for two years, and then she moved to Dubai to work for her current employer. Fatima finds her work very rewarding and feels a great sense of satisfaction, and yet she struggles with a complex set of pushes and pulls.

Fatima started her career when there was a push to hire more women for professional jobs, a government-sponsored initiative similar to several others in the Gulf states; the effort has been successful to a point. "Women have no problems at the more junior levels," she said. "But at senior levels, it's a boys' club."

Religious women were at a particular disadvantage, she found. On more than one occasion she heard male colleagues discussing a decision she should have been involved in. When she asked why she had not been included, they responded, "We discussed it while you were at a religious commitment." But it wasn't only religion that kept her from the key discussions and deals. "These negotiations happen over a coffee, a smoke, an informal gathering where women can't be present." Fatima also found out that some of these deals were discussed with "team members who are my subordinates and should be hearing about these decisions from me and not before me."

Despite long days that often go until midnight, Fatima feels a great sense of satisfaction in her work. But the undermining and circumventing behaviors are wearing on her. She is tired of constantly having to overcompensate for not being able to be where the deals she needed to be front and center on were being negotiated. And even then, there's no guarantee that she'll be involved in those deals. Fatima said she's heard repeatedly, "If you're going to represent the commercial front of the business, we're looking for a certain type of individual." Those individuals are all a certain type of man.

A COMPLEX WEB OF PULLS

In spite of the remarkable social and economic changes in the UAE over the past two decades, age-old traditions persist with great tenacity. Women in the UAE face a unique set of constraints deriving from Arab tradition and culture regardless of education or achievement. These include the expectation that women and men be segregated in all spheres of life except in the home, and a great premium placed on a woman's modesty and reputation.

The Force of Tradition

In many Arab families, the central expectation for daughters is that they marry and have children. Marriages continue to be defined by a traditional division of labor, with men as breadwinners and women as keepers of the family and caretakers of the home. The traditional emphasis on marriage and children is evident in our survey findings: 72 percent of female respondents over thirty are married, and 70 percent have children.[10] (In the United States, by comparison, 55 percent of Gen X and Boomers have children.)

Concerns about reputation have a huge influence on an Arab woman's career choices, dictating where, when, and how she works. Many educated Emirati women encounter disapproval of women working in the first place. According to Meenaz Kassam, a professor at the American University of Sharjah, many Emirati families still feel that "women from good families don't work" and fear that a working wife implies that her husband cannot provide for her.[11] Although these views are not as prevalent as in the past, they still impact a sizable percentage—one university administrator puts it at about 20 percent—of female Emirati graduates.[12]

More generally, we found the women in our research were deferential to the dictates of their families or husbands, basing their choice of whether to work on the approval of others. Even those with supportive families gravitate toward professions that pose the least threat to their reputation, such as education, health care, or the civil service. A recent government mandate requiring all university students to engage in an internship before graduation is directed at the lingering stigma, with the hope of easing the path for educated women to enter the job market.[13]

Traditional social pressures are magnified for single women. Not only are unmarried Emirati women not allowed to live alone, but also their mobility is highly restricted and their independence limited. Shamsa, an ambitious twenty-one-year-old Emirati university student, aspires to a career in communications. In an interview with the local press, Shamsa describes a strict code of conduct that she must follow: she may not leave the house without her mother's permission; when she goes out, she must be accompanied by a domestic worker so as not to be alone with their driver, a foreign-born man; her father must approve of the work she will pursue. Luckily for Shamsa, her father backs her in her aspiration to work in the public sector. Gaining permission to work for a private company, where opportunities are greater, would be a tougher proposition. "They want to make sure I'm working in a respectful environment, where they know the people," she explains.[14]

With a formidable range of social and cultural prohibitions, single Emirati women remain, in spite of their qualifications and aspirations, restricted in their most fundamental life choices. "Educated women in the UAE end up with the short end of the stick," lamented Sultan Sooud Al-Qassemi, a fellow at the Dubai School of Government, in a recent opinion piece.[15]

Family First

Women face distinct additional pressures related to motherhood. In our survey, 38 percent of respondents report feeling pressure to drop out of the workforce upon the birth of their first child, and 89 percent experience maternal guilt, the highest number for the countries considered. We also find that 46 percent of college-educated women with children are not employed, compared with 31 percent of childless women, a difference that is indicative of the maternal pulls that keep women out of the workplace.

In a society where family ties are of paramount importance, it is assumed that family priorities will prevail over work needs. Even if a working Emirati woman has domestic help, she is expected to be, as one woman described it, "a perfect wife, a perfect mother, a perfect cook, with a perfect career at the same time."

Women who choose to be working mothers, aiming for perfection on all fronts, report marathon days that start well before dawn, as early as 4:30 or 5:00 a.m. Although nannies ease the burden, parenting duties, such as helping with homework, and taking children to and from school, remain the province of women. The domestic sphere remains highly gendered in the division of labor—one woman expressed appreciation for her husband taking his own teacup to the kitchen—and working mothers are left with little room to breathe between work and home. Exacerbating the situation is the concern in the Middle East that women's jobs and ambitions do not overshadow those of their husband. "Women are largely expected to be there for their husbands and the family when the head of the family comes home," notes an INSEAD researcher.[16]

Family pressures extend well beyond the nuclear family. May al-Dabbagh, the Director of the Gender and Policy Program and a research fellow at the Dubai School of Government, explained, "When working women get home, they are confronted by other responsibilities, kids and parents and social obligations. And these social obligations trump any work-related networking or socializing. For example, if you don't attend a second cousin's wedding, you are sending a message that you don't care about family."

The other important piece of the family equation is elder care: some 70 percent of women surveyed report having elder care responsibilities. The care of one's parents is a basic social obligation in Arab culture. Beyond the fact that there are almost no institutional care options for the elderly, 95 percent of respondents would not consider placing their elders in an assisted care or institutional facility. In the words of an Ivy League-educated Saudi woman, "Across the Arab world, it is part of the expectation of what children do: they take care of their parents when they grow up." The alternative is literally unthinkable, says May al-Dabbagh. "Thinking of [elder care] as a burden—you would be considered a really bad person."

The UAE population is a young one, and elder care concerns have yet to surface as a major pull. As in many countries, women typically bear a disproportionate share of the responsibility; one number that hints at the importance of elder care duties is that 64 percent in our sample currently provide their parents with monetary support. Elder care as an issue is sure to gain in importance in the years ahead, and employers that offer culturally sensitive solutions will be the ones best able to hold on to talented women.

PUSH FACTORS AT WORK

For Emirati women, reconciling traditional social expectations with their ambitions is a continued concern, and the UAE workplace presents its own set of challenges. Three aspects of work in particular can push talented women out of the workplace: the rise of extreme jobs, restrictions on travel, and gender biases.

Extreme Jobs

Our survey data shows that women in the UAE appear to have relatively manageable hours: thirty-nine hours per week at local companies and fifty-three hours per week at multinationals. The large gap has implications for multinationals' ability to compete for female talent, particularly in view of the steep demands on women's time on the family front. Furthermore, the average length of the workday is on the rise: 43 percent of our female respondents working full-time reported working more hours than they had three years earlier, and the increase was substantial—an additional ten hours per week.

The UAE workweek differs significantly in its structure from that in the West, something that catches many multinationals by surprise. The standard workweek for the public sector, schools, and many businesses runs from Sunday through Thursday, with Friday and Saturday as the weekend, or in some cases Saturday through Wednesday, with Thursday and Friday as the weekend. Some sectors and businesses operate on workweeks that are five and a half or six days long. The way the workday is structured also varies, with some operations having a continuous "single shift" workday from 9 a.m. to 5 p.m., and others operating on two shifts, a morning shift from 8 a.m. to 1 p.m., followed by a break and an afternoon shift from 4 to 7 p.m. During the holy month of Ramadan, in which Muslims fast from dawn to dusk, the working day is reduced to six hours, and although legally this schedule should apply to all staff, many companies apply it only to Muslims. Breaks within the workday are mandated by the government to ensure that employees have time for prayers, with the law prohibiting more than five hours of work without a one-hour break.[17]

These differences add to the workload of women who work at multinationals having a global span of operations. The women in our focus groups reported juggling calls set by colleagues elsewhere that not only were inconvenient owing to time differences but that also cut into the UAE weekend, which begins on Thursday evenings. "It's more challenging here than in every other place, since we have to adapt to the time zone of corporate headquarters and those are rarely in our own region," explained one focus group participant in Dubai.

Another woman in the same group complained, "Today, there's a conference call starting at 5:30 p.m. that's scheduled to last three hours. Why is it starting at 5:30? Because the little mister in New York who is commuting from Connecticut can't get to the office at 8 in the morning. I'm sorry, but do the conference call from home. It seems that the flexibility and compromises come only from one side. Asking New York to have the same kind of flexibility would certainly help."

Handling conference calls after hours and on weekends can have a cumulative impact that is wearing. One executive, for instance, related that her workdays stretched late into the evening to accommodate the nine-hour time difference with her company's headquarters in New York. "It's demanding healthwise and familywise," she said of the toll extracted by her extended days. "So many days I wish I could stop at six or seven p.m. I am not planning to keep doing this for long."

Restrictions on Travel

Exacerbating the pressures of the onerous daily schedule in the UAE are two other elements: protracted commutes and work-related overnight travel. Although only one in ten workers in the UAE is reported to have daily commutes longer than ninety minutes, the negative fallout is greater for women who, as daughters or wives, typically have little say in choosing their place of residence.[18] Where a woman lives depends on her family's or husband's needs, seldom her own. We heard examples of professional women enduring daily commutes between Abu Dhabi and Dubai, a distance of more than sixty miles, or from other Emirates to either Abu Dhabi or Dubai, where the jobs are concentrated.

In a society in which the codes of conduct for women are strict and limiting—even speaking in public to men to whom they are not related is frowned upon—work-related travel can be a serious difficulty.[19] It is commonplace to hear accounts of groups of young Emirati men following and harassing young women who are alone. Even educated, adult women are expected to be accompanied at all times, either by chaperones or, in the case of work, by drivers, employees, and colleagues. Unless a father or a brother is willing to tag along, a single woman is not able to get on a plane or stay in a hotel.

In the UAE, the difference between men and women in the number of nights spent away from home for work purposes was greater than in any other country. As a consequence, women—expatriates and locals alike—tend to concentrate in sectors where responsibilities are by and large local: medicine, law, hotel administration, advertising, public relations, and education.

Bias in the Workplace

Given that gender boundaries are strictly defined, the presence of gender bias at work in the UAE is hardly a secret: 32 percent of women and 18 percent of men in our survey feel that women are treated unfairly in the workplace owing to their gender. We heard a broad range of examples of discrimination, from the subtle to the egregious. Alia, a small-statured, robed Emirati woman who holds a doctorate in psychology, spoke of the slights she had endured in the course of her work. "In one job I had to assess pilots, and one man in his fifties looked at me and said, '*You* will give me my assessment?'" She believes these types of comments stem from the discomfort many Middle Eastern men have in dealing with intelligent and highly competent women. "My work is felt as an ego challenge. They respond by undermining me and knocking down my ideas."

In the workplace, women in the UAE also come up against deeply rooted notions about women's roles. These range from invasive questions in interviews that would be illegal in many countries to actual discriminatory practices. We heard of women being asked up front about their marital status ("Why should I hire you or invest in you since you are just going to go off and get married?") or, in the case of married women, whether they were planning to have children. Others were made to take pregnancy tests and, if pregnant, given a temporary job contract instead of a permanent one. One expert in the field noted, "The basic practices that can protect women from discrimination are entirely absent."

A great deal of business and relationship-building in the UAE takes place in informal after-hours settings, such the *majlis*, a sort of segregated male-only salon, or gender-segregated football games, sporting events, and social events. "These are spaces where a lot of the important

Expatriate Women: An Uneasy Compromise

Expatriate women are not exempt from the rules and conventions of this deeply conservative society.

Female expatriates of Arab or Muslim background who have no family nearby are perhaps the ones who suffer most from cultural constraints. Rula, an unmarried Jordanian sales manager who lives alone in the UAE, describes her situation. "It's a very exceptional thing to do," she says. "My parents are constantly explaining why their daughter is a single professional, living alone in Dubai. It makes me feel very guilty." To combat the deep suspicion and stigma associated with women living away from their families, single professionals from neighboring countries often resort to moving their relatives—sisters, parents, brothers—to the UAE to live with them as chaperones. At the end of our conversation, Rula mentioned her own plans to relocate her parents to Dubai to live with her and, as she put it, "make up" for her independence.

Unmarried women in Dubai also face serious legal risks. A single Turkish woman, a manager at a global pharmaceutical company, describes her anxieties stemming from her personal status. "My boyfriend lives in the U.K., and when he visits, he's legally not allowed to stay with me. I could get reported to the police, and there would be the possibility of imprisonment for us both." Another issue: "Since I am Muslim and he is Christian, we're not allowed to get married in the UAE. It's been a struggle to keep the relationship going."

We heard many accounts of the difficulties expatriate women professionals encountered when they ran up against UAE cultural mores. A British executive sent to her company's regional headquarters in Dubai had her first brush with the restrictions on women even before setting foot in the UAE. When applying for a work visa to the UAE, she was shocked to learn she was required to submit an approval letter from her partner, granting her "permission" to travel to the UAE to take on her new role.

Caroline, a Canadian professional, had an equally jarring experience when she tried to obtain a dependent visa for her husband, who did not have a job lined up in the UAE. "To work here, you have to be under the sponsorship of a company. No job, no Dubai." There are zones where foreign companies can sponsor their employees, but the zone where Caroline's employer is located doesn't allow women to sponsor their children and husbands. "I was given a really hard time when I tried to sponsor my husband—he only got a one-year visa," she recalled. "The Emirati official practically hissed at me: 'Husband the sponsor, wife three years. Wife the sponsor, husband one year.'"

Worse, her husband wasn't allowed to work. "And if you don't have a work permit, you will be deported," Caroline says. Her husband finally submitted a request through another sponsor. It was accepted, and he now has a work permit. But the experience was scarring. "They acted as if I were a prostitute," she says. "As a visitor you don't see this. They actually have a lot of respect for foreigners. But when you go deeper, the country is still very conservative."

Beyond the indignities associated with operating within so openly unequal a system, expatriate women also come up against more mundane annoyances. Tradesmen—electricians, plumbers, and so on—may not show up on time, if at all, to an appointment made by a woman. Obtaining a driver's license or hiring a nanny is complicated for expatriate women unless their husbands are also residents. Women report difficulties in renting a house or an apartment alone; in Dubai, for instance, the renting of villas by single individuals is banned. Exacerbating these problems, employers accustomed to hiring male expatriates with stay-at-home wives who attend to personal matters do not provide female professionals any start-up time to arrange housing, find schools for children, or find domestic help.

"My daughters asked me, 'Why aren't you reacting more?'" said a North American senior marketing director for a global pharmaceutical firm. "I say, 'We're in a foreign culture and we have to respect the rules.'"

networking is done, all the brainstorming sessions and sharing of inside information," says May al-Dabbagh. As a result, women find themselves excluded from important brainstorming and decision-making discussions, and they feel marginalized in the workplace. Based on focus groups with working women in the UAE, we heard many variations of the intentional exclusion of women, such as the case of a male manager who scheduled all important meetings at 5 p.m. when his key female staff had to leave to pick up their children from school. Another focus group participant told us of businesses where women were relegated to back-office roles, with client-facing roles reserved only for men.

Although one can argue that there's a female version of the *majlis* where women can socialize with each other, al-Dabbagh points out that when women get home from work, they're often overwhelmed by maternal, filial, and social obligations, all of which trump work-related obligations. "You work long hours and you're going to do something work-related after work?" she says. "For many women, networking is not a priority because it competes with other, more important priorities."

In spite of the fact that most women in the UAE are extraordinarily ambitious and driven, a full one-third find that problems of bias at work are severe enough to make them scale back their careers or even quit. Others strive to go the extra mile—prove themselves by working harder than their male colleagues, a tiring and draining effort that is not always sustainable in the long haul.

The Lure of the Public Sector

In the UAE, the government sector has long been the foremost career choice for Emirati women: the sector employs 40 percent of the Emirati labor force and is overwhelmingly female, with two of every three employees a woman.[20] The reasons are obvious: job security, limited work hours (9 a.m.–2:30 p.m.), ample benefits, and salaries equal to or greater than those in the private sector. This makes the competition for local talent in the Emirates an uphill battle for multinational corporations. As a result, Emiratis make up 54 percent of employees in federal ministries but account for less than 1 percent of private sector staff.[21]

"Locals definitely prefer the public sector due to the hours, benefits, and the prestige," commented one of our focus group participants. Her observation was confirmed by our survey findings: 48 percent of college-educated women in the Emirates view the public sector as a very desirable place to work, more so than multinationals headquartered in the West. Beyond the benefits already mentioned, the public sector offers Emirati nationals more days off and is also seen to invest in the development of Emirati talent.

Aisha al-Suwaidi, director general of the Dubai Women Establishment, chose a public sector career after working for a global multinational in North America and Europe. Her official working day starts at 7:30 a.m. and ends at 2:30, a schedule that allows her to spend quality time with her two small children. The short government working day notwithstanding, al-Suwaidi is highly motivated and ambitious, carving out early-morning and late-night hours between her job and family responsibilities to study for a postgraduate degree. Her days are no less arduous perhaps than those of her peers in the private sector, because she performs the lion's share of parenting and housekeeping in her family. However, the kinder schedule of her public sector job allows her to both pursue her ambitions and fulfill her traditional role.

The UAE government itself views the overwhelming preference for public sector jobs among Emiratis—and Emirati women in particular—as a major concern. The nation's continued reliance on expatriates and foreigners to drive the private sector is considered untenable in the long term.

In 2009, the Emirates Foundation launched an initiative called Tawteen to demystify the private sector for educated Emirati women and their families. The program was based on the findings of a study showing that Emirati women shy away from private sector careers for three key reasons: lack of job security, lack of opportunities close to their place of residence, and lack of appropriate child care arrangements.[22] Tawteen tries to underscore the positive aspects of the trade-offs women make to enter the private sector, namely the exposure to global practices and access to world-class training. A parallel program to encourage private sector companies to hire and retain Emirati women is on the drawing board.

In the short term, though, the public sector in the UAE remains a strong contender for top talent. In the words of one foreign employer, "Emiratis already know that what they can obtain in the public sector is going to be far better than in the private sector."

CONCLUSION

Until a few years ago, in the words of an expatriate working for a multinational corporation in Dubai, "The only education an Emirati woman needed was how to withdraw money from the bank." Today, the UAE government views women as a vital national resource.

Despite the daunting hurdles they face in and out of work, educated Emirati women are eager to take advantage of the unprecedented opportunities opening to them. Many look to their employers to help support their ambitions as they crack the mold of traditional expectations. Time and again, the women in our study mentioned how much they would benefit from programs and initiatives that help them break out of their shells and combat the workplace biases and stereotypes documented here. Mentors, affinity networks, access to leadership training, all conducted in an atmosphere of cultural sensitivity—with these tools, companies can tap in to a vast well of talent.

Part Three

Action Agenda

Forward-thinking companies are already beginning to respond to the realities of professional women in emerging markets. Although no one company has "cracked the code," that is, entirely solved the challenges faced in attracting, developing, and advancing women, the examples we uncovered are encouraging on a number of fronts. Many of the most successful programs start locally or at the grass-roots level, rather than attempting a wholesale transfer of initiatives from established markets. They also provide innovative models and learnings that might apply in the Western context. The roadmap for fully realizing female talent in emerging markets involves three essential action steps.

The first area of focus is *becoming a talent magnet*, i.e., establishing a reputation for being a standout employer of talented women. Whether by tapping into unconventional talent pools or targeting disciplines where they are underrepresented, companies can gain access to a phenomenal resource pool for which there is as yet little competition.

The second area is *claiming and sustaining ambition* among talented women. Many professional women downsize their ambitions or opt out of the workplace altogether in the face of escalating personal and professional pressures. By making women feel valued and providing them with targeted skills and opportunities they need to succeed, companies can do a much better job of developing female leaders.

The third area involves *dealing with pulls and pushes*, keeping in mind the priorities for women in the emerging markets context.

The following chapters describe 30 women-focused programs being implemented by multinational corporations in BRIC/UAE markets.

8

Becoming a Talent Magnet

As multinationals expand and solidify their presence in emerging markets, they have a rare opportunity to gain a powerful advantage in the cutthroat competition for top talent. Being known as a standout employer has an enduring impact on a company's image and reputation, enabling it to attract and retain the brightest and best right from the start and over the long haul.

Companies can create the conditions that allow talented women to flourish—that keep them motivated and feeling valued—by paying attention. Our data makes it clear what educated and ambitious women want from their employers: intellectually stimulating work, plentiful opportunities to learn and develop, smart colleagues and a supportive work environment, fair compensation and reliable job security. When employers satisfy this side of the value proposition, they will be repaid in above-average levels of engagement, commitment, and loyalty. Here, we look at eight organizations that have become talent magnets:

- Bloomberg: *Women Moving Markets*

- Ernst & Young: *Inclusive Recruiting Strategy*

- Goldman Sachs: *New Markets Mobility Exchange*

- Google India: *Women in Engineering Award Program*

- HSBC: *Flexible Work Arrangement*

- Infosys: *Infosys Women's Inclusivity Network (IWIN)*

- PepsiCo India: *Breaks into Beginnings*

- Siemens: *BRIC* and *ME*

BLOOMBERG:
Women Moving Markets

In 2010, Bloomberg made a formal commitment to increase its overall coverage of women by adding individual profiles, feature articles of interest to women, and columns written by and addressed to women.

In retrospect, says Amanda Bennett, executive editor of projects and investigations, "Women Moving Markets," the rubric for the shift in emphasis, was an idea whose time had come. "We do profiles of women in the news anyway, so why not increase the number of profiles of women of significance to all of our clients? Everybody in the Bloomberg universe should know of Sheryl Sandberg, who is the COO of Facebook, or Irene Rosenfeld, the CEO of Kraft, who faced down Warren Buffett, her largest shareholder, to make an acquisition she wanted. There are lots of women to focus on, not just because they're women but because they're worthy of coverage."

The new lens will be directed to all aspects of newsgathering:

- *Polling:* "We never broke out the results by gender before, but we do now," says Bennett.

- *Demographic coverage:* Bennett envisions broad investigations into such topics as how China's one-child policy affects the country's growth, how women's increased access to capital in developing markets will affect GNP growth, and how the increased educational ambitions of women in Arab countries will change the workforce and local economy. "We're looking at women's issues that will be of interest to all readers, men and women," says Bennett.

- *Columns:* In addition to opinion columns written by Margaret Carlson and Amity Shlaes, there will be more contributions from women analysts who are experts in their own fields and whose comments move markets.

All stories will be coded so that a simple search for "new information and women" on the Bloomberg site will produce all women-oriented stories.

"There's no opposition," says Bennett. "It's not even controversial. When we asked the people who do the polling to split the results by gender, they said, 'Sure.' When we said, "There are ten women in Brazil and eight women in India whom everyone ought to know about, everyone said, 'Sure.' This is not rocket science. It just requires someone who notices in the first place and says, 'I'm really interested in this. Let's get it done.'"

Because the initiative is still in the development phase, Bennett and her deputy, Lisa Kassenaar, chose to engage Bloomberg's women reporters first. To their surprise, at the first meeting, the women moved to include their male colleagues, too. That's fine with Bennett, who looks forward to the time when female-focused news coverage will no longer be "a 100-percent women-driven issue" and will occur "as much by osmosis as by fiat." Pragmatism also has a part: "Since we have more men reporters than women, more men will have the opportunity to do these stories."

Bennett and Kassenaar meet weekly to approve stories and suggest new assignments. They're in the process of setting specific numerical goals to measure coverage, based on the number of female-focused stories that ran in 2009 and the number they'd like to achieve in 2010. "Once we get our baseline down, we'll see that the amount of coverage we currently offer is pretty feeble," Bennett says. "It will be easy to double or triple what we're doing pretty quickly."

Bennett anticipates a lot of impact, thanks to the wide coverage of Bloomberg outlets, including the Bloomberg terminal to the Web site, television, radio, news feeds to local affiliates, and *Bloomberg Business-Week*. "We can't guarantee where a story will end up, but if we double our output of profiles on women or increase our female focus in small but meaningful ways or do more stories on gender-related global issues, those will begin to seep out everywhere."

ERNST & YOUNG:
Inclusive Recruiting Strategy

It's not an easy task to grow a business from scratch, especially where the competition for talent is as fierce as in India. In 2001, Ernst & Young coordinating tax partner Sharda Cherwoo and her team did it through an inclusive recruiting strategy.

The challenge: launch a global shared-services center in India. Cherwoo, a New York-based native of India, was asked to lead all aspects of management for the Ernst & Young facility in Bangalore, including recruiting more than five hundred associates over a three-year period.

Ernst & Young is well known in the United States for its progressive, people-focused workplace policies. Cherwoo brought that same focus and philosophy to the facility in India. With knowledge of the local culture, her team began implementing people practices such as transportation services (a significant issue in India) as well as on-site health care services. Given the cultural significance of caring for aging family members and children, Cherwoo and her team expanded the group health care policy to include child and elder care assistance. Her team also implemented an innovative loan policy that helped staff and their family members with housing and education expenses. To this day, there has been a 100 percent payback rate on the loans.

Cherwoo notes that her experience in recruiting for the global shared-services center highlighted a unique opportunity to build a diverse and inclusive workplace culture from the ground up. She personally interviewed all candidates and insisted that her recruiters use unbiased interview questions even though there are no laws in India prohibiting employers from asking discriminatory questions. "Talent comes from all places, and we worked hard to focus on a candidate's potential rather than their pedigree or the school they attended," noted Cherwoo.

With eighteen thousand applicants on the first day for the first one hundred jobs, a strong recruitment strategy was essential. Cherwoo credits recruiting the right kind of staff members as the key to the facility's success. She and her team deliberately recruited local rather than expat talent and targeted applicants having a broad range of educational and professional backgrounds, not only those from the top schools. They also looked for people with the right attitude who were team-oriented, innovative in their thinking, and willing to learn and grow. "You're making more of an impact that way," Cherwoo says. "For ... the leadership team [and me], it became a matter of getting great people and creating an environment of empowerment that benefited everyone—our people, clients, and the community."

In addition to recruiting efforts, Cherwoo and her team placed great emphasis on soft-skills training and innovation (there is a specific quarterly award for innovation). She also brought in top-name local CEOs and leaders to give inspirational presentations. Everyone—from the mailroom workers to top managers—received the soft skills training, which was geared toward creating an environment of leadership, empowerment, and innovation.

Using these and other policies designed to create an equitable workforce, Ernst & Young India managed to attract a staff that was 55 to

60 percent female. Nearly ten years later, the core leadership team and HR processes that Cherwoo put into place in 2001 still remain, and Ernst & Young India's global shared-services center is recognized as an award-winning, inclusive work environment. Equally important, the strategy has helped the company maintain an extraordinarily high retention rate. In an industry with typically high staff turnover, that's a crucial competitive advantage.

GOLDMAN SACHS:
New Markets Mobility Exchange

Early in his career at Goldman Sachs, Robin Vince, then based in London, was asked to pack a bag and spend six months in New York. "It was a great experience to see the business from a slightly different angle," he says, "to form new relationships, to see the technology and tools and market practices in this new location, and then have the benefit of importing some of the best practices back to my home location."

Four years later, Vince was asked to move to New York permanently to run the very business he had sampled earlier. "I know my career would not have turned out the same way had I not spent those six months" in New York, says Vince, now Goldman Sachs's head of operations. "It was an invaluable part of the foundation that ultimately helped me build a successful career."

It was so invaluable, in fact, that the investment bank hopes to replicate the experience through the New Markets Mobility Exchange program. The program, to be launched in 2010, will choose fifty to sixty individuals in this year's graduating class of the firm's operations analyst program to spend up to six months working in Goldman Sachs's offices, including Brazil, Russia, India, China, and other key hub locations.

"Countries like the BRICs and other growth markets are central to our strategy over the medium and long term," explains Vince. "We need to reduce the barriers and improve the comfort people have interacting with people from different cultures." His view is that if people get accustomed to mobility early in their careers, they will be more open to mobility later. By offering this opportunity to people in their early twenties—still young enough to be unencumbered by spouses, children, and career expectations—Vince hopes they will gain "the experience and sensitivity to doing business in places they are less familiar with, bring the value of their own experience to bear on those situations, and reimport the experience back to their home location."

The firm operates analyst academies—a three-year training program for recent college graduates—in Goldman Sachs's global offices, including Salt Lake City, New York, Jersey City, Bangalore, Tokyo, Hong Kong, and London. New Markets Mobility Exchange is an aspirational program, targeted at people who are successful at what they already do and are familiar enough with the Goldman Sachs culture to leverage their skills in different locations. Participants are nominated based on who might benefit most from the experience, who has the curiosity and appetite for adventure, and who has the foreign language skills.

Managers nominated 120 applicants from a pool of 500 trainees. They selected a Korean national currently working in Tokyo to be transferred to Seoul, an American fluent in Portuguese to spend time in São Paulo, and an analyst of Russian origin to go to Moscow. Almost 60 percent of the program participants are women.

"One of the factors is building a pipeline of returning nationals," notes Meriel Ward, vice president and co-head of the operations HR generalist team. "Growing the future leadership pipeline in smaller local offices is a big part of this program." To ensure that none of the participating offices suffers head count shortages, all managers who send someone in the program also receive someone. All participants are assigned a "buddy" to help them integrate into their destination office, as well as a mentor; senior-level sponsors are responsible for ensuring that host managers know what to expect and for ensuring the program's success in their region. Both home and host managers team up on feedback and performance reviews so that the participant doesn't "get lost" during the program.

The most complicated part of the program was matching participants and destinations, said Tami Rosen, managing director and divisional HR head for operations. The relocation process is similar to setting up a short-term assignment: each person is assigned a corporate apartment, gets a round-trip ticket plus one home-leave trip, and receives immigration assistance and a per diem based on the location.

Rosen expects the program to be a major selling point in attracting new recruits. Although the program has not yet been launched at the time of this writing, it is already included in the marketing material on college campuses and, she says, has been well received. In fact, the program is already changing the focus of the recruitment effort for the analysts' program. "Now we aim to hire people in every one of our offices with diverse language skills," she says, noting that 80 percent of the trainees in the Salt Lake City office speak at least one language other than English. "It will make it easier down the road for them to go to different locations."

"We're a human capital company, so investing in our people is our version of research and development," concludes Vince. "It's particularly appropriate to have this type of investment, crossing borders and cultures, in those markets that are growing. And there's an enormous amount of commercial value by making a big firm feel just a little bit smaller and more connected."

GOOGLE INDIA:
Women in Engineering Award Program

Diversity is a core value at Google worldwide. But a few years ago, the human resource team responsible for engineering in India wanted to find an exciting new way to translate this commitment into action. The result is a pioneering award program that promotes diversity both within the company and across an emerging market. Now in its third year, the Google India Women in Engineering Award celebrates young women in college or graduate school who have chosen to pursue a career in engineering or computer science. Sixteen women won the $2,000 award in 2008, and nine in 2009, for their academic excellence and demonstrated leadership skills.

Originally, Google managers thought about helping encourage young Indian girls to study math and science. But they soon opted for a more specific, targeted goal: celebrating the dedicated young women who are pursuing a career in these male-dominated fields. "We asked, 'What could we do to create some kind of immediate impact?'" says Jayashri Ramamurti, head of human resources for engineering at Google India and a creator of the program. "It made sense to start in a small way, as a first step."

Surprisingly, there was initial resistance from some of the women whom Google was trying to laud. When Google representatives toured fifteen to twenty campuses to promote the nascent program in 2007, many would-be applicants said, "Don't single us out." Like many females in science or technical fields, the young engineers did not want to call attention to their gender. But after learning about the broad, long-term goals of the initiative, more than 270 applicants stepped forward in 2008, the first year of the program. "It was crucial that we talk to the girls, to let them know why we're doing this," says Ramamurti. Her team also worked hard to get buy-in from senior management and from the many Google engineers who serve as judges for the competition.

The awards are given at an expense-paid professional retreat, at first held for one day in Bangalore and then expanded to include a day as well in Hyderabad, the other base for the company's engineering operations in India. Winners and finalists alike attend presentations by Google engineers and outside experts and participate in fun and games. Although the program is in its infancy, the reaction within Google, from the press, and from award winners has been highly positive. Anjali Sardana, a 2009 winner and PhD candidate at the Indian Institute of Technology Roorkee, says that the award inspired her to keep pursuing her dreams. "Not only did the award encourage me to stay in my field, it has made me confident and given me the spark to mentor" other younger women engineers, says Sardana, who notes that she's had to work harder and faster than many male students to prove herself. "Patience and perseverance have worked for me."

HSBC:
Flexible Work Arrangement

When HSBC surveyed its 6,500-plus employees in India on the topic of engagement three years ago, one issue shot to the top of the list: work-life balance. The company was already known for implementing revolutionary ideas in this space. In 2006, for example, it was the first in the industry to cut the workweek from six to five days. With its Flexible Work Arrangement (FWA) initiative, launched in February 2008, HSBC took the issue a giant step further.

The program, offered to any employee who has been with the bank for three months, encompasses three options:

- *Staggered hours:* When all employees were required to be at work by 8:30, many had to leave home at dawn to allow enough time for India's infamous traffic jams. With staggered hours, employees can choose the time most preferable for them to arrive or leave, as long as they work a regular nine-hour day and those hours cover the peak period between 10 a.m. and 4 p.m. Being able to come in at 9:30 "gives me a lot of flexibility," says Nikunj Upadhyay, vice president of organizational development. "I can exercise or do yoga. That hour is very valuable for just taking care of myself."

- *Part-time work:* Depending on their role, some employees can choose to work part-time or share their job. Other than a correlated reduction in salary, there's no penalty; part-time workers still receive health insurance and other benefits.

- *Telecommuting:* This option enables employees to work from another branch, from home, or even from a location elsewhere in the country. HSBC provides the laptops and technology to access the company system. Upadhyay especially appreciated being able to telecommute when she was being treated for a medical condition by a doctor in Pune, a city about one hundred miles from her home office in Mumbai. "It gave me that flexibility to work, so I didn't need to apply for sick leave," she says.

Implementing the program required a deliberate change in the mind-set of line managers. "It's been a challenge to get them to accept that just because an employee works from a remote location doesn't mean they're losing an employee," recalls Upadhyay. HSBC held workshops to identify managers' concerns, allay their fears that they would lose control of their teams, and explain how best to manage in a more flexible environment.

Two years later, the program has proved to be a solid success in more ways than originally anticipated. Approximately six hundred employees—almost equal percentages of men and women—have availed themselves of one or more of the FWA options. Internal studies reveal that productivity has gone up in about 88 percent of employees and has remained the same (i.e., it has not gone down) in the rest of the workers.

By making working hours less rigid, HSBC has also been able to respond better to customers, many of whom also no longer conform to conventional schedules. "If a customer calls at 8 a.m. or 7 p.m., there's a better chance of being able to speak to a manager," notes Tanuj Kapilashrami, HSBC's head of human resources. "That is the kind of differentiated service that pulls in customers and translates into increased brand loyalty."

As more women, working couples, and younger employees change the traditional workforce demographic, mature organizations like HSBC hope that programs that enable staff members to take control of their working style and break the stereotypical office roles will brand them an employer of choice, helping them attract and retain their top talent. In fact, since FWA was implemented, notes Kapilashrami, "We have the lowest attrition record in the industry."

INFOSYS:
Infosys Women's Inclusivity Network

In the early years of the new millennium, Infosys, the Bangalore-based information technology giant whose name is practically synonymous with India's booming business process outsourcing industry, was running out of young engineers. Like every other company in the burgeoning field, it was engaged in a fierce war for the best and brightest university graduates. Unlike many of them, Infosys specifically targeted women as a solution—not only to expand the potential pool of top talent but also to tap in to a wider range of intellects. "Diversity brings in creativity and innovation," explains Nandita Gurjar, senior vice president and group head of human resources. "We are a very large organization, large enough to form a society on our own, and we want to make sure that the Infosys society reflects the greater society."

The Infosys Women's Inclusivity Network (IWIN) was launched in 2003, when 17 percent of the Infosys employees were women. Today, 34.1 percent of the workforce is female—in absolute numbers, more than thirty-six thousand women. Women make up 40.3 percent of entry-level workers, 24.2 percent of midlevel managers, 6.5 percent of senior managers, and 6.2 percent of top-tier leaders, nearly double the number of six years ago.

The key reason for those impressive figures is IWIN. The program has three aims: to persuade more high school girls to study engineering in college; to attract more female engineers to Infosys; and to make it easier for women to maintain their careers at the company after having children.

The core element of IWIN in making Infosys a female-friendly environment was identifying the stress points at which women tended to leave the organization and creating policies that helped them deal with those stresses. Surveys showed that many Infosys women dropped out after getting married; the numbers skyrocketed after the birth of their first child and were almost universal after the second. "There was no formal process of retaining women employees or attracting former employees who had left to have children and might want to come back," says Gurjar.

IWIN began by introducing a one-year child care sabbatical with the option of working part-time for the next two years. The part-time option permits employees to work either half-days or a few full days per week. A satellite office in the center of Bangalore enables prospective and new mothers to avoid traveling to the suburban main campus. "It can cut a commute by 50 percent," says Gurjar. Flexible work schedules and telecommuting are also available.

Approximately 96 percent of the part-time employees are working mothers, Gurjar reports. During sabbaticals, women can stay connected with their teams and catch up with technology advances that occurred during their leave. They are also put on projects, with a strong monitoring system in place for their first two months back to spot problems and accelerate learning. In addition, if a returning mother feels that her job is too stressful, the WithInfy internal job posting network helps her find alternative career opportunities so that her skills aren't completely lost to the company.

Every year, the company asks women to identify three things it can do to make Infosys more attractive to women and make it easier for them to do their jobs, says Gurjar. "We do all of them."

For example, expectant mothers asked for parenting workshops and health programs. Infosys provides daily Pregnacare yoga and fitness classes on the main campus. There's an online referral service for hospitals, pediatricians, day care centers, nannies, and schools. Nursing stations supported by women lactation experts and a doctor on call are set up in all the offices. Similarly, all the offices have day care centers within four kilometers; most are equipped with Web cameras so that mothers can check in remotely throughout the day. Employees use office shuttle buses to drop their children at day care free of cost.

Because a major challenge for working mothers is "me" space, Infosys campuses are equipped with supermarkets, beauty salons, drugstores with prescription services, banks, recreation facilities, and canteens that offer take-out meals. "In the Bangalore office, the canteen offers eighteen different cuisines," Gurjar notes. "Many people carry food home."

Concierge services assist with tax returns, insurance advice, telephone hook-up, and other mundane tasks that can stretch a long day to the breaking point. Although many of these services are used as much by men, Gurjar says, "During the times when a woman is feeling overwhelmed by family and work, these are things that help her get over the hump."

As a result of these programs, the number of women returning to work after maternity leave increased from 59 percent to 88 percent in the past five years; the total number of working mothers tripled during that time.

IWIN recently expanded its offerings to include life counseling for young women—60 percent of its entry-level women join the company directly from university—as well as professional support for women facing harassment at home.

The company hopes these policies will persuade more high school girls to decide to study science and engineering. To get the word out, it routinely brings large groups of high school girls from all around the country to Infosys campuses. "They see our workforce, learn about the customers, the management, the possibilities," says Gurjar.

The company's ultimate goal is to have women make up at least half of the workforce, if not more. By creating a work environment that both attracts and retains them, IWIN helps make Infosys a magnet for women.

PEPSICO INDIA:
Breaks into Beginnings

Pavan Bhatia likes to cite a dramatic metric to prove the value of gender diversity: after women were put on the bottle inspection station in one PepsiCo India plant, productivity went up 20 percent. Women have "a natural focus on cleanliness," explained Bhatia, vice president of human resources, India region. Men "were more tolerant about dirty bottles going through."

PepsiCo India ramped up its diversity initiative five years ago. As in the bottling plant, the results were quickly apparent. "From the shop floor to the executive committee, the perspective in discussions and ideas was entirely different and added a tremendous amount of value," Bhatia recalls.

From 2006 to 2008, PepsiCo India increased the percentage of women on its payroll from 5 percent to more than 20 percent. Currently, women account for 25 percent of the senior leadership team in India, up from 10 percent in 2005. It's a good start, says Bhatia, but not nearly enough. "We're just halfway through the journey."

To make more progress along that path of becoming an employer of choice for women, PepsiCo India recently rolled out a variety of programs and policies aimed at all levels of employees.

Breaks into Beginnings is an on-ramping recruitment program aimed at women who want to resume their careers after taking a break. Teaming up with Jobstreet, a leading recruitment agency, and IndiWo, a woman-centered Web site, in 2008, PepsiCo advertised opportunities from entry-level positions to senior manager roles, from part-time openings to full-time jobs. The response was tremendous: in four months, more than seven thousand women submitted resumes, of whom one thousand were qualified.

Although the actual conversion rate was very low—only three women were actually selected—Breaks into Beginnings publicized PepsiCo's commitment to women in its workforce. Aware that off-ramped women are a rich talent target, the company is now working out ways to make the program even stronger.

Meanwhile, the company is also enhancing its flexible work arrangements for its existing female workforce. Maternity policies now include an extended leave of six weeks in addition to the basic government-mandated maternity leave of twelve weeks. (There is, as yet, no paternal flextime.) From nonexistent three years ago, flextime and temporary leaves of absence are now available to help women manage crises at home. "It's not only about being able to attract female employees, but being able to retain them," Bhatia explains. "In certain cases, where we would have lost women because we were being inflexible, we started keeping them."

As more women climb the career ladder in India, there's more focus on providing support through role models and experience-sharing platforms. One topic raised by the Diversity Council was how women balance their dedication to work and their dedication to their family. To show how important she considers this issue to be, PepsiCo CEO Indra Nooyi dedicated two hours of a recent visit to India to talk with fifteen senior employees about her own experiences balancing career and motherhood. "It's in examples like this, where the senior leadership shares advice, that we build capability and perspective," says Bhatia. "Now we have all of them playing a lead role in helping others to cope with stress and guilt and to advise on what really works to succeed at PepsiCo."

Sharing solutions to one problem has led to greater openness about others. A focus group of women employees pointed out that the convention of hosting international visitors with formal dinners took time away from their families. Although the interactions were important, why did they have to occur after working hours? they asked. Why not have lunch instead?

Within three months, at least 35 percent of dinner meetings were converted to lunch interactions. "For me, it was a small 'aha' moment, but it made a big difference to the women who wanted to be at these meetings," says Bhatia. "And from an organizational perspective, it helps showcase our talent"; the more women who can attend, the better. "It's a simple solution but it makes a huge difference"—and will help make PepsiCo an employer of choice for Indian women.

SIEMENS:
BRIC and ME

The global economic balance of power is shifting rapidly toward new engines of growth, led by the BRIC nations and the Middle East. But talent is in short supply in emerging markets, and the leaders of agile multinationals understand that they must do all they can to nurture skilled, experienced professionals in these regions. That's why in autumn 2009, Siemens launched BRIC/ME, its latest diversity initiative, a unique network of young talent from the BRIC and Middle Eastern nations.

One of three powerful networks rolled out in the past year by the engineering giant to revitalize its approach to diversity, the BRIC/ME Network was created to engage talent in key regions in unprecedented ways. "These countries are not only important export markets," said one executive. "We can also benefit from their expertise and different perspectives." Of the 2,700 Siemens employees worldwide who have been identified as top talents, some 350 are based in BRIC or Middle Eastern markets.

To kick off the new network, Siemens unveiled a unique approach to engaging future innovators in these regions: an internal talent competition. The company invited all 350 people in their BRIC and ME offices to generate innovative ideas on business areas crucial to their fast-growing regions. Categories included how Siemens could better develop customers or regional workforces, adapt to local needs, or position itself in these markets.

The business pioneers, who were on average age thirty-six, generated 140 ideas. Then the twenty-five men and women with the best ideas gathered in Munich in October 2009 in teams of five and developed the suggestions into rough project proposals presented to members of the managing board. The composition within the teams reflected diversity of nationality, business background, gender, and expertise. Working virtually on an IT collaboration platform and also in physical meetings, team members finalized their suggestions over four months, with the guidance of senior business executives who were assigned to them as coaches. Finally, each team selected one developed idea to present to the managing board in March 2010 for possible later execution by the company. Ideas were judged on their level of innovation as well as the team's powers of persuasion.

With the BRIC and Middle Eastern countries set to generate half of world GDP in the next five years, Siemens is determined to fully tap the expertise and creativity of its up-and-coming talent in emerging markets. By shining a spotlight on the innovators and emerging leaders in these areas of the globe, the company sends a crucial signal to customers, employees, and suppliers alike: diversity—in all senses of the word—is a business imperative for Siemens.

9

Claiming and Sustaining Female Ambition

Confounded by the escalating pressures of extreme jobs, the dissonance between conflicting social and professional expectations, and confusion about where they stand in a cultural tug-of-war, many talented women downsize their ambitions for themselves. This is a huge and significant issue. An employer cannot promote a woman if she is not strongly vested in this endeavor.

How can ambition be rekindled and nurtured? How can a woman gain the confidence and skills to feel comfortable—and excel—in a leadership role?

Ensuring that talented women in emerging markets feel valued is of fundamental importance in multinational organizations, particularly those headquartered in the United States or Western Europe. Networking and relationship building, which are essential to strengthening engagement and commitment, help women develop the ties, visibility, and organizational know-how essential to their professional success. This chapter looks at twelve programs dedicated to claiming and sustaining female ambition:

- Boehringer Ingelheim: *Extended Business Trips*
- Cisco Systems: *Power Camp*
- Citi: *Latin American Banker Mobility Program*
- GE: *Women's Network*
- Genpact: *Female-Friendly Policies*
- HSBC: *Cross-Functional Development Panel*
- Intel: *Women at Intel Network*
- Lenovo: *Women in Lenovo Leadership*
- Novartis: *Executive Female Leadership Program*
- Pfizer: *Global D&I Action Teams*
- Siemens: *Ambassador Program*
- Standard Chartered Bank: *Women in Leadership Program*

BOEHRINGER INGELHEIM:
Extended Business Trips

Gaining international experience and visibility can be a challenge to men as well as women in multinational corporations. Knowing this, Boehringer Ingelheim created a short-term assignment program to augment its long-term offerings and allow its less-mobile employees to gain international exposure.

Boehringer offers two types of international assignments. The first requires employees to spend one to eight years on assignment. Families are expected to come along on these traditional longer-term postings.

Within the past few years, Boehringer has also implemented a short-term assignment program called the "extended business trip."

Extended business trips are regulated by tax laws, which limit employees' time in the country to 183 days (six months). These trips range from three to six months. In addition to providing development opportunities, extended business trips allow for knowledge transfer on a short-term basis. In one case, a woman from Germany was brought to the United States to provide coverage for a U.S.-based employee who was on maternity leave. Extended business trips are offered around the globe, with the focus currently on the Americas. Participants are all high-potential employees ranging in level from director to senior manager. Boehringer provides participants with housing and transportation in the host country.

In 2008 Boehringer refined the guidelines for the program to better accommodate participants who have family obligations. "We've become much more flexible in terms of how we address family issues, both with the extended business trips and with our long-term assignments," says Gwendolyn Doden, recently retired corporate vice president of human resources for the Americas.

To that end, the company now provides support for the family members of participants on extended business trips. In the case of dual-career couples, the partner usually stays home; however, the company provides for monthly visits between the home and host countries. Visits may last for up to ninety days, although they are generally for a much shorter period. "Separation is difficult, but it's a lot less stressful than having to uproot your entire family, especially if you're only going for a year," Doden says.

In some cases, participants' family members may join them on extended business trips. One woman's stay-at-home husband came with her on assignment in Latin America. Child care and elder care may also be provided. When one woman from Venezuela went on an assignment to Ecuador, Boehringer brought her mother along. When a German woman on assignment at Boehringer's U.S. headquarters in Ridgefield,

Connecticut, brought her two-year-old with her, the child was able to attend the on-site child care center.

The flexibility of the extended business trip has made it extremely appealing to employees who have traditionally been less mobile, such as women with child care and elder care responsibilities. The program benefits men and women, with about one-quarter of participants in the United States and Canada being female and a nearly equal gender break-down in South America.

CISCO SYSTEMS:
Power Camp

One of the difficulties in developing and sustaining talented women in emerging markets is the lack of female role models. Cisco found this especially true in the smaller countries in the Asia-Pacific region. "I'm working with countries that have very few women at the leader level," says Tracy Ann Curtis, senior manager, inclusion and diversity, Asia Pacific and Japan.

Cisco already supported a growing constellation of Connected Women employee resource groups (ERGs) across the region. In coun-tries with few female senior managers within the company, the Con-nected Women ERGs take on the important task of building an infrastructure for female leadership by looking for role models *outside* the company: women leaders in customer or partner companies are invited to discuss their career paths and give mentoring advice.

Development and networking between Connected Women ERGs are also encouraged, allowing Connected Women ERG leaders in, say, Korea to get to know their counterparts in Hong Kong, Australia, and Singapore. "Bringing them together to develop their skills and build a sense of community is just as important as what they are doing locally in their countries," Curtis explains.

In 2009, Cisco amplified the Connected Women's work to a new level by launching Power Camp. A two-day event appended to the annual meeting, Power Camp had as its goal to empower talented women to articulate their goals, identify the personal obstacles that get in the way of attaining them, teach strategies to surmount those barriers, and develop an ongoing community of support.

Created by Center Stage Group, Power Camp offers a safe place for women to share their challenges and concerns with their peers, as well as receive intense one-on-one feedback to gain greater awareness of the personal obstacles that prevent them from making progress. For example, Curtis recalls, culturally a more reserved and indirect style of communicating may be preferred, especially among many Asian women, many of whom may speak English as a second or third language and are not as easily fluent in English as other languages. Consequently, they may not be seen as having managerial presence or being leadership material if they have not adopted a more direct and assertive Western communication approach. "The broader context was, Are you seen to have a credible voice, and what's required to have a credible voice? What are the challenges you create for yourself that you need help removing?"

Ten women were invited, with participants coming from Hong Kong, Taiwan, India, and Australia. Everyone was paired with a buddy, and each team committed to hold a monthly meeting to continue to push their agenda and act as change agents with their Connected Women ERG. Cisco's WebEx and TelePresence technology enabled the geographically separated pairs to have the kind of intimate, authentic dialogue that supports personal growth and development.

One of the participants was Curtis's own direct report, Radhika Muthukumaran. Curtis was aware of visible changes. "As her manager, I saw a difference. She really stepped up from the time she finished Power Camp. She became much more confident, and she expanded her network. She wasn't just talking to people in India. Now she had a colleague in Australia and could pick up the phone and say, 'Here's what I'm facing. What would you do about it?'"

Buoyed by the success, Cisco's ERG in Singapore held its own Power Camp, and more Power Camps are on tap for the future. "Given the evolution of distance learning and the strength of our technology, we are working to leverage our technology tools and host mini Power Camps,"

Curtis says, focusing on specific modules rather than holding a full two-day meeting. By using teleconferencing technology to expand beyond the geographic region, Cisco can use Power Camp as an important tool in developing women leaders throughout the emerging markets and building bridges across geographies for tighter, more effective networks of support.

CITI:
Latin American Banker Mobility Program

In 2009, in response to employees' requests for increased lateral development opportunities and international exposure, Citi instituted the Latin American Banker Mobility Program. The program offers short-term international assignments to its Latin American bankers, providing them with exposure to Citi's other offices in the region.

The Banker Mobility Program targets high-potential bankers at the middle-management level. Managers are asked to nominate direct reports who have specific developmental needs that have been identified in their personal development plans and can be addressed with an international placement. For example, one participant requested a placement in a bigger market so that he could gain experience working with more-developed products.

Assignments typically last three months. During the assignment, participants temporarily replace a banker in another Latin American country. They assume all of that individual's responsibilities and work as a part of his or her team. Additionally, the participant is assigned a mentor in the area where the assignment is located; the mentor offers feedback and guidance. The participants' goals for this assignment are to learn specific products or practices that can be developed or strengthened in their home countries, improve their current banking skills, and share their own knowledge in the new market.

The program works primarily as a swap; participating offices both send and receive a banker so that there is always backup. In this way, the program creates a chain of movement within Citi's Latin American offices. A banker from Venezuela may go to Costa Rica; a banker from Costa Rica may go to Peru; in turn, the Peruvian banker may go to Venezuela.

Elluany Rodriguez, who works in Citi's Costa Rica offices, took the place of a banker in Peru for three months. Her goal was to understand best business practices in Peru, where Citi's offices represent a bigger market than they do in Costa Rica. "The people in Peru were wonderful. They made is so easy for me to work there," she says. Rodriguez was able to bring what she learned back to Costa Rica, and she credits her recent promotion to systems VP to the Banker Mobility Program.

The program's first year saw eight participants. Maria Ordonez, HR generalist for Latin America, anticipates that ten to twelve people will participate in 2010. Through the program, participants improved both their managerial and their technical skills. After the program, participants work with their managers to keep up the skills they have learned and continue to make progress on their goals.

GE:
Women's Network

China is GE's largest hub in Asia. The number of women in its workforce—about 35 percent—is one of the highest, and 25 to 28 percent of the leaders are women. Yet despite these promising figures, says Liu Li, senior vice president of marketing for GE Capital, "women's representation at the senior level is an issue." Many of the senior leaders are American, based either in the United States or China. GE Women's Network (GEWN) aims to change that.

Launched in China in 2000, GEWN now has twenty-eight chapters located throughout Asia. The network initially focused on work and lifestyle issues. However, it has since shifted its focus to career development, with an emphasis on the cultural hurdles that hold women back. "This is almost like a business," says Li. "We have all these highly structured initiatives. Every year we come up with an annual plan and we review the activities on a quarterly basis."

At this year's Asian Female Talent Forum, an annual networking event for fifty senior-band women with the potential for executive promotion, GEWN tackled the issue of self-confidence. "It can be a barrier that keeps some of our Asian female leaders from moving forward," says Jacqueline He, HR manager of GE China.

The two-day event in Tokyo offered a rich amalgam of training sessions, networking, and inspiring by example. The training was tailored to enhancing the skills Asian women need to develop if they want to grow and succeed in a multinational corporation: effective communication, assertiveness, and the ability to make strong presentations. "This training is about how to achieve goals by influencing and engaging other people, to get your results in a skillful way," says He. "The ultimate goal is to help our members grow continuously, both professionally and personally, within GE."

Intercultural communication skills are crucial, says Li. "Dealing with Chinese customers and colleagues is different," she notes. "There are many times you communicate indirectly. But when you communicate with American and European colleagues and leaders within the company, you have to be assertive." The forum offers plenty of opportunities to practice and receive feedback and encouragement. "This is a good way to develop self-confidence," says He.

One of the most significant lessons learned is how these skills can be used within the wider context of the corporation. "It's not just about Chinese doing business with other Chinese," Li now points out to the young Chinese women she regularly mentors through GEWN. "How are you going to be accepted by leaders who are mostly American and male? You still need to keep in mind your internal customers—you have to sell your ideas to them, make them accept them, and be recognized by them."

All forum participants are expected to share with their direct reports what they've learned from senior leaders, coaches, and trainers so that junior team members can leverage their insights, nurture their team, and benefit more people. "Every female staff member knows there's a tremendous platform they can leverage," says He. "All these resources are there, and they should take the initiative to grow themselves. There's no excuse for not doing so."

GENPACT:
Female-Friendly Policies

Genpact pioneered the outsourcing industry in India, China, and Eastern Europe, starting in 1997 with a handful of employees in its India office. Those were the days when the industry was still finding its footing, and Genpact, eager to quickly grow its employee base, was open to hiring inexperienced professionals, believing that the right kind of training and development could help them develop into corporate leaders.

The gamble paid off. Genpact, now a giant corporation with more than forty-one thousand employees, is known for its people-centered practices. Interestingly, it continues to bet on and succeed with a commitment to attracting and promoting raw talent, especially women.

Early on, Genpact management realized that gender diversity, especially in the senior ranks, would be critical to the firm's performance. As client companies have become more gender diverse, having women in senior leadership roles is crucial to winning business. Furthermore, becoming known as an employer of choice among highly educated women helps maintain Genpact's famously low turnover rate, a significant competitive advantage in India's tight talent market.

The company has a stated goal of having an executive cadre that is 25 percent women and hiring women at the rate of 50 percent for the management level. In 2009, it reached 26 percent women hires above the assistant vice president level, and it continues to work at raising the numbers. Genpact offers financial incentives to search firms that successfully place senior women, but its greatest magnet is building and sustaining a female-friendly culture. To that end, Genpact has developed programs that meet the needs of women in many innovative ways.

- *Promoting and sustaining ambition:* Genpact has two powerful programs. Genpact Women's International Network (GenWIN) is a global affinity group for women that addresses their individual needs and increases their exposure by providing various networking opportunities; and the WeMentor initiative identifies and pairs 150 high-potential middle-management women with experienced leaders in the company to assist and guide them on various professional fronts.

  Genpact believes that such programs help build global perspective through sharing of best practices and experiences among all members. For the company, too, these programs fulfill a business need by helping tap in to a wide pool of skilled employees, encouraging the culture of diversity and boosting retention with the number of high-profile career opportunities and stretch assignments that drive motivation.

  As further proof of its commitment to helping women excel, every year Genpact invites high-potential women to present key organizational priorities at their annual conference of senior leadership and top clients, where they meet company executives and major clients.

- *Encouraging flexible work arrangements:* From the beginning, Genpact has been committed to allowing the maximum flexibility for its employees and has instituted several flexible practices such as working from home, flextime arrangements, extended maternity leave, and sabbaticals to support the well-being of its employees and help them achieve a healthy work-life balance. At the senior levels, performance is judged more on output than face time, and Genpact believes in walking the talk. Indira Screymour, VP of human resources, currently oversees six direct reports, three of whom work from home 100 percent of the time, coming into the office only for important meetings. This flexibility is instrumental in ensuring her team is happy, energized, and productive.

- *Building family support:* India remains a conservative society, and some families still are uncomfortable with women working, especially when they are required to work at night. To prevent family pressures from pulling women off their career paths, every month Genpact hosts family days. Spouses and parents are invited into the office, where senior leaders speak directly with them about the business and the importance of each employee's contribution. Family members are encouraged to ask questions and raise concerns. These meetings are now considered one of the reasons for Genpact's low attrition rate.

- *Ensuring safe commutes:* Like many Indian companies, Genpact runs shuttles to and from the office from designated pickup and drop-off points. For night-shift employees, the company offers something unique. Employees working after hours are given car service to and from their homes, accompanied by a private security guard responsible for their safety. This added measure reassures employees and their families and has set an industry standard that many other companies have followed.

These policies as well as other small gestures, such as twenty-four-hour concierge services and on-site utility stores, show Genpact's women that the organization is willing to support and sustain them and help nurture and fulfill their ambition. As a result, Genpact has one of the lowest rates of turnover, an important advantage in the fierce competition for talent in India's outsourcing industry and one of the secrets to its success.

HSBC:
Cross-Functional Development Panel

Like every multinational corporation expanding into China, HSBC wished to ensure that its growth plans would not be stymied by a shortage of top talent. "The competition for talent in Mainland China is ferocious," explains Melvin Fraser, group organizational development senior specialist. "Unless you have a differentiated proposition, you can face challenging attrition rates."

At the same time, there was concern that the widespread financial services firm, with more than eight thousand branches in eighty-eight countries and territories around the globe, was so big that up-and-coming talent was inadvertently becoming siloed. "Some colleagues may have worked for the retail banking business for five years but don't have a clear understanding of how operations works," says Carol Zhang, senior talent, resourcing, and organizational development manager at HSBC China.

The Cross-Functional Development Panel aims to address both issues. Launched in 2010, the program singles out high-potential middle managers in its China region for customized career guidance from senior leaders, advice that endorses the benefits of experience across different functions.

Each quarter, eight candidates are chosen based on their performance, their line manager's recommendation, and their area of expertise. They prepare a career biography detailing their experience, their accomplishments, their personal and professional aspirations, and their immediate, three-year, and five-year career plans. The candidates then present their stories and advocate their career interests to a panel of three senior leaders from other functions who serve as talent managers.

The ensuing conversation is both wide-ranging and specific, says Zhang. If the candidate states a goal of becoming the head of a particular business unit, the talent managers probe the rationale: Why are you interested in this position? What experience will you need to qualify for it? How will it benefit your future career? "Traditionally, our people follow the instructions of their line manager or boss," says Zhang. "Through this conversation, we try to have the talent understand why they need to engage with people at different levels—their peers, their team members, their senior leaders—in order to drive the process of their own career management."

The conversation, though only one hour, can be empowering. "We find that many of our people here are very good at execution, but their aspirations are still a little humble," Zhang notes. "The panel pushes them to think more and further. We share with the talent that they can be bolder in their career objectives and braver about taking senior leadership roles. We encourage them to exceed their expectations."

The panel also focuses on the pushes and pulls of the candidate's personal life. For example, one woman had two young children. Her background was in IT and operations, but she wanted to get frontline exposure, a more demanding position. The panel wanted to understand how she would manage work-life balance in the face of such change. She explained her motivation for driving this change. In three months, she was given the opportunity to transfer to a frontline job.

Although the candidates and panel meet only once, "it's not the end of the story," says Zhang. The panel's feedback is shared with the candidates' line manager so that both can work on a career plan. "We work closely with the line manager to monitor their development," Zhang says. "It could be for another assignment or for a workshop or training to support their development needs."

Six months after the first meeting, each candidate sits down with one of the original panel managers to report on progress and line up next steps. These meetings serve a dual purpose: in addition to maintaining the momentum, says Zhang, "the talents have the chance to develop sponsors in other parts of the organization and increase their overall visibility."

HSBC employee engagement surveys show that Gen Y and young Gen X employees are looking for active support to move their careers forward. The Cross-Functional Talent Panel offers a proposition that strengthens engagement among the newest tranche of talent while also driving overall business performance.

INTEL:
Women at Intel Network

The goal of Intel's global women's initiative is to ensure that Intel is a great place to work for women—worldwide. But making this happen is a highly local process, says Kim Warren, manager of women's initiatives for the department of global diversity and inclusion. Intel seeks to understand how the challenges facing women in China may differ from those confronting female employees in Russia or Europe. That's why the company's thirteen-year-old Women at Intel Network (WIN) is going global—in a grassroots way.

Since 2007, the employee networking group, which is open to all employees regardless of gender, has added fourteen international chapters. China was the first to initiate a chapter outside the United States, with a group in Chengdu. Offshoots in Shanghai and Dalian soon followed. In spring 2008, nearly three hundred participants from across the country attended the first Chinese WIN Leadership Development Conference in Shanghai Zizhu science-based industrial park, attending sessions on achieving work-life balance, managing stress, and growing technical skills. In addition, women in Russia and Brazil are working to start local branches of the global networking group.

In practice, WIN chapters endeavor to strike a balance between global aims and local needs. Chapter chairs from around the world hold virtual meetings each quarter to establish global goals in areas ranging from membership to professional development, which are then adopted according to local priorities and cultural contexts. "Each site implements what's best for them," says Warren. Each time a new chapter is started abroad, in-country representatives work with U.S.-based managers to establish rules and guidelines that fit local needs. New WIN chapters are paired for about a year with established U.S. "sister" branches so that the newcomers can learn best practices.

In the long run, the company hopes to offer women in emerging markets the kinds of careers that they may not easily obtain in male-centered cultures, says Rosalind L. Hudnell, director of global diversity and inclusion. "Companies such as Intel are leading the way to achieve, inside of our organizations, what the world has yet to accomplish," says Hudnell. "In the end, the more successful we are within our walls, the more positive change we will see in society as a whole."

LENOVO:
Women in Lenovo Leadership

As a company with one of the highest percentages of women managers in the high-tech industry, Lenovo has long recognized the contributions women make in helping the company meet its business objectives. "We have a lot of extremely talented, capable women," says Barbara Dower, executive director of human resources, North America. "We have such a unique history at Lenovo—where Eastern and Western cultures meet." Lenovo, China's largest PC maker, acquired IBM's global desktop and notebook computer business in 2005. "We created WILL to bring forth women's leadership from both of those heritages, share experiences, and learn from each other."

Women in Lenovo Leadership (WILL) was launched in 2007 to address key priorities that support women's growth and contributions to the company. A global program with regional leaders in Australia/New Zealand, Brazil, Canada, China, France, Western Europe, the United Kingdom, India, Japan, and the United States, WILL encompasses events, programs, and HR processes to enhance work-life balance, mentoring, networking, and leadership development.

Although the core agenda is clearly aimed at nurturing and supporting high-potential women who want to move through the management pipeline, the range of programs offers something for everyone. For example, an executive roundtable in September 2010 focused on how senior women balance the demands of their personal and professional lives; held in Buenos Aires, it was open by call-in to Lenovo women in Argentina, Brazil, Chile, and Peru. Other programs offered in 2010 included a series of parenting workshops in Beijing, networking events, breakfasts with representatives from local companies and customers, and a seminar on global opportunities for women in Lenovo.

"Some of the programs come from the top down, where we see a need for women to develop certain needs or skills," says Dower. "But they also come from the women themselves. They'll say, 'I'd like to do mentoring. What are some suggestions for a mentoring program?' Or they'll arrange for a speaker or a meeting on a specific topic," such as a seminar on using social media for networking and development.

Mentoring is hard-wired into the company's ethos, Dower says, so as executive women travel around the world, they regularly schedule roundtable discussions at each location they visit. "There's a lot of willingness on the part of the senior executive team to be available and to communicate openly," notes Dower. A recent panel discussion featured four newly appointed women executives candidly answering questions about their career paths, the challenges they've encountered, and the choices they've made.

WILL also participates in global women's events that raise the visibility of Lenovo as a female-friendly employer, including IT diversity forums, community activities, and networking events. In 2010, it initiated the Fran O'Sullivan WILL Scholarship program, named for a recently retired senior vice president, which will award $5,000 to any U.S.-accredited college where a woman has a declared major in math, science, or computer engineering. "It's a way to show commitment to women in technology," says Dower.

As WILL moves into its fourth year, Dower is especially proud of how the program has tapped in to a bottomless well of enthusiasm. "It's not something that HR does. It's really self-sustaining. It continues to have life because the women in Lenovo have an interest in supporting it."

NOVARTIS:
Executive Female Leadership Program

As the Healthcare Businesswomen's Association reports, only 17 percent of senior management jobs at pharmaceutical, health care, and biotechnology companies are currently held by women.[1] Novartis's goal is to see its female professionals fill more general management positions and ultimately bring more balance to the company's executive committee, where one of twenty-three current members are female.

"We wanted to be innovative in coming up with methodologies to create a program that not only gets women to the top of the house, but addresses the visible and invisible barriers that preclude them from reaching the seniormost levels of the organization," reflects Michelle Gadsen-Williams, vice-president and global head for diversity and inclusion at the Novartis Group and Novartis Pharma AG.

On May 17, 2010, with the sponsorship of David Epstein, division head of Novartis Pharmaceuticals, and the company's executive committee, Gadsen-Williams and her team launched the twelve-month Executive Female Leadership program, aiming to prepare female participants for high-level positions, increase their exposure to senior leadership, and maximize their workplace contributions. Pinpointing pharmaceutical employees at a critical juncture in their careers, the initiative offers them the support they need to move ahead and trains them to succeed in key roles, ultimately diversifying the pipeline.

For its test group, the company selected thirty high-potential women at the level of vice-president, all with proven track records in the commercial or technical side of the pharmaceutical division and boasting an average tenure of five to ten years. Nominated by executive committee members, the women represent a global swath of talent stretching from Europe and North America to Africa, Asia, and South America. "We wanted the best and the brightest," says Gadsen-Williams.

Real-world training is at the program's core. From the outset, participants divide into six groups (meeting virtually or at a central location) to work on high-level projects that are real business priorities for the company. They complete relevant tasks on their own time and provide their executive committee member with regular updates. After one year, they present a final report.

Participants also receive mentoring from senior leaders who serve as members of the executive committee. To ensure that these relationships are effective, facilitators from the program's strategic partner, Duke Corporate Education/Cook Ross, may check in occasionally, along with members of the internal team. Complementing such guidance, the company will soon introduce instructional webinars in which female leaders discuss their own paths toward success.

To provide participants with more support, the women are also matched by geographic region with executive coaches from an external group, with whom they meet via teleconference monthly (or, at minimum, every six to eight weeks). This relationship is a "safe space" within which they can discuss any personal concerns, challenges, or career barriers. Potential topics might include maintaining the balance between motherhood and a leadership role, finding the right time to start a family, and dealing with workplace issues that might prevent their advancement.

Every three months, the participants spend a week in Basel, Switzerland, where they refine their leadership skills. At first, they focus on the self, learning to sustain high performance, demonstrate leadership behavior, and act as role models. Their focus then turns toward their colleagues, as they learn how to manage a culturally diverse workforce or lead a high-performing team. Finally, their attention shifts to the business itself. They might learn how to operate in a B2B world or how to cultivate a global mind-set.

While in Basel, they are frequently joined at gatherings by executive committee members or division head David Epstein. By blocking out space on his calendar to attend meals and meetings, Epstein demonstrates his commitment to making the program a priority and to advancing the women who work for him.

With at least a few months to go, feedback from the program is extremely promising. "I was honored to be a part of this group," said one female participant. Added another, "From this point on, I want to do more to engage men and women in understanding what leadership is all about." And from a third woman, "This was the best leadership course I've ever had."

As a participant in the program, Vice President Dagmar Rosa-Bjorkeson, head of the company's multiple sclerosis business unit, is working with an international, cross-functional group of VPs on a project for the president of the Latin American division, Carlos Garcia. The women conduct research into patient–customer behavior (which includes recording video "journeys" and spending time at pharmacies) to develop actionable insights for that region's marketing plan.

Getting support from the executive committee while on the program makes an important difference, Rosa-Bjorkeson says. And it's not just because they understand what she's doing. "Their involvement symbolizes a true commitment to developing more women so they will end up on the global executive committee," she explains. "Without that, this would be just another development program." Rosa-Bjorkeson also singles out the coaching she receives, which helps her address leadership issues and manage personnel. "For me, it's very valuable; I have not had such consistent coaching before, in such a dedicated way."

"We give women the tools, skills, and resources to make them more effective than they currently are," confirms Gadsden-Williams. Ideally, she would like to see at least three women graduates of the program be promoted into the corporate executive group (the leadership tier at Novartis). She also intends to launch an alumni association to keep participants and executive committee members engaged in the effort to help women advance.

Rosa-Bjorkeson says she would definitely sign up for alumni meetings. "There's a wealth of support, knowledge, and real business value in just knowing this group of women. That, to me, was the best part of the whole thing."

PFIZER:
Global D&I Action Teams

Pfizer has devised an innovative means of developing its leaders to work cross-culturally to create an inclusive work environment. In 2009–2010, its "global D&I (diversity and inclusion) action teams" served as an experiential learning exercise for high-potential managers. Team members worked together across national boundaries and cultures to solve a specified problem set in a global work environment. The initiative was central to Pfizer's talent strategy of "making sure that our colleagues have not only the skill set, but also the experiences they need," says Sandra Bushby, director of global diversity & inclusion.

The action teams were composed of more than 250 high-potential managers from fifty countries within the company's Emerging Markets business unit who had been identified as "agents of change" within Pfizer. The action teams covered all areas of the diversity spectrum, including gender, ethnicity, age, and even function.

The teams were first brought together at Pfizer's Global Emerging Markets Leadership Summit, which was held in Dubai in the summer of 2009. Following the summit, the action teams returned to their home regions to embark on an experiential, action-learning process and execute their projects. The engagement of the teams expanded the lessons of the summit beyond simple in-class training to real-world action and results.

For nine months after the summit, members of each action team worked together virtually, cross-country and cross-culturally to implement a team inclusion initiative that would result in a heightened focus on diversity and inclusion. The action teams were created so that the colleagues represented different countries within each region. Each team was given one of five key focus areas and asked to identify a strategic direction that would have a measurable impact on the creation of an inclusive work environment and could be launched within three months. The focus areas included developing leaders who maintain a D&I focus in a financially constrained environment, becoming an employer of choice, developing global cultural awareness, minimizing unconscious bias, and enhancing colleague engagement. The teams were instructed to have a first-level benchmark measure within six months, a measure that they would work together to implement. In April 2010, the teams recommended to the leadership team of their business unit whether or not to go forward with their projects.

Throughout the process, the teams were reminded that it was not the project implementation that was most important but rather their experience in implementing the initiatives. A final recommendation for the business unit not to go forward with the project was still considered a win. Along the way to their final recommendation, teams faced embedded action learning that, if not navigated, became "derailers," such as cultural collaboration, working across geographies, establishing performance standards and accountability processes, leveraging existing resources, working with ambiguity, and collaborating with key stakeholders. One of their biggest challenges was building virtual teams whose members could network with each other and cross-pollinate one another's ideas within the matrix structure of Pfizer. Region and country managers provided support and motivation for the teams operating in their areas.

Despite the intentional hurdles, many projects have been recommended and even piloted as a result of the work of the global D&I action teams. One team developed the broad implementation of a Cultural Navigator program, which trains employees to deal with cultural differences. Dubai is now investigating how to best integrate privacy rooms on an action team's recommendation. An Asia-based team recommended that a diversity and inclusion lead be created to help coordinate their diverse region.

Not all of the action teams produced workable results, but Bushby emphasizes that the experience of the teams was of paramount importance. "The team members have a huge 'aha' moment at the end where they realize that this wasn't about, say, formal diversity training. The whole key learning was about them learning to lead inclusively in an experientially based way," Bushby explains. "They've just experienced what it's like to be a region president working to create a sustainable, globally inclusive work environment, and those constraints that are working against making that happen, so that they can better understand now how to solve that."

Patrick van Ginneken saw how the action teams expanded his colleagues' understanding of the value of diversity when he coordinated five teams in Pfizer's Emerging Markets Europe region. "The eye-openers for a lot of our colleagues were the unconscious bias, and also the understanding that diversity is an issue that goes much broader than the numbers of how many males and females you have in your organization," he says. Van Ginneken now advocates for diversity experience as part of the onboarding process for Pfizer colleagues. "Diversity is something that should be part of our leaders' DNA."

SIEMENS:
Ambassador Program

Diversity at Siemens isn't simply a department or a policy. It's a business imperative, realized through a global web of innovative efforts to attract and retain the best and brightest, regardless of background, and nurture a diversity mind-set in all that Siemens achieves. A key pillar of such efforts is a vibrant series of networks, carefully built to engage employees throughout the 163-year-old company in bringing diversity to every aspect of their work.

With 139 members—including 52 women—based in thirty-four countries, the newly created Ambassadors Network is the most recent addition to the company's expanding roster of diversity networks, joining GLOW (Global Leadership Organization of Women) and the BRIC–Middle East Talent Network. Also planned is a network aimed at connecting engineers from different generations.

Selected for their outstanding careers, track records as role models, and excellent people skills, the ambassadors serve as active champions of diversity in their home countries and globally. They act as crucial sounding boards and advisers to managers who are formalizing and cultivating diversity efforts. The ambassadors also personify the power of diversity given the breadth of the personal and professional challenges they have faced during their careers. "These are individuals who have made it and have continually moved out of their comfort zones," observes one executive. "We encourage others to approach them as mentors."

In South Africa, a diversity ambassador who is also a member of GLOW worked with other local female executives to start ALOW, the African Leadership Organization of Women. ALOW addresses the specific concerns and needs of the female talent pool in their region. Ambassadors in Southwest Europe meet quarterly, bringing talent of all backgrounds together for career development and other advancement efforts. In addition, the European emissaries are starting an analysis of local diversity baselining in their region. In China, ambassadors are creating ways to provide job rotation and exchange opportunities to encourage mixed experiences among local employees.

Through these and other grassroots efforts, Siemens's new global ambassadors are working to communicate the business case for diversity. Just as international diplomats represent their countries broad, so Siemens's ambassadors are the first-line voices of diversity in the company's offices worldwide.

STANDARD CHARTERED BANK:
Women in Leadership Program

With eighty thousand employees spread over seventy markets, Standard Chartered is one of the world's most international banks. And with a high percentage of women in its workforce—for example, 67 percent of the overall employee base in Mainland China is made up of women, including 51 percent of middle management—the company has been strengthening the pipeline of high-potential women targeted for senior management roles.

In 2007, Standard Chartered invited women middle managers from Asia, Africa, and the Middle East to a Global Women's Forum in Dubai. Many of the attendees had never previously had the opportunity to discuss career development issues with their female peers because they typically found themselves to be a minority in traditional management development programs. "Feedback in Dubai was that this is fantastic, but we need to offer the opportunity to many more women," recalls Kari Reston, head of group diversity and inclusion.

A focused two-day program was then piloted in 2008, followed by four programs in 2009: two for women managers in Korea, one for their peers in Africa, and one for their colleagues in the Middle East. "We wanted the program to be grounded in the culture and dynamics of the local environment," Reston explains. "What's relevant in Korea versus Kenya can be very different."

With strong positive feedback, the bank decided to bring the previously outsourced program in-house, where it could be aligned to Standard Chartered's strengths-based approach and dovetail with the bank's overall diversity and inclusion agenda.

The program was also expanded to reach even deeper into the talent pipeline: in addition to a two-day program targeting women just below the senior management level, there's now a shorter version for junior- and mid-level managers one step below them. Eight other programs were offered in 2010 across Europe and Asia. "This was designed to be both high-touch and yet quite scalable," says Reston.

Participants represent a geographically and functionally diverse group of high-potential and high-performing managers at a certain level. Before the program begins, each has a conversation with her manager to discuss strengths and critical career issues. Each manager has already been contacted by the country CEO to underline the program's credibility and ensure the manager's support. The women receive a personal telephone call from one of the program administrators to answer any questions and ensure they will get the most out of the experience; a video from senior executives reinforces the significance of the program.

The two days are composed of a series of facilitated discussions: on developing and articulating a career vision; on identifying challenges and self-limiting beliefs; on learning to negotiate and overcome those obstacles; on defining the concept of strategic visibility; on strengthening one's resilience to rebound from the downdrafts that hit every career. "There are no PowerPoint slides—this isn't a skills training course," says Reston. Peer coaching sessions train the women to support their colleagues. By the end of the program, each woman has come up with a robust and sustainable action plan, both for her own career and for supporting those of others.

Many of the sessions divide participants into small groups, a tactic to foster peer support among the women. These close-knit groups have also seeded larger networks among the alumni, networks that have resulted in the creation of women's networks in, for example, China and Kenya. These alumni groups, in turn, stay connected through face-to-face meetings, online discussions, and periodic teleconference calls on various topics of interest.

In addition to metrics showing significant post-program increases in participants' clarity concerning their future and their understanding of what will be needed to reach their goals and aspirations to senior management roles, the reaction from participants has been unequivocally enthusiastic. In a typical response, one participant from Hong Kong wrote, "It made me understand what is needed to reach a senior management position." Managers have been equally impressed. "Her communication skills have improved a lot, and she is working with more confidence," said one participant's boss. Said another, "After running so hard in their current position in the organization, the program gave her and other participants a clear direction and the confidence to set up an ambitious career goal."

As one mark of the program's success, Reston reports that there's no longer a need to seek out support from countries to hold the program. "Numerous markets have been coming to us, persuading us to hold programs there next."

10

Dealing with Pulls and Pushes

Women in the BRIC countries and the UAE face unique family-rooted pulls and social and work-related pushes that conspire to derail their career ambitions and cause them either to settle for dead-end jobs or leave the workforce entirely. These factors are highly specific to the context of the emerging markets, reflecting entrenched cultural perspectives and modern global complexities.

Responding to these challenges with imagination, sensitivity, and flexibility can be a tall order. What solves the problem in one country may have little impact in another. Training mostly male senior managers to become aware of the difficulties and to respond appropriately takes time and dedication. Finding solutions involves a delicate balance of a global mind-set and local knowledge. In this chapter, we look at ten organizations that have successfully managed these pulls and pushes:

- Booz & Company: *Middle East Flexibility*

- Cisco Systems: *Extended Flex Program*

209

- Deutsche Bank: *India Diversity Council*

- Ernst & Young India: *Innovative Workplace*

- GE India: *Assertiveness for Work Effectiveness Program*

- Goldman Sachs India: *Work/Life Skills*

- Google: *A Safe and Comfortable Commute*

- Pfizer India: *Creating a High-Performance Community*

- Sodexo: *Women's Networks in China*

- Wipro: *WoW*

BOOZ & COMPANY:
Middle East Flexibility

The calculus of work-life balance is especially challenging for consultants at Booz, whose clients demand their attention 24/7. It's even more so in emerging markets and the Middle East, where family-rooted forces that can derail talented women from their career tracks have unexpected pull.

Booz doesn't have a formal flexible work practice for the region, but that doesn't mean the company isn't aware of and sympathetic to the difficulties confronting some of its high-performing women employees, many of whom would otherwise leave the workforce. Instead, the firm takes a flexible approach to flextime, leaving it up to the manager to customize a plan for each employee and have the two of them work out the details together. Although nebulous in concept, this approach has had tremendous success in practice.

As a consultant, Joanne Alam traveled five days a week. "Our projects take us anywhere across the region, from Jordan to Dubai to Syria. That's the nature of the job," she explains. But when she became pregnant with her first child in 2006, she says, "I knew I couldn't keep traveling if I wanted to be there for my children. I love the firm, I love the people and the nature of the work, but that's my priority." Regretfully, she tendered her resignation.

Her project manager, Karim Sabbagh, a Booz partner, had another idea. Rather than lose one of his top talents, he suggested Alam apply her brainpower to a new and different opportunity: starting up a marketing communications department in the region. She could put in a 60 percent schedule and gain the flexibility to work from her home.

Having forged relationships with the partners when she was doing client-facing work made it easy for Alam to slip into this new role. "Booz by nature is very virtual, so partners often don't see each other for months," Alam notes. "We build the relationships by productivity. We don't always have to see each other in meetings."

Three years later, the marketing communications department has tripled in size and Alam has been promoted twice, most recently to senior manager. The projects she oversees have expanded from having a regional to a global reach. Rather than feeling marginalized for working part-time, she feels her career has plenty of room to grow. "I can see myself in two or three years becoming director of marketing communications."

Arine Hadidian, too, was ready to resign when a close family member became ill and the Oman-based consultant wanted to stay close by in Beirut. She was unaware of the possibility of flextime until her manager suggested it. Now based in Beirut as a global business operations manager, she feels she has built many of the same skills and relationships she would have developed as a consultant while traveling only once every four to six months. "I don't see flextime as an obstacle to career advancement," she says. "Just because you're there only half the time doesn't mean you can't come up with something of value, and my manager understood that."

Being flexible about flextime has been a win-win policy, enabling Booz to attract and retain talented women and giving women new opportunities to nurture their ambition and continue to build their careers. That translates into the kind of loyalty and commitment money can't buy. "It really made a difference for me to be able to take care of my personal life without having to drastically change my professional life," says Hadidian. "It helped me get through those hard times—and it meant the world to my family that I could be with them. I'm very proud to be a Booz & Company employee."

CISCO SYSTEMS:
Extended Flex Program

Flexible work arrangements are a standard part of the vocabulary for employees at Cisco offices in North America and Europe. But when the global telecommunications giant, whose workforce numbers sixty-five thousand worldwide, decided to extend flex options to Asia, it encountered challenges with translation.

"In Asian regions, there is still a high value on face time and the number of hours worked," explains Tracy Ann Curtis, senior manager, inclusion and diversity, Asia-Pacific and Japan. "With these policies, we're pushing a cultural expectation that's very different. We are not just adopting a policy but a complete mindshift."

Nonetheless, it was a fundamental change the company realized would be necessary if it wanted to remain an employer of choice. "A third of our new hires come from India and China," says Curtis. "These are Gen Ys—'freshers,' as we call them in India—and expect to work in new and different ways based on their natural rhythms, not confined to an office for eight, ten, or twelve hours a day."

A readiness assessment revealed surprisingly little push back from senior leaders. Bangalore's notoriously congested roads had already turned many of them into fans of telecommuting. The challenge was in breaking through the permafrost of middle managers—the level where the cultural values linking hard work, face time, and relationship orientation were most entrenched. The company created a Web site, scheduled Q&A sessions, and brought in senior Asia-Pacific leaders to explain why flexible work should be seen "as an opportunity to push a new leadership mind-set," Curtis says. In Asia's traditionally hierarchical environment, having senior role models "is one card that's really important to play in this part of the world."

With momentum established, the next step was to create a road map to implement flextime. Training programs were set up for employees to explain the responsibilities involved in taking up flexible work practices and for managers to help them learn how to manage a flexible workforce. "It's the manager's discretion as to whether the job profile supports flexible working," says Radhika Muthukumaran, project manager for global inclusion and diversity.

Phase I—telecommuting, flexible time, and part-time—was rolled out in India, Australia, New Zealand, and Singapore in October 2009. (Because each country in the Asia-Pacific region has different government guidelines regarding flextime, Cisco must conduct a legal review for each of the fourteen countries in which it operates in that region. Consequently, the road map for China, Korea, and Hong Kong has a longer timeline.) Phase II aims to introduce the concept of off- and on-ramps and remote work that had already been successfully implemented in North America and Europe in 2009.

Building on the insight that people have different needs at different points in their lives, Cisco's Off/On-Ramp Program allows workers to take unpaid breaks of twelve to twenty-four months. When ready to return, they have ninety days to find a job within the company. "If no job is available, they have to leave. That's the risk the employee takes," Muthukumaran says. Once an opening is identified, employees go through an on-ramp training program to get up to speed on their business function.

When the Extended Flex initiative was introduced in the United States, about a dozen people applied for and were approved for extended leave in the first round. With no upper limit on the number of program participants, Cisco expects that figure to increase, especially in Asia. "We expect two to four percent of the workforce at any given time to take any of the work options," says Muthukumaran. Although the program will undoubtedly appeal most to women who want to stop working temporarily after their children are born, the company plans to make the program available across all populations—allowing employees to take time off to resolve elder care issues, pursue a graduate degree, or refocus their careers as they see fit. "It's all about the employee value proposition—what are we offering employees to stay engaged," says Curtis.

DEUTSCHE BANK:
India Diversity Council

When Deutsche Bank human resource leaders set up a high-level Diversity Council in India, some senior managers had little or no understanding of the concept. "In a lot of emerging markets, the whole agenda is new," says Anu Sarkar, regional manager of diversity in Asia-Pacific. For many, diversity "is a buzzword coming from the U.S. and the UK." But starting fresh has a plus side, notes Sarkar, one of the organizers of the council when it was created in March 2008. "We didn't have any legacy. It was like a green field for us to get launched on this journey," she says, adding, "We don't mind going slow."

The ten-member, cross-divisional council may be proceeding cautiously, but its early impact has been widely felt. With the help of the human resource team, the Diversity Council increased maternity leaves in India by one month (to a total of four months) and added an optional extra phase-back program for new mothers. As a result, mothers can work a variety of half-time schedules, such as three full days or five half-days weekly, for two months after their main maternity leave ends. With the council's help, HR and diversity leaders also introduced a maternity coaching program for new mothers and their managers in the Asia-Pacific region. Before, during, and after their leaves, mothers get four to five hours of career-oriented telephone coaching on handling the transition, including an hour with their spouse if they wish. Separately, managers are offered two hours of coaching.

The council also has been active in helping create the bank's first mentoring program for senior women leaders in India. As of fall 2009, the fledgling program had paired fifteen senior Indian women with an equal number of managing directors, both male and female. A similar program launched in Japan in autumn 2009, and others are planned for Singapore, Hong Kong, and Australia. To retain senior management and promote generational diversity, the company also boosted the workforce retirement age in India to sixty from fifty-eight.

For now, the Diversity Council is focusing on issues related to female advancement and gender. But going forward, diversity will be broadly defined and the council may explore policies related to disability and generational diversity, says Sarkar. In a country with a tight labor market and a young workforce, diversity is a crucial way for the bank to remain an employer of choice. By 2020, 35 percent of Indians will be ages fifteen to twenty-four, and the country will be well on its way to overtaking China as the most populous nation on the globe. In coming decades, employers in India must address the needs and concerns of talented young Indian women or risk falling behind in a crucial global market.

ERNST & YOUNG INDIA:
Innovative Workplace

Ernst & Young India regularly holds an open house Family Day at its office in Bangalore. Twenty-five to thirty family members gather for show-and-tell sessions about the work environment and their day-to-day experiences. In particular, Family Day appeals to the parents-in-law of the company's married female employees by demystifying the work of their daughters-in-law. In fact, after his visit one father-in-law wrote to a partner, "My daughter-in-law will be working at Ernst & Young forever."

Family Day is part of the proactively inclusive work environment in Ernst & Young's India office. The company has instituted a number of cutting-edge policies aimed at retaining women and other talented employees. To address transportation challenges, Ernst & Young offered minivans to do door-to-door pickups and drop-offs for their employees, a service it subsidized by half. About 90 percent of the users of the vans were women. The company set up an on-site playroom with a desk for mothers of small children to use when they returned from maternity leave. Finally, it remodeled the office space "with a woman's eye," creating a relaxation room in the reception area with a TV and cushions.

But Ernst & Young India isn't only a great place for women; it's a great place for anyone to work. The company has made a concerted effort to create a lively, upbeat atmosphere to make Ernst & Young a place where people love to work. Employees are encouraged to "put their hearts in everything they do," and they joke about a "heart potion" being mixed into the coffee and tea that are served in the office. They even hand out paper hearts to give their colleagues kudos for a job well done. The hearts are known as RAVEs, shorthand for "a random act of value and excellence." Throughout the office, employees have pinned them to boards at their desks. The company also has a bell in the office that employees are encouraged to ring when a major milestone is achieved.

Other examples are contests that encourage employees to make the physical workspace their own. One sought inspirational quotations to post in the workspace. Another asked employees to submit paintings to decorate the office. The paintings were a major source of pride for employees.

As a result of its innovative workplace, Ernst & Young's India practice secured a spot in *Businessworld India*'s list of Great Places to Work. The office climate has been a boon for retention. Employees are so happy at the company that they have stayed even after competitors offered to increase their salaries.

GE INDIA:
Assertiveness for Work Effectiveness Program

When leaders of the women's network at GE India asked for an assertiveness training program, the organization's leadership took action. The program that resulted, the Assertiveness for Work Effectiveness

Program (AFWEP), was started in 2004 with the help of a consultant who specialized in assertiveness training.

The program was initially open to women of all levels at GE, who were placed in the program through their managers. With the consultant's help, GE India adapted a model of assertiveness that fit with the company's specific corporate culture. Activities included role playing and discussions about assertiveness in the workplace and were designed to address the issues that the women in the group were dealing with. Topics included assertive communication, dealing with aggression, and social power. The program focused on improving the women's interactions with their managers, peers, and direct reports. Participants also have the option of one-on-one sessions with a facilitator, in which they refine their action plan for assertiveness.

After several sessions, the men at GE India heard about the positive feedback from the program and wanted the chance to participate as well. In response, GE began offering mixed-gender and men-only sessions to interested employees.

Now the program is targeted at men and women of all levels who have a need to be more assertive. Each group has fifteen to twenty participants. Since the start of the program, some eight hundred people have participated out of the approximately twelve thousand employed in the GE India offices. About 80 percent of the participants have been female.

AFWEP sessions are offered multiple times each year, and feedback from men as well as women has been wonderful. GE is currently trying to adapt the program for its employees in China and in other emerging geographies.

GOLDMAN SACHS INDIA:
Work/Life Skills

At any given moment, approximately 4 percent of the nine hundred women employed in Goldman Sachs's center in Bangalore, India, are out on maternity leave. As more women continue to join the workforce, that number is expected to rise.

But despite the firm's generous maternity leave policy—four weeks on top of the government-mandated twelve weeks, plus the option of setting up a flexible work arrangement (FWA), such as a half-day schedule or working from home—a troubling number of women were leaving the workforce.

The problem, explains Viji Rajagopalan, vice president of employee relations and co-head of the Women's India Network (WIN), was "the cultural overlay of India." Women in India play a dual role, balancing their career aspirations against their responsibilities as primary care providers for their children and an extended family of parents and in-laws.

"There is definitely more support available today than before, but the challenges continue to be more here than I've seen in other parts of the world," says Rajagopalan. "India is booming as the IT development center that supports the rest of the world. But we don't have the infrastructure, like child care centers that are open beyond 6 p.m. There are no certified nannies, so you have to hire and train an uneducated housekeeper while you're working full hours." Furthermore, with many entry-level people migrating to Bangalore to start their careers, the traditional support of a relative at home doesn't exist.

To keep new mothers from being overwhelmed, in 2009 the firm launched Work/Life Skills, a cross-divisional maternity mentoring program that pairs new mothers with experienced working mothers who explain maternity benefits, discuss how to return from maternity leave, and provide hands-on advice on balancing motherhood with a full-time career. The company has bolstered these efforts by actively encouraging managers to provide flextime, either formal or informal work-from-home options, and extended maternity benefits to make it easier for women to return to work. "The feedback has been very positive," says Rajagopalan, noting that there are now as many women volunteering to mentor as there are new mothers.

A key element of the program involves training managers, most of whom are men, to be supportive of the needs of their female reports. "Before I went out on maternity leave, my manager and I talked about what would work for me and what wouldn't when I came back," recalls Rohini Eapen, vice president in operations. "If there were late-evening calls I couldn't take, it was okay as long as I communicated that in advance. The team is very sensitive to this as a matter of routine. It works like clockwork."

Increasingly, the traditional mind-set is changing as global attitudes percolate through the workplace and men in two-career marriages with children see how flextime arrangements can work for them. Goldman Sachs is further accelerating the change by seeding its India office with a higher proportion of expatriates on long-term assignments, many of whom come with their families, who serve as informal role models. "They not only bring their own personal experience but bring a cultural infusion from other Goldman Sachs offices and different sets of expectations of how the firm has supported them in New York, London, or elsewhere," says Tony Russell, managing director and head of human capital management in India. "That helps educate local managers about ... how we think about it as a global firm."

With a large population of young men and women who will doubtless soon marry and have children, providing advice and support through the childbearing and child-rearing years is crucial to attracting and retaining the workforce Goldman Sachs needs to succeed in the subcontinent. "We know we need to have something in place to keep the best talent," says Cindy Wright, vice president in operations India and co-head of the Women's India Network.

GOOGLE:
A Safe and Comfortable Commute

Getting to work is so stressful for women in India that, according to a USAID survey, it's a primary reason for them to consider quitting their jobs. As mentioned earlier, public transportation is often a gauntlet of taunting, catcalling, pinching, groping, and other indignities. Driving one's own car may be safer, but enduring an hour each way of slow traffic, with its nerve-gnawing bouts of automotive chicken and horn-blasting stoppages, saps energy and takes a toll on productivity. And with gasoline costing about $5 per gallon, it's expensive.

Most high-tech firms in India routinely provide transportation for their employees. The big ones usually offer buses and commuter vans that shuttle employees from train stations and other prearranged stops to and from their campuses. Google goes one step further by offering shared cabs for all of its more than twelve hundred workers—men and women—at its sites in Hyderabad, Bangalore, and Gurgaon.

The company outsources the service to contractors, which provide trained drivers and clean, air-conditioned cars—usually white Tata Indicas that, for safety reasons, do not carry the Google logo or any other form of branding. "Having air conditioning is very important, especially since the climate is typically hot and humid, so employees are fresh and rested during their commute," says Keerthana Mohan, Google's diversity and talent inclusion manager, Asia Pacific.

The system is personalized and flexible. Every morning, Mohan is picked up at her doorstep, joining two other people who live on the same route to the office and have been assigned to commute together as a threesome. In Google's larger offices, a transport supervisor sets the pickup and drop-off schedule, and employees can opt for a convenient time slot; at its site in Bangalore, where Mohan lives, she and her cab-mates agree on when they want to go into the office. It takes about sixty to ninety minutes to cover the fifteen kilometers (ten miles) to work. The car isn't equipped with Wi-Fi—wireless service isn't universally available in India—but she can plug a data card in to her laptop and connect with the Internet or take meetings via teleconference. "Typically one person takes a call while the others may log in or get some shut-eye," Mohan explains.

The cab and its driver are on contract to Mohan's group for the full day. Although the group usually leaves at 6:30 p.m., the cab is available to her whenever she needs it, including into the evening on occasions when she may have a late meeting. Indian labor law precludes women working after 8 p.m., but most states exempt IT and outsourcing firms from the restrictions as long as they follow certain mandated safety measures. For example, if a woman leaves work alone after 8 p.m., she must be accompanied by a security guard as well as a driver. If she leaves with other employees, the male employee gets dropped off last, no matter where his home is located on the route. "The woman is never alone in the car with the driver," says Mohan. In addition, both she and the transport supervisor have the driver's identification number and the supervisor knows what time she plans to leave, so she is always tracked.

The shared cab service extends to Google's Hyderabad employees who use the company-subsidized child care facility. The taxi picks up the parent and child—sometimes there will be more than one pair, depending on the route—and waits while the child is dropped off; then it takes the parent to work. The route is reversed with the same driver at the end of the day.

Almost all IT firms provide after-hours transportation for free, but many have employees pay a discounted rate for the service during ordinary work hours. Google, however, subsidizes the entire service. "The employee doesn't have to pay at all," says Mohan.

"It's so convenient, not to have to drive to work each day," she adds. "And it's fuel efficient, too."

PFIZER INDIA:
Creating a High-Performance Community

India's rich talent pool of high-performing professional women is a key element in almost every organization's plans to succeed in this enormous, dynamic, and rapidly expanding economy. Yet despite their advanced education and soaring ambitions, many of India's high-potential women struggle with work-life balance issues that choke their capabilities, thwart their careers, and, in many cases, cause them to drop out of the workforce.

With the world's eleventh-largest economy targeted as a top growth market, Pfizer initiated a special effort to recognize and engage its high-potential female talent in India. The program has three goals, as explained by Amy Schulman, senior vice president and general counsel, and executive sponsor of the company's Global Women's Council:

- Help Pfizer develop and retain top female workers by ensuring that they feel valued and supported.

- Strengthen the connections among and between Pfizer's high-performing women and their women customers, creating a virtuous circle of support and loyalty.

- Put together a pilot program that can be used in developed and emerging markets.

In a pioneering integration of two sets of needs, Pfizer India identified ten of its top women in sales and marketing, as well as ten of its most important female customers: physicians in private practice, high-profile hospitals, medical technology, and other fields running the gamut of Pfizer's markets. Each was interviewed individually and invited to participate in a focus group in which the women discussed their career goals and the challenges and opportunities they face in fulfilling them.

There was a common narrative of blazing ambition often blocked by cultural barriers. In addition to the usual issues of work-life balance, professional Indian women must perform a complicated balancing act that pits their career aspirations against social expectations. Although an extended family network usually moderates the child care issues facing many of their counterparts in developed economies, Indian women are disproportionately responsible for elder care. Often, the demands of sales jobs are not understood by family members, so women come under a lot of pressure to give up their careers to take care of aging relatives. Safety and security issues that hamper women's ability to travel or work at night also make it difficult for them to do their jobs.

By providing the opportunity to share their experiences, the debut discussion group encouraged Pfizer's rising stars and their customers to connect, celebrate each others' successes, and discuss difficulties, with the underlying recognition that they aren't toiling on their own but are part of a larger community whose efforts are valuable and worth supporting.

Pfizer's next step was to hold a one-day workshop in April 2010 to address these cultural issues, as well as to teach career women and their customers the leadership skills that will help them raise their careers to the next level. The workshop was supported by Kewal Handa, managing director of Pfizer India, as well as Pfizer board members and senior women in India. Workshops were held in Mumbai and Delhi. "It's not about Pfizer," says Schulman. "It's about leadership."

SODEXO:
Women's Networks in China

From the moment they enter grade school, Chinese girls are taught that they are equal to boys. But once they enter the workforce, the reality is quite different. Despite similar—and often better—educational qualifications, Chinese women have not moved up the management pyramid in the same proportions as men. Sodexo China aims to shift the balance when it launches women's networks in Beijing, Hong Kong, and Shanghai in 2011.

A global provider of food and facilities management services, Sodexo already hosts women's networks in some of the eighty countries where it operates. The idea for a Chinese version was sparked when Rohini Anand, Sodexo's global chief diversity officer, attended a diversity conference in Beijing in November 2010. Impressed by the energy radiating from the Chinese women executives who attended and participated, she asked Grace Han, executive director for health care and seniors, to organize a network that would encourage female employees to strengthen their leadership capacity. "Chinese women have a lot more opportunities than before to take higher positions in the organization," says Han. "They have the capability, but they lack confidence."

Sodexo's women's networks will take a new approach to building confidence. At the Beijing conference, Anand and Han brainstormed with their counterparts at other multinational corporations. All were interested in promoting a women's network in China. "We had the same goal, so we said, 'Why not work together?'" Han recalls. The result: rather than limit the groups to the Sodexo China universe, each regional network will form a strategic partnership with a major multinational corporation operating in China. "This is a brand-new concept not just for Sodexo but for large international companies," notes Han.

All these corporations are Sodexo China clients, so they are already familiar with the others' cultures and standout women. "We will have events across companies to create a platform for both companies' women, so the participants will get to know more women and see more opportunities," says Han. "If they see more women who are successful, we can help build their confidence." The first joint event is scheduled in Shanghai in June 2011 with a Sodexo client.

At each event, senior women and men from both companies will be invited to share stories about their successes and challenges. "We want to have our people know more about other firms," says Han. "Another advantage is that the network will provide a good platform for high-potential women to make connections with senior executives and find a sponsor or mentor, particularly someone who can help them navigate work-life balance challenges." Although Han hopes the networks will attract high-potential women, especially those working in the business lines and operations, she points out that they're not limited to one gender. "We'd also like men to attend and to be sponsors."

The networks promote Sodexo's aim of pushing more women through its management pipeline, but they have the potential for a much broader field of benefits: through the strategic partnerships, they will open the horizon of opportunities for women at all of the companies.

WIPRO:
WoW

Buzz—that's what women senior executives at Wipro sought in launching a first-ever women's initiative in 2008 at the Indian technology giant. Women leaders on the company's Diversity Council wanted "the whole company hearing and thinking about the Women of Wipro (WoW) initiative," recalls Sunita Cherian, a general manager in talent engagement and development and a key player in the WoW launch. "We wanted to get people excited."

Women of Wipro was created to enable women to strategically build a career at the global IT services provider headquartered in Bangalore. Although women make up nearly 30 percent of the 100,000-strong workforce, they make up only 5 percent of management at the vice presidential level or higher, and fewer than 20 percent of managers overall. But times are changing, and the business case for women's advancement is clear, company chairman Azim Premji told reporters at the launch of the group. "There is no doubt that having more women in an organization can help in making it more profitable," he said.

To build buzz for the new group, founding organizers first pursued low-hanging fruit—that is, projects that both help women concretely and raise internal awareness of WoW. In 2008, WoW began sponsoring a series of ongoing self-defense workshops for women employees across India. Additionally, the group developed brochures on personal safety for new employees across the company.

In 2008, WoW also began sponsoring on-site vacation camps for employees' children across the country. The camps boost productivity for mothers who face long daily commutes and a dearth of reasonable child care options during the long spring school holidays. By bringing their children to on-site camps, mothers also get to spend extra time together while commuting and even over lunch, says Kavita Mathu, whose eleven-year-old daughter participated in a camp at a Wipro site near Bangalore. "The children felt a sense of pride and involvement at the end of the workshop as they got an idea of where we worked and what we did."

To understand how to further help women employees, WoW next undertook an in-depth research project, interviewing 120 high-potential women who were current or former Wipro employees or who worked at similar firms. The results showed that "painting all women with the same brush is not the final answer," says Cherian. "Different interventions are required at different life stages."

During the early stages of their careers, for instance, women benefit from being exposed to varied, challenging roles and female role models, the findings suggest. Success stories teach young women that "if these women can, I can," says Cherian. As a result, WoW has begun sponsoring a robust array of mentoring experiences, career advice blogging, outside speakers, and other inspiring programs.

During the next, more family-centered stage of their careers, many women need flexibility, the research findings revealed. So WoW worked to alert female employees of the availability of extended maternity leaves, which allow as much as six extra months' unpaid leave following the standard three months' paid leave. Now, 90 percent of women who take maternity leaves take a full nine months off, says Cherian. In addition, WoW began a program to keep women on leave better informed of company developments via a digital newsletter and other communication. This connection has helped persuade 75 percent of women who take extended leaves to return to the company.

"The extended leave helped my life immeasurably," says Reena Pereira, partner on the talent engagement and development and human resource team. Pereira gave birth to her first child in September 2008 and extended her leave until February 2009. By staying out six months, she was able to spend focused time with her child before hiring and training a nanny. Plus, the newsletter gave her the "courage" to return to work. "It gave me the reassurance that there are many working mothers who have balanced their careers and homes, and I will be able to do it too!"

WoW is also working to ensure that female employees have the child care they need. WoW members help the company search for top-notch day care centers near Wipro campuses and then negotiate subsidized rates for employees. The day care centers even pick up and drop off employees' children.

In later career stages, veteran women need empowerment, especially in the male-dominated IT industry, WoW's research revealed. As a result, WoW worked to reshape the company's annual succession planning to bring more women into the leadership pipeline. Now, the company's main succession plan, which is reviewed by the chairman and covers every managerial role, specifically includes a section on women. In addition, the company is hiring senior female talent from outside the company to increase the number of high-level role models for its female workforce.

The Leapfrog Opportunity

With their phenomenal pace of growth and change, emerging markets are fertile ground for the development of new approaches to attracting and managing talent. Rather than being constrained by an entrenched business-as-usual mind-set, companies moving into these geographies have the chance to get their talent models right from the start, to leapfrog legacy practices and create new approaches that encourage and enable highly qualified women to succeed in these dynamic markets.

Adding to an urgent need for innovative solutions is the fact that educated women in emerging markets are ahead of the curve in unexpected ways. The vast differences in socioeconomics, culture, and demography can make it easier for a woman to pursue and sustain a career in São Paulo than in London. Companies that understand the nuances of doing business in emerging markets can further leverage that resource through inclusive, women-friendly people practices.

A closer look at the leapfrog opportunity provides a context for existing action agendas and lays the foundation for further cutting-edge initiatives in the future.

THE BLANK SLATE PHENOMENON

"Ten years ago when I was flying from São Paulo to Rio, we had a female pilot. The men on the flight thought the plane would crash," recalls Samara Braga, a Brazilian economist. "On a recent flight, they announced a female pilot and everyone clapped."

What a difference a decade can make! So much change in so little time speaks to the dynamic nature of emerging markets; it also creates a blank slate environment—a drive for institution-building and an openness to new ideas among highly skilled professionals.[1] A senior Indian executive underscored the need for a different approach to doing business in emerging markets. "If you are profit-making in an established economy, you go with the assumption that whatever you think is true, everything is right. But in emerging markets, you have certain ethical, social, cultural conditions—so sensitivity is required to figure out what works and how to balance those sensitivities with issues of effectiveness and economy."

A nuanced understanding of the cultural and social influences is essential to doing business effectively anywhere; yet the "think globally, act locally" mantra that is the cornerstone of many a successful business strategy rarely extends to managing talent. It is often assumed that gender trumps culture and that the menu of solutions that works for attracting and developing female talent in the West—centered on topics such as child care—will work, with minor amendments, for women in emerging markets. In reality, educated women in emerging markets seek support for the professional challenges particular to their context.

"There has to be an understanding of how people live—the daily realities of raising a family and what is important, what the specific challenges are," advises a senior HR manager speaking of the Indian context. In fact, the same advice holds true across the BRIC and UAE economies.

SHIFTING GENDER ROLES

Companies are often surprised by how much they stand to learn from emerging markets about managing female talent. The key message here: women in emerging markets can in no way be assumed to be "behind" their Western peers.

For one thing, rapid economic growth has triggered a vast shift in gender roles, particularly among urban professionals, for whom an unprecedented range of professional opportunities has opened up in the past two decades. The millennial generation of women in emerging markets is also making its mark, bringing a global outlook and distinct set of work-life expectations to the workplace.

A growing number of women in emerging markets outearn their spouses; in Brazil, China, and the UAE, they constitute at least one in five of our sample. The contribution women make to household income has become indispensable as living costs escalate in emerging markets, especially in urban areas. Consider that seven of the thirty most expensive cities in the world are in Russia, China, and the UAE.[2]

On the cultural front, the majority of women in emerging markets do not report any social pressure to quit work at critical life stages, such as getting married or the birth of their first child. The notable exception is India, where traditional values remain tenacious. Yet even in this most tradition-bound of societies, change is imminent. An Indian finance executive contemplates her choice to be a working mother: "My husband says, 'There's no way you are leaving your job. You're way too driven, you're well qualified, and you have ambition.'"

Many multinational organizations assume that female professionals will refuse international job opportunities, negatively impacting their leadership prospects. Our findings squarely counter this view. In fact, most women in emerging markets express a strong interest in taking on an international assignment. We probed this theme further by asking married women in the sample how open their spouses would be to relocating for them; the majority claimed their spouses would be willing to move, and in India, China, and Brazil, women's responses to this question were surprisingly close to those of men. One female executive of a global engineering giant in Russia eagerly anticipates the opportunity to expand her horizons: "In the next few years, I would like to return to headquarters in Europe to take on an operational role, and then maybe later, I'd like to go on to another region, perhaps Asia."

MILLENNIALS AND THE REWARDS REMIX

Companies are hiring so many Millennials in emerging markets that the average age of their employees is plummeting. How do Millennials differ from their predecessors, and how are they changing the talent equation in emerging markets? To begin with, today's young women, recently graduated from university and entering the workforce, have a world of potential role models to choose from—literally. Thanks to the Internet, Twitter, and Facebook, the boundaries of their imagination have dissolved. The gender-neutral communities on the Web allow them to draw inspiration from women—and men—all over the globe and not only from their own countries and cultures. At the same time, having grown up in exponentially expanding economies, they have a sense of limitless possibilities leashed only by their skills and the size of their ambition.

"The idea of equal opportunity came to be in the previous generation, but the opportunities were more limited," says Adeline Wong, who heads up human resources for Booz & Company's Greater China practice. "This current generation realizes that if they try, they actually can achieve a lot more."

Throughout the BRIC nations and the UAE, the word that older career women consistently use to describe educated twenty-somethings is "confident." Samara Braga sees tremendous self-assurance among young women at work, where she is the financial markets leader for Ernst & Young in São Paulo, Brazil, as well as in her own family. "My daughters, both of whom work for multinational corporations, are more relaxed about telling their bosses what they want and don't want to do. I see this in all different professions—women are feeling more comfortable about saying no and pushing the envelope more. It's a major change."

That has profound repercussions for employers. Millennials are already a sizable portion of the workforce in emerging markets: one-third in India and Brazil, and one-quarter and one-fifth in Russia and China, respectively.[3] Their attitudes toward work, careers, and life are a departure from prior generations' and are already prompting employers the world over to reevaluate the value proposition on offer. Years of economic growth and the concomitant talent crunch have given recent university graduates a sense of being hot commodities, making Millennial women more selective in terms of job placement or career choice than their female counterparts were a decade earlier. Today's ambitious graduates aren't looking for a job; they want to shape a satisfying career. "Their career aspirations are very focused, very stated," observes Anjali Hazarika, head of talent management for Oil India. "They are also more eager to invest in training and development opportunities. Somewhere at the back of this is the mind-set that if men can have these opportunities, so can they."

Although there's no diminution of their competitive spirit, the new crop of talent takes a different approach to work, aspiring toward a more balanced work-life equation. Unlike women of prior generations, who reconciled themselves to significant trade-offs in their personal lives to succeed professionally, women of the new generation feel that they can succeed on their own terms. As Samara Braga observes, in contrast to the dedication and sacrifices women of her generation made, "the young generation feels they have the right to do less."

These comments mirror the Center for Work-Life Policy's recent research on Gen Ys in the United States, United Kingdom, and China. Growing up under the shadow of their parents' "all or nothing" work world indelibly marked this cohort, prompting a strong commitment to choice, flexibility, and work-life balance. Gen Ys across geographies share not only common desires but also a common value set. This is clearest in our findings around the "rewards remix," the fundamental shift in the definition of a satisfying career. Gen Ys in China, for instance, rated recognition, great colleagues, a range of interesting experiences, and a steady rate of advancement as more important than financial compensation, much like their peers in the West.[4] Similar sentiments come through strongly in our interviews with Generation Y women across the BRIC economies and the UAE.

Our research also points to a convergence of attitudes between Millennial men and women. Consider the fact that 88 percent of Gen Y women and 85 percent of Gen Y men consider work-life balance important.[5] Adeline Wong already hears young Chinese men fretting about work-life balance. "I hear male colleagues saying, 'I don't get to go home as much as I like. I want to spend time with the kids.' They have support at home, but they want to spend quality time with their kids." The message is clear for employers: corporations that can offer this rewards remix are more likely to attract and retain the top talent in this region.

TOWARD A NEW PARADIGM

Vinita Bali, CEO of Britannia India, one of the country's largest food companies, recently introduced a mandatory 50/50 male/female candidate slate for every job at the company. Rather than replicate the "fix the women" approach common to corporate gender initiatives in the West, Britannia is aiming for changes in its core business culture by increasing the representation of women across levels. This is one of the many ways in which companies, recognizing the business benefits of a more inclusive corporate culture, are reshaping traditional work paradigms in emerging markets.

Consumer product companies are especially aware of the importance of gender inclusion; with women making 80 percent of consumer decisions globally, the consumer is no longer king, but queen. Female perspectives and representation are essential to any company that is directly customer facing. As Michael Silverstein and Kate Sayre note in *Women Want More: How to Capture Your Share of the World's Largest, Fastest-Growing Market*, their analysis of the growing clout of women in the global market for goods and services, "The rewards for women that serve women well will be enormous."[6]

This argument increasingly holds true regardless of industry as women gain influence across disciplines and sectors. "When you think about health programs and medical research, about building partnerships with governments and hospitals, there are huge opportunities for educated, motivated females to create careers at Pfizer," says Jean-Michel Halfon, who recently retired as president of Pfizer's fast-growing, emerging-markets business unit. "Organizations that want to distinguish themselves in developing all their talent have to be good at understanding the motivation of women leaders, embracing differences in leadership styles, and recognizing the constraints often imposed on women by organizational cultures." He adds, "It's not enough to focus on specific tactics. Leadership has to change the culture of the organization."

For multinationals that are just beginning to build scale in emerging markets, the immediate opportunity is to ensure that management levels have at least a critical mass of women. "Without 20 percent critical mass, the system doesn't change," observes Murali Kuppuswamy, senior human resources manager, Drilling and Production, GE Global Oil and Gas. "Where women constitute over 20 percent of the total leadership pool, things change dramatically." He cites the example of ICICI Bank, which not only is headed by a woman but also is renowned in India for being a talent magnet for top women.

Flexibility

What are the top workplace priorities for women in emerging markets? Heading the wish list is flexibility—of schedule, location, and total hours worked. Women already recognize the benefits; they're just waiting for their employers to catch on. "If you provide good results, if you're self-oriented, self-motivated, and self-disciplined, why not provide the opportunity to work on a flexible basis?" asks one Russian manager.

The potential for flextime to increase efficiency and productivity was often noted in our study as an antidote to the everyday inefficiencies and obstacles still prevalent in daily life in many developing economies. In countries where the transit infrastructure has not kept pace with rapid growth, traffic jams are an unavoidable aspect of the urban environment. Beyond mere inconvenience, these highly unpredictable and time-consuming commutes also impact productivity and morale. As a solution, many women seek the relief of periodically working virtually or having flexible hours.

One common concern about promoting workplace flexibility is the specter of a mass exodus of staff to home offices or a drastic scaling back of weekly hours—changes that could paralyze day-to-day business. Contrary to these assumptions, however, our data reveals that employee flexibility needs are relatively modest and manageable. The majority of men and women prefer full-time work arrangements over reduced hours, with some flexibility at the edges—for example, flexibility in the structure of the day (flextime) or one day a week working from home.

The appetite for flexibility among men in emerging markets should also be noted; more than half in the CWLP survey chose nontraditional full-time arrangements as their preferred mode of working. This data bolsters the case for mainstreaming flexibility, for framing it as a business solution rather than a gender-specific one. Providing the types of flexibility at the edges sought by men and women in emerging markets can be a competitive advantage in countries where few employers currently offer alternatives to the rigid, traditional full-time work model.

Rethinking the Traditional Career Model

The prevalence of nontraditional or scenic career paths in emerging markets makes it imperative for multinationals to be creative and flexible in their approach to guiding the careers of their high performers. Our data shows that 30 to 50 percent of educated women in

BRIC countries have taken an off-ramp, indicating that discontinuous careers are more prevalent than usually assumed. In each country, 10 to 20 percent plan to take a time-out from the workplace in the future. In other words, a significant portion of the female talent pool in emerging markets has off-ramped (or plans to) in the course of their careers.

Sunita Thawani's story is in many ways typical of talented women who off-ramp. She left a budding law practice in New Delhi when she married and followed her husband to Jamshedpur, an industrial town that's home to many of the Tata conglomerate's industries. For the next twelve years, she raised two children but deeply missed her profession. She started a small jewelry business, but, she says, "it gave me no pleasure, no satisfaction. It was just for the sake of doing something because I was so bored sitting at home."

Then, when she accompanied her husband to a company conference, an opportunity arose. The CEO of Tata Steel addressed company wives, enjoining them to keep their husbands happy so that the men could contribute more to Tata. Thawani raised her hand and asked, "How can I keep my man happy if I'm not happy?" The question eventually led to a job interview. "I had lost confidence, but my father and husband kept my ambition fresh. They told me, 'You can do it, you can do it.'" With her innate curiosity to learn, hard work to catch up on the lost time, and her husband's enthusiastic encouragement and support—he tutored her in economics and business environment every night after the children went to bed—Thawani got back up to speed. Today, she describes herself as "a very confident head of the legal department."

In addition to her work, she has become a voice for qualified women who want to return to the workforce. "Times are changing. Women now want to come back, and husbands want the qualifications of women to be utilized. If companies offered opportunities, I'm quite sure that the women sitting out now would not be sitting out for so long."

Women take off-ramps for a variety of reasons, typically when pull factors in their personal lives and push factors at work combine to create a perfect storm of unsustainable pressures. Would women in emerging markets off-ramp in such large numbers if alternative options were available?

We asked this question in our survey, and the answer is a resounding no! Our results show that 81 percent of female professionals who had off-ramped would have stayed in the workforce had an alternative work arrangement been available to them. The most attractive of these options are seasonal work arrangements, telecommuting, and job-sharing.

Another means of bolstering the pipeline of female talent in emerging markets is to tap in to the rich pool of educated women who have off-ramped. If our sample is any indication, the opportunity is a significant one: an overwhelming majority (96 percent) of BRIC and UAE women would like to pick up their careers. With few avenues for reentering the workforce—at least without incurring a disproportionate loss of income, seniority, or responsibility—this talent pool remains vastly underleveraged. Off-ramped women suffer further from the perception that they have lost cutting-edge skills because of their time-out, particularly in industries such as technology where the pace of change is enormous.

One solution is to offer periodic retraining to bridge knowledge gaps as an integral part of the on-ramping process. The best on-ramping programs—many of which fell by the wayside during the 2008 financial crisis—offered mentoring, networking, and career management to support the reintegration process. However, none have offered the types of skills and knowledge-based training many on-rampers desperately need. Prohibitive costs and complexity are obvious issues, and yet the leaders we interviewed suggested a number of creative ways to tackle the skills gap. One idea was for a consortium of companies in emerging markets to join forces to offer on-ramping and retraining programs of sufficient scale to make economic sense; another was to partner with a business school or trade association to develop a curriculum catering specifically to the needs of boomerang professionals.

THE ROAD MAP FOR CHANGE

Many leading-edge multinationals are introducing forward-thinking inclusive practices and programs. These examples of action on the ground in emerging markets are encouraging and, in some cases, serve as models for managing female talent well regardless of geography. However, these efforts are by no means comprehensive or complete, and a great deal remains to be done. Some of the top priorities—for instance, mainstreaming flexibility and introducing on-ramps—remain largely unaddressed in these markets, representing a vast talent opportunity for multinationals.

As companies build their presence in emerging markets, getting their talent models right the first time around will ensure that they attract and retain the most talented women available. Our hope is that business leaders will take note and actively engage in the leapfrog opportunity—that they will acknowledge the full potential of educated women in emerging markets and will create the processes and practices that will enable these qualified and ambitious women to flourish on their own terms. In a rapidly evolving business environment, it's the surest guarantee of gaining a lasting competitive advantage.

APPENDIX

METHODOLOGY

Our research consists of a series of surveys in six geographies. Qualitative data was collected through focus groups, our Virtual Strategy Session tool, and numerous one-on-one interviews.

The surveys were conducted online in Brazil, Russia, India, China, and the UAE in October 2009, reaching a total of 4,350 women and men (a minimum of 1,000 people in each of four countries—Brazil, Russia, India, and China—and 200 in the UAE). Qualified respondents were country residents with at least a bachelor's degree equivalent. The surveys were translated into the local languages.

The sixth national survey, which included selected questions from the emerging markets questionnaire, was conducted in the United States in February 2010 of 2,952 currently employed men and women in certain white-collar occupations with at least a bachelor's degree. Data in this survey was weighted to be representative of the U.S. population of college graduates on key demographic characteristics (age, sex, race/ethnicity, household Internet access, metro status, and region). The base used for statistical testing was the effective base.

The national surveys were conducted by Knowledge Networks under the auspices of the Center for Work-Life Policy, a nonprofit research organization. Knowledge Networks was responsible for the data collection, and the Center for Work-Life Policy conducted the analysis.

In the charts, percentages may not always add up to 100 because of computer rounding or the acceptance of multiple response answers from respondents.

CHARTS

This appendix includes many data points from our research on the BRIC geographies and the UAE. It is intended to provide a broader context for comparisons and the analysis of country-specific themes.

Chapter 1: Unprecedented Advantages

FIGURE A-1

Percentage of school-age population enrolled in tertiary education

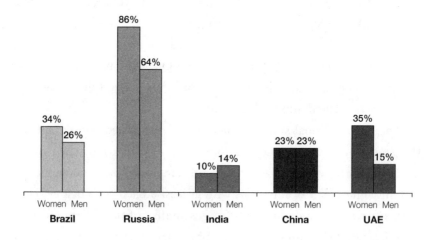

Source: World Bank Education Statistics Database.

FIGURE A-2

Graduate degree holders in sample

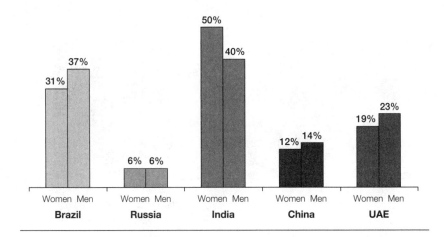

FIGURE A-3

Women with high level of ambition, by age

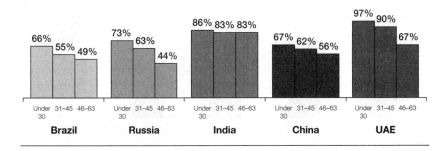

FIGURE A-4

Women's attitudes toward work

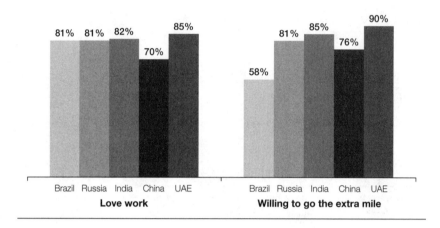

FIGURE A-5

Women's loyalty to current employer

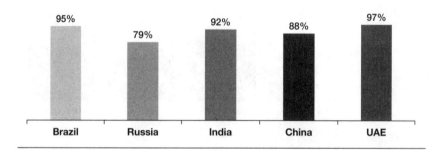

FIGURE A-6

Top work motivators for women

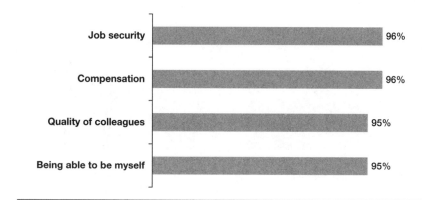

Job security — 96%

Compensation — 96%

Quality of colleagues — 95%

Being able to be myself — 95%

Chapter 2: Pitfalls and Trip Wires

FIGURE A-7

Child care options, full-time working mothers

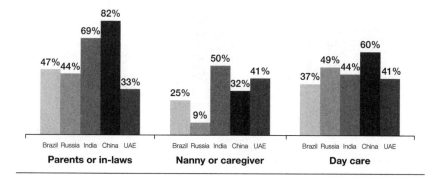

Parents or in-laws	Nanny or caregiver	Day care

Parents or in-laws: Brazil 47%, Russia 44%, India 69%, China 82%, UAE 33%

Nanny or caregiver: Brazil 25%, Russia 9%, India 50%, China 32%, UAE 41%

Day care: Brazil 37%, Russia 49%, India 44%, China 60%, UAE 41%

FIGURE A-8

Cultural pressure to "drop out"

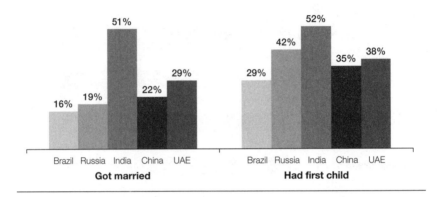

FIGURE A-9

Elder care responsibilities and options

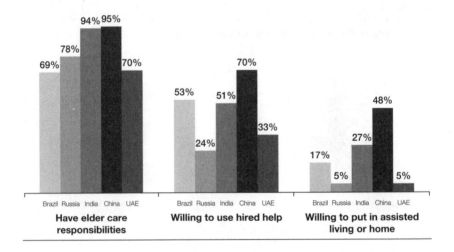

FIGURE A-10

Percentage of women providing monetary support for parents

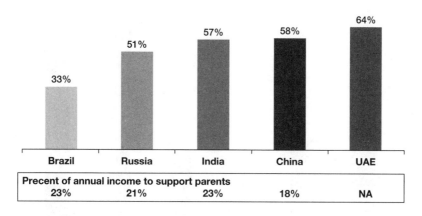

Precent of annual income to support parents				
23%	21%	23%	18%	NA

Data for UAE not available given restrictions on tracking salary levels.

FIGURE A-11

Percentage of women who share a household with parents

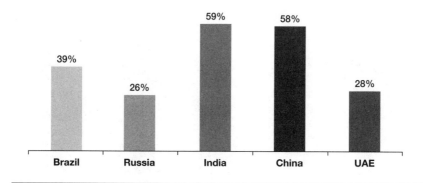

FIGURE A-12

Women working full-time who outearn their spouses

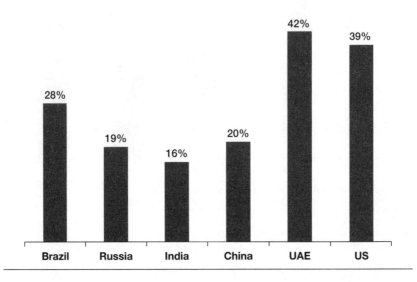

FIGURE A-13

Average work weeks (in hours): full-time working women

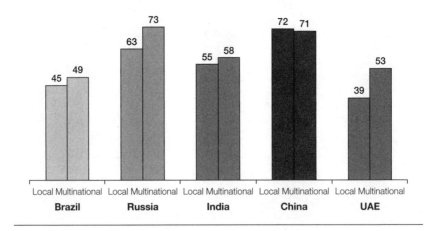

FIGURE A-14

Full-time working women: percentage working more hours than three years ago

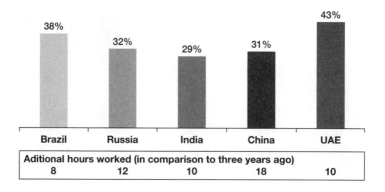

Aditional hours worked (in comparison to three years ago)				
8	12	10	18	10

FIGURE A-15

Percentage who believe that women are treated unfairly because of gender

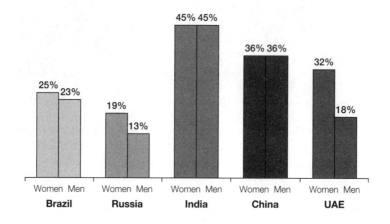

FIGURE A-16

Women's interest in international assignments

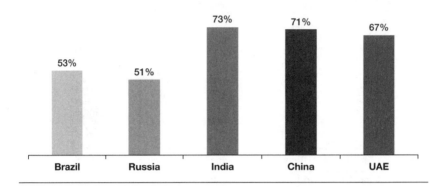

FIGURE A-17

Barriers to travel for women

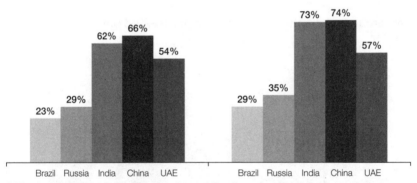

Difficulty getting visa for international travel Family and societal disapproval of women traveling alone on business trips

FIGURE A-18

Women who experience safety concerns on a regular basis

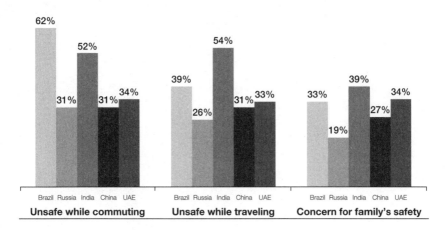

Brazil Russia India China UAE	Brazil Russia India China UAE	Brazil Russia India China UAE
Unsafe while commuting	**Unsafe while traveling**	**Concern for family's safety**

FIGURE A-19

Women's desire to work in the public sector

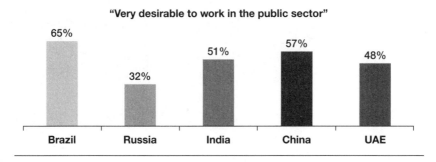

"Very desirable to work in the public sector"

Brazil	Russia	India	China	UAE

FIGURE A-20

Why is the public sector attractive to women?

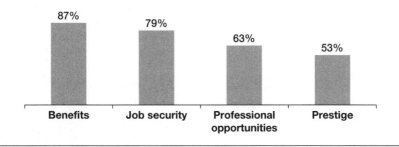

NOTES

Introduction

1. Jim O'Neill and Anna Stupnytska, "The Long-Term Outlook for the BRICs and N-11s Post Crisis," Goldman Sachs Global Economics Paper No 192, December 4, 2009, 6, 8.

2. World Bank Education Statistics Database.

3. "Women in Emerging Markets," Catalyst Quick Takes, April 2009. Women make up 43 percent of workers in Brazil, 49 percent in Russia, 28 percent in India, and 44 percent in China.

4. Nicholas Kristof and Sheryl WuDunn, *Half the Sky: Turning Oppression into Opportunity for Women Worldwide* (NY: Knopf, 2009).

5. Jim O'Neill, "We need Brics to build the world economy," *Times* (London), June 23, 2009; O'Neill and Stupnytska, "The Long-Term Outlook for the BRICs," 3.

6. Based on 2009 figures, data from Goldman Sachs, most recent available as of May 17, 2010; PricewaterhouseCoopers, "Convergence, Catch-Up and Overtaking: How the balance of world economic power is shifting," January 2010.

7. Douglas A. Ready, Linda A. Hill, and Jay A. Conger, "Winning the Race for Talent in Emerging Markets," *Harvard Business Review* (November 2008): 63–70.

8. According to Michael Paul Sacks and Kerry G. Pankhurst, eds., *Understanding Soviet Society* (London: Routledge, 2002), in 1988 nine out of ten women aged twenty to forty-none were employed—a figure higher than in any other industrialized nation.

9. See, for instance, Nishchae Suri and Stella Hou, "The War for Talent in India and China," *Hewitt Quarterly Asia-Pacific* 5, no. 1 (2006); *Achieving High Performance in a Multi-Polar World*, Accenture, 2008; Ready et al., "Winning the Race for Talent in Emerging Markets."

Chapter 1

1. Ricardo Hausmann, Laura D. Tyson, and Saadia Zahidi, *The Global Gender Gap Report 2010* (Geneva, Switzerland: World Economic Forum, 2010).

2. World Bank Education Statistics Database.

3. Michael Wines, "China Dismisses Its Minister of Education," *New York Times*, November 2, 2009.

4. "When More Is Worse," *Newsweek*, August 9, 2008.

5. McKinsey Global Institute, *The Emerging Global Labor Market*, June 2005, 32.

6. Phil Baty, "Rankings 09: Asia Advances," World University Rankings 2009, *The Times Higher Education*, October 8, 2009.

7. "Financial Times Global MBA Rankings 2010," *Financial Times*, 2011.

8. Ibid.

9. Christine Heenan, "Harvard Center Shanghai opens its doors," *Harvard Gazette*, March 20, 2010.

10. *The World Factbook 2009* (Washington, DC: Central Intelligence Agency, 2009).

11. Mercer, "Worldwide Cost of Living Survey, 2009–City Ranking," London, July 7, 2009.

12. Towers Perrin, *Global Workforce Study, 2007–2008*, "Closing the Engagement Gap: A Roadmap for Driving Superior Business Performance."

13. Ben Hirschler, "Firms Bet on Emerging Markets," *Reuters*, September 23, 2008.

14. Bruce Einhorn and Ketaki Gokhale, "Bangalore's Paying Again to Keep the Talent," *Bloomberg Businessweek*, May 24, 2010, 14.

15. Ibid., 16.

16. Sylvia Ann Hewlett, *Top Talent: Keeping Performance Up When Business Is Down* (Boston: Harvard Business Press, 2009).

Chapter 2

1. "The Sponsor Effect" research study, Center for Work-Life Policy, 2010.

2. Window2India, "NRI families: Caring for aging parents in India."

3. Tom Washington and Sergei Dmitriyev, "Almost Home," *The Moscow News*, April 17, 2008.

4. Population Division of the Department of Economic and Social Affairs of the United Nations Secretariat, *World Population Prospects: The 2008 Revision* (New York: United Nations, 2009).

5. Richard Jackson, Keisuke Nakashima and Neil Howe, *China's Long March to Retirement Reform* (Washington, DC: Center for Strategic and International Studies), 2009, 2.

6. Sylvia Ann Hewlett, Carolyn Buck Luce, Sandra Southwell, and Linda Bernstein, *Seduction and Risk: The Emergence of Extreme Jobs* (New York: Center for Work-Life Policy, 2007).

7. Dubai Online, "Working Hours," http://www.dubai-online.com/jobs/working-hours.htm.

8. "IBM Global Commuter Pain Study Reveals Traffic Crisis in Key International Cities," press release, *IBM 2010 Global Commuter Pain Survey*, June 30, 2010.

9. Jim Yardley, "Indian Women Find New Peace in Rail Commute," *New York Times*, September 15, 2009.

10. "The Family Friendly Workplace Model," USAID Health Policy Initiative, February 2, 2009.

11. Yardley, "Indian Women Find New Peace in Rail Commute"; "Rail Budget 2010: Six New Ladies' Special Trains," *One India News*, February 24, 2010.

12. "Brazil City Ready to Introduce Women-Only Buses," *MSNBC*, November 17, 2006; Andrew Shields, "Ladies' Taxis in the UAE," *Move One*, March 2, 2010.

13. "Brazil City Ready to Introduce Women-Only Buses."

14. "Pink Taxi Service in Moscow," *Russia Info-Centre*, March 30, 2007; "Pink Taxis in Moscow," *Lilith-ezine.com*.

15. Shields, "Ladies' Taxis in the UAE."

16. Sylvia Ann Hewlett, Peggy Shiller, and Karen Sumberg, *Sin Fronteras: Celebrating and Capitalizing on the Strengths of Latina Executives* (New York: Center for Work-Life Policy, 2007), 8.

Chapter 3

1. Cited in John Paul Rathbone, "South America's giant comes of age," *Financial Times*, June 28, 2010.

2. International Monetary Fund, "IMF Executive Board Concludes 2010 Article IV Consultation with Brazil," Public Information Notice (PIN) No. 10/111, August 5, 2010.

3. Quoted in "Passport to Brazil: A summary of the opportunities and challenges," Ernst & Young, 2010, 1.

4. "Brazil's President Exits with a Protracted Victory Lap," *Wall Street Journal*, December 31, 2010.

5. Iuri Dantas and Arnaldo Galvao, "Brazil Central Bank Sees Faster Growth and Inflation," *Bloomberg Businessweek*, June 30, 2010. Unemployment may end 2010 at a record 7 percent low, the Central Bank forecast.

6. Ibid.; "Sustainable Brazil: Economic Growth and Consumption Potential," Ernst & Young, 2010.

7. Cited in "Revolution, BRIC by BRIC," 20-First blog, May 17, 2010.

8. "No Rio, mulheres já ocupam metade das vagas das melhores empresas para se trabalhar," *O Globo*, March 2, 2010.

9. "Latin American Women Gain Edge," *Wall Street Journal*, December 24, 2010.

10. International Labor Organization, LABORSTATA, data for 2007 or most recently available; Grant Thornton, "International Business Report," [Grant Thornton], 2009; *Breaking Through the Glass Ceiling: Women in Management Update 2004* (Geneva International Labor Office, 2004), 14. See also Irene Chang, "Blazing Trails in Brazil," *Working Mother*, June 2008.

11. Tessema Tesfachew, Saadia Zahidi, and Herminia Ibarra, *Corporate Gender Gap Report 2010* (Geneva: World Economic Forum, 2010).

12. World Bank Education Statistics Database.

13. "Pesquisa mensal de emprego," Instituto Brasiliero de Geografica y Estatica, 2009.

14. Quoted in "Salto Quantitativo," *Estado*, May 31, 2009.

15. United Nations Population Division, "World Population Prospects: The 2008 Revision."

16. Elizabeth Jelin and Ana Rita Díaz-Muñoz, "Major trends affecting families: South America in perspective," report prepared for United Nations Department of Economic and Social Affairs Division for Social Policy and Development Programme on the Family, April 2003, 26.

17. Richard Jackson, Rebecca Strauss, and Neil Howe, *Latin America's Aging Challenge: Demographics and Retirement Policy in Brazil, Chile, and Mexico* (Washington, DC: Center for Strategic and International Studies, March 2009), 10.

18. Sylvia Ann Hewlett, Diana Forster, Laura Sherbin, Peggy Shiller, and Karen Sumberg, *Off-Ramps and On-Ramps Revisited* (New York: Center for Work-Life Policy, 2010), 17.

19. Cited in Sharon Lobel, "Work-Life in Brazil," Boston College Center for Work & Family Executive Briefing Series, 3.

20. Mercer, "Worldwide Cost of Living Survey, 2010–City Ranking" (London, June 29, 2010).

21. Quoted in "Seja una mamae executive," *Revista Mulher Executiva*, July 2010.

22. Miguel R. Olivas-Luján, et al., "Values and attitudes towards women in Argentina, Brazil, Colombia, and Mexico," *Employee Relations*, vol. 31, no, 3, (2009): 227–244.

23. Marlise Simons, "Brazil Women Find Fertility May Cost Jobs," *New York Times*, December 7, 1988.

24. "Diversity at Work: Blazing Trails in Brazil," *Working Mother.*

25. Sharon Lobel, "Work-Life in Brazil," Boston College Center for Work & Family Executive Briefing Series, 3.

26. Cited in Andrew Downie and Sara Miller Llana, "Latin America's Worst Wage Gap for Women and Minorities? Powerhouse Brazil," *Christian Science Monitor*, October 13, 2009.

27. Quoted in "Mulheres ainda tem pouco reconhecimento no trabalho," *Portal Exame*, April 24, 2010.

28. Overseas Security Advisory Council, *Brazil 2009 Crime and Safety Report: Sao Paolo*, April 27, 2009.

29. Bureau of Consular Affairs, "Brazil Country Specific Information."

30. "Country Commerce: Brazil," The Economist Intelligence Unit, September 2009.

31. Ieda Novais, personal communication with author, August 30, 2010.

Chapter 4

1. Stephanie Baker, "From Russia with Cash," *Bloomberg Markets Magazine*, April 7, 2010.

2. "Making a Clean Sweep," *Irish Times*, September 6, 2006.

3. Ibid.

4. "Women in Emerging Markets," Catalyst Quick Takes, 2009.

5. Robert L. Engle, Luodmila N. Usenko, and Nikolay A. Dimitriadi, "Work-Life in Russia," Boston College Center for Work and Family Executive Briefing Series, 2010, 5.

6. PricewaterhouseCoopers, "In Russian business women keep watch over finance and personnel," press release, March 3, 2010.

7. World Bank 2008.

8. World Bank Education Statistics Database.

9. Phil Baty, "Rankings 09: Asia advances," World University Rankings 2009, *The Times Higher Education*, October 8, 2009.

10. McKinsey Global Institute, "The Emerging Global Labor Market," June 2005, 32.

11. Dane Mitchell Donato, "The Soviet Union's Mother Heroes," April 10, 2002.

12. Glenn E. Curtis, ed., *Russia: A Country Study* (Washington, D.C.: Federal Research Division, Library of Congress, July 1996).

13. Tamara Liyalenkova, "Retirement-Home Fire Underscores Plight of Russia's Elderly," Radio Free Europe/Radio Liberty, February 7, 2009.

14. Federal State Statistics Service, *Marriages and Divorces 1992–2008*, 2009.

15. Ljubica Vujadinovic, "Russia: Domestic Violence Against Women on the Rise," *All Voices*, November 25, 2010.

16. The Legal Communications Ltd., "Divorce," http://www.russianlawonline.com/divorce-russia.

17. *The World Factbook 2009* (Washington, DC: Central Intelligence Agency, 2009).

18. Keith Gessen, "Letter from Moscow: Stuck: The meaning of the city's traffic nightmare," *New Yorker*, August 2, 2010.

19. "Russian crisis sparks Moscow crime wave—prosecutor," *Reuters*, February 16, 2009.

Chapter 5

1. "Sonia, ICICI's Kochhar among top 20 powerful women," *Express India*, August 20, 2009.

2. Ricardo Hausmann, Laura D. Tyson, and Saadia Zahidi, *The Global Gender Gap Report 2010* (Geneva: World Economic Forum, 2010), 9.

3. World Bank Gender Statistics Database (December 2010) and World Bank, Education Statistics Database.

4. Heather Robinson, "Women in the Indian Workplace," *Diversity Executive*, March 14, 2010.

5. "From Gandhi to Gucci: A Tale of Two Indias," *Financial Times (Economics Blog)*, January 20, 2010.

6. Somini Sengupta, "Inside Gate, India's Good Life; Outside, the Servants' Slums," *New York Times*, June 9, 2008.

7. World Bank Education Statistics Database.

8. "IITs, IIMs Largest Source of Business Leaders," *Economic Times*, March 20, 2009.

9. Rina Chandran, "Talent Building Key Challenge for India Firms," *Reuters*, August 11, 2009.

10. "HR Managers Work on Salary Hikes to Calm Antsy Workers," *Live Mint (Wall Street Journal)*, January 17, 2010.

11. Typically parents live with their son's family, so the actual number of people living in multigenerational households (i.e., with in-laws) is higher.

12. "Next Big Spenders: India's Middle Class," *Businessweek*, May 19, 2007.

13. Population Division of the Department of Economic and Social Affairs of the United Nations Secretariat, *World Population Prospects: The 2008 Revision*.

14. "Women in India have made their mark," *Rediff News*, March 06, 2008.

15. Jim Yardley, "Indian Women Find New Peace in Rail Commute," *New York Times*, September 15, 2009.

16. "The Family Friendly Workplace Model," USAID Health Policy Initiative, February 24, 2009.

17. Messaoud Hammouya, *Statistics on Public Sector Employment: Methodology, Structure and Trends* (Geneva: International Labour Office, 1999), 12.

18. Maarten van Klaveren, Kea Tijdens, Melanie Hughie-Williams, and Nuria Ramos Martin, *An Overview of Women's Work and Employment in India* (Amsterdam: University of Amsterdam/Amsterdam Institute for Advanced Labour Studies, 2010), 58.

19. S. C. Mishra, "Is Sarkari Naurki recession-free?" *Article Alley*, February 24, 2009.

20. "India will add 110mn people to workforce by 2020: Study," *Economic Times*, July 28, 2010.

Chapter 6

1. World Bank Gender Statistics Database (December 2010).

2. "China GDP grew about 10 percent in 2010—Vice Premier," *Reuters*, January 8, 2011.

3. Dominic Wilson and Raluca Dragusanu, "The Expanding Middle: The Exploding World Middle Class and Falling Global Inequality," Goldman Sachs Global Economics Paper No. 170, July 2008, 10.

4. Luisa Kroll, "The World's Richest Self-Made Women," *Forbes*, June 14, 2010.

5. "Four in ten businesses worldwide have no women in senior management," press release, Grant Thornton, 2007.

6. "China's Powerful Women," http://www.china.org.cn/china/2008-03/08/content_11976795.htm.

7. "China's Women Struggle for a Foothold in Power," *Reuters*, March 7, 2010.

8. Didi Kirsten Tatlow, "Setting the Space with Toughness," *New York Times (The Female Factor)*, January 26, 2011.

9. Andrew Jacobs, "China's Army of Graduates Struggles for Good Jobs," *New York Times*, December 11, 2010.

10. World Bank Data Catalog, http://data.worldbank.org/data-catalog.

11. American-Chamber of Commerce in Shanghai, *2009 China Business Report*.

12. Diana Farrell and Andrew Grant, "Addressing China's Looming Talent Shortage," McKinsey Global Institute and McKinsey & Co., 2005, 5–6.

13. Financial Times Global MBA Rankings 2010, *Financial Times*.

14. Shen Jingting, "MBA Study Can Be a Risky Investment," *China Daily*, April 21, 2010.

15. Nancy J. Adler, "Pacific Basin managers: A 'gaijin,' not a woman," *Human Resource Management* 26 (1987): 173.

16. "IBM Global Commuter Pain Study Reveals Traffic Crisis in Key International Cities," press release, IBM 2010 Global Commuter Pain Survey, June 30, 2010.

17. Jacobs, "China's Army of Graduates Struggles for Jobs." See also "Educated and Fearing the Future in China," *New York Times*, March 7, 2010.

18. "More Than 770,000 People Sit for Nationwide Government Recruitment," *People's Daily Online*, November 30, 2008; Wang Wei, "No Return to the Iron Rice Bowl," *China Daily*, December 3, 2009.

19. Quoted in Tarun Khanna, *Billions of Entrepreneurs: How China and India Are Reshaping Their Futures and Yours* (Boston: Harvard Business School Press, 2007), 13.

20. Cited in Yu Tianyu, "Businesswomen Show Mettle in a Man's World," *China Daily*, May 24, 2010.

Chapter 7

1. Data refers to the year 2009. World Bank, "Gross domestic product 2009, PPP & Population 2009," World Development Indicators database. Per capita values were obtained by dividing the PPP GDP data by the Population data.

2. *Women in the United Arab Emirates: A Portrait of Progress* (United Arab Emirates: Ministry of State for Federal National Council Affairs, 2008), 8.

3. World Bank, "Labor participation rate, female (% of female population ages 15+)" in 2008, most recent data available.

4. Ricardo Hausmann, Laura D. Tyson, and Saadia Zahidi, *The Global Gender Gap Report 2010* (Geneva: World Economic Forum, 2010).

5. *Women in the United Arab Emirates: A Portrait of Progress*.

6. See Serra Kirdar, "United Arab Emirates," in *Women's Rights in the Middle East and North Africa*, Sanja Kelly and Julia Breslin, eds. (New York: Freedom House, 2010): 517–543; and "The United Arab Emirates: Women's Rights in Progress?" Association for Women's Rights in Development, March 25, 2010.

7. See, for example, *Women in the United Arab Emirates: A Portrait of Progress*.

8. Joe Saddi, Karim Sabbagh, and Richard Shediac, "Measures of Leadership," *Strategy and Business* 59 (Summer 2010).

9. Helena Smith, "From Iraq to Oman, the Future Is Female," *Observer*, April 23, 2006.

10. Survey sample insufficient in size to allow a breakout of findings for Emiratis versus non-Emiratis.

11. Alison McMeans, "Emirati women held back from the workforce," *National*, May 24, 2010.

12. Rania Moussly, "Minority of Emirati Women Still Struggle to Work and Study," *Gulf Daily News*, January 31, 2010.

13. Katty Marmenout, "Women-Focused Leadership Development in the Middle East," INSEAD faculty and research working paper, 2009.

14. Kara Alaimo, "Families Vie With Boom Economy for Emirati Women," *WeNews*, April 9, 2006.

15. Sultan Soooud Al-Qassemi, "Expectations Haven't Advanced With UAE Women," *Huffington Post*, May 14, 2010.

16. Marmenout, "Women-Focused Leadership Development in the Middle East," 20.

17. UAE Labour Law, reproduced by Gulf Talent, January 2007, 16.

18. "UAE workers 'spend more time commuting,'" *TradeArabia*, August 9, 2010.

19. Heather Sharp, "Dubai women storm world of work," *BBC News*, August 4, 2005.

20. *Women in the United Arab Emirates: A Portrait of Progress*, 6; Embassy of the United Arab Emirates in Washington, DC, "Women in the UAE," 2009.

21. "Pay rise for public jobs has private sector wary," *The National*, December 22, 2009.

22. Reena Amos Dyes, "Helping Emirati women join the private sector," *Emirates 24/7*, April 29, 2009.

Chapter 9

1. Healthcare Businesswomen's Association, "Healthcare Businesswomen's Association and Booz Allen Hamilton announce results of groundbreaking study and best practices for recruitment, retention, and advancement of women," November 8, 2007.

Conclusion

1. Joe Saddi, Karim Sabbagh, and Richard Shediac, "Measures of Leadership," *Strategy & Business* 59 (Summer 2010).

2. Mercer, "Worldwide Cost of Living Survey, 2010—City Ranking," June 29, 2010.

3. Booz & Company analysis; US Census Bureau International Database, August 2009.

4. Sylvia Ann Hewlett, Maggie Jackson, Laura Sherbin, Peggy Shiller, Eytan Sosnovich, and Karen Sumberg, *Bookends Generation: Leveraging Talent and Finding Common Ground* (New York: Center for Work-Life Policy, 2009), 28.

5. Ibid., 18–20.

6. Michael Silverstein and Kate Sayre, *Women Want More: How to Capture Your Share of the World's Largest, Fastest-Growing Market* (New York: Harper-Collins, 2009), 3.

INDEX

ABOUT THE AUTHORS

Sylvia Ann Hewlett is the founding president of the Center for Work-Life Policy (CWLP), a Manhattan-based think tank where she chairs the Hidden Brain Drain, a task force of sixty-five global companies committed to global talent innovation. She also directs the Gender and Policy Program at the School of International and Public Affairs, Columbia University. She is a member of the Council on Foreign Relations, the Century Association, and the World Economic Forum Council on Women's Empowerment. Hewlett is the author of eight *Harvard Business Review* articles, ten critically acclaimed books, including *Off-Ramps and On-Ramps* (Harvard Business Press, named as one of the best business books of 2007 by Amazon.com) and *Top Talent: Keeping Performance Up When Business Is Down* (Harvard Business Press, 2009), and she's a featured blogger on Harvard Business Online. Her writings have been published in the *New York Times, Financial Times, Foreign Affairs,* and the *International Herald Tribune,* and she has appeared on *Oprah, Newshour with Jim Lehrer, Charlie Rose, Today,* and *BBC World News.* In 2011 she received the Isabel Benham Award from the Women's Bond Club and the Woman of the Year Award from the Financial Women's Association. Hewlett has taught at Cambridge,

Columbia, and Princeton universities. A Kennedy Scholar and graduate of Cambridge University, she earned her PhD in economics at London University.

Ripa Rashid, executive vice president, heads up intellectual capital strategy and emerging markets research at the Center for Work-Life Policy, has worked across Europe, the Americas, and Asia-Pacific and has held senior diversity roles at Booz Allen Hamilton and Met Life. Prior to her focus on talent management, Rashid spent more than ten years as a management consultant at Booz Allen Hamilton, PricewaterhouseCoopers, and Mitchell Madison Group, where she served global clients in media and financial services. She is coauthor of "The Battle for Female Talent in Emerging Markets" (*Harvard Business Review*), *The Battle for Female Talent in India* (CWLP, December 2010), and *The Battle for Female Talent in China* (CWLP, March 2011). Forthcoming publications include *Top Asian-American Talent*. Rashid has also authored numerous white papers on global talent management and gender advancement strategies, and she has been featured by *Fox News, Bloomberg, Newsweek*, and China Radio International. She holds an AB cum laude in astronomy and astrophysics from Harvard University, an MA in anthropology from New York University, and an MBA from INSEAD.